Entrepreneurship and Social Capital

Entrepreneurship and Social Capital

Relationships and Start-ups in Indian ICT Industry

Anirban Sengupta

RAWAT PUBLICATIONS

Jaipur • New Delhi • Bangalore • Guwahati • Kolkata

ISBN 978-81-316-0787-9

Published by
Prem Rawat for **Rawat Publications**
Satyam Apts, Sector 3, Jawahar Nagar, Jaipur 302 004 (India)
Phone: 0141 265 1748 / 7006 Fax: 0141 265 1748
E-mail: info@rawatbooks.com
Website: www.rawatbooks.com

New Delhi Office
4858/24, Ansari Road, Daryaganj, New Delhi 110 002
Phone: 011 2326 3290

Also at *Bangalore, Guwahati* and *Kolkata*

Typeset by Rawat Computers, Jaipur
Printed at Chaman Enterprises, New Delhi

Dedicated to my parents
Professor (retired) **Apurba Kumar Sengupta**
and **Late Anjana Sengupta**

Contents

Preface

A long-standing and intimate relationship between business and community has been historically recognized. Whereas on the one hand, community has facilitated development of business, on the other, business has played an important role in enabling community. It is important to note here that community, as a category, has also been understood differently in terms of levels of diversity, concentration in a geographical location, and emphasis on primordiality. However, in all these forms, community has shaped business across the world by supporting entrepreneurship and/or by setting principles of ethics. While there remains little or no doubt about the structural significance of community with reference to business, it overshadows the importance of entrepreneurial agency in the entire process. This book is an attempt to explore ways in which entrepreneurs engage with their structural locations for the purpose of business.

In spaces of businesses over which specific cultural communities have historically developed considerable dominance, structural locations of an entrepreneur is understood in terms of primordial ties. However, in newer spaces of business where dominance of cultural communities is not clear, the meaning of structural location is open to interpretations. That makes it particularly interesting to explore the facets of entrepreneurship in a new and dynamic business space like information and communication technology industry. It helps in reflecting on the multiple meanings of structural locations and forms of entrepreneurial engagement with them.

What makes a business space like information and communication technology distinct is the scope to understand structural location of entrepreneurs not just as considerably fixed socio-economic background, but as a dynamic space open for innovation. Educational or professional attainments of entrepreneurs considerably shape their structural locations and entrepreneurs play critical role in making use of these positions. Interest in understanding entrepreneurial engagement with their structural locations makes social capital a suitable perspective for this work.

Understood largely as resources evolving out of social relationships, social capital here is used as a framework to explore how individual entrepreneurs capitalize the social relationships in which they are immersed. Some of these relationships are primordial in nature, whereas others evolve out of professional/educational achievements of entrepreneurs. This book focuses on entrepreneurship in information and communication technology industry in India. Being an emerging economy, the contours of this industry in India are still being explored, and therefore opens up possibility for newer manifestations. Being a highlighted industry in India, the success stories of first generation entrepreneurs making their small enterprise grow big and respected internationally have received considerable media and research atttention. However, in this process, the experience of entrepreneurship in numerous small and medium organizations in this industry, which form the majority, has been left relatively undocumented. While the present work covers luminaries of this industries, the focus remains on the small and medium entrepreneurs.

This book attempts to understand entrepreneurship with reference to engagement of business with customers and 'business ecosystem', an umbrella term popularly used by entrepreneurs to imply aspects like financial investment, physical infrastructure, human resource, partnership, and relationship with government. In each of these contexts significance of relationships is explored through the framework of social capital. Forms of social capital that have been found to be relevant for this context include reference, goodwill and support, all evolving out of relationships. However, it has also been pointed out that business is not just about relationships. There exist different spheres of business where relationships play little or no role. Entrepreneurship, thereby, evolves as a creative process where entrepreneurial agency plays a critical role in taking a conscious decision about utility of relationship for facilitating the processes of business development. While conscious decision-making process appears significant, serendipity remains critical for business. The book aims to argue that the continuous interplay among structural forces, entrepreneurial agency, and serendipity is critical for understanding the diverse trajectories of development of individual enterprises. Social capital plays a decisive role in understanding this engagement.

The research which forms the content of this book would not have been possible without the cooperation of entrepreneurs whom I interviewed. I am indebted to them for the time that they provided despite their busy schedule and the patience with which they answered all my questions. I am also thankful to Mumbai Chapter of The Indus Entrepreneurs (TiE) and Mumbai Entrepreneurship Meetup Groups for allowing me to participate in their events and also, at times, introducing me to entrepreneurs whom I could interview. Without having any background in business, it would have been difficult for me to engage with entrepreneurs if I did not get the opportunity to interact with numerous entrepreneurs at these events, whom I formally never interviewed.

The initial thought about pursuing this research developed in conversation with Professor Leena Abraham. I take this opportunity, therefore, to thank her for sowing the seed of the research idea. One person without whose critical comments, motivation, and support this research would have been impossible is Professor N. Jayaram. If readers of this book find it useful, it is thanks to the rich academic discussions that I had with him at different stages of this research. Without his encouragement I would have never thought of writing this book. This research was facilitated by the short visiting fellowship that Entrepreneurship Development Institute had offered me for conducting this research. This fellowship provided me with an opportunity to utilize library resources of the institution and consult many faculty members working in the area of entrepreneurship. The support that I received from Tata Institute of Social Sciences, Indira Gandhi Institute of Development Research, and Institute for Social and Economic Change also facilitated this research. This research was also made possible thanks to the academic support that I received from faculty members at various other academic institutions and moral support that my friend, colleagues, and students extended.

I am deeply thankful to Rawat Publications for deciding to publish this research. Their painstaking efforts at editing the content has made it read better.

My parents Professor (retired) Apurba Kumar Sengupta and Late Anjana Sengupta always wanted me to be an academician. While I never shared their vision till I accidentally got into teaching, today I feel glad about their plan for my future. I, therefore, dedicate this book to my parents. How I wish mother was around to see this book.

Vandana, my wife, has been a keen and patient participant through the entire process of this research listening to the various challenges that I faced and extending appropriate advices. Without her enthusiasm and support, this book would not have been completed. This pursuit was also facilitated by encouragement and support received from my elder brother Angshuman Sengupta and sister-in-law Sudipta Sengupta. The playful time that I got to spend with children in the family my daughter Ipshita, niece Adrita, and nephew Anomitro made it easier to write this book.

Anirban Sengupta

1

Introduction

Business Venture and Social Capital

Globalization has been influencing all aspects of life in recent times. Concerns about its impacts have given rise to many long-drawn academic and political debates. As a concept 'globalization' lacks a precise definition. Economically, globalization may be understood as a process, which is bringing about mobility to many previously immobile or less mobile essentials of production like location, organization, and capital. It has facilitated a functional integration of internationally dispersed economic activities, leading to the creation of global production chains and reconstruction of existing distribution chains. Globalization implies that the world is being converted into a shared space by technological and economic forces in a way that developments taking place in one part of the world may have profound influence on the experiences of people living in other parts (Held, et al., 1999).

Internationalization, in the form of international trade in various commodities, has existed since many centuries. Such internationalization enhanced considerably with the inception of industrialization in the eighteenth century Europe, which led to a search for market in different parts of the world. However, even at that time, international trade was primarily limited to exchange of raw materials and finished products. Production process was essentially completed within a single national economy. The economic scenario started changing rapidly since the 1950s, when many Western countries began opening up their economies. For them, national boundaries no longer acted as barriers in the economic production process (Dicken, 2000). Some decades later, similar liberalization was introduced in many developing and underdeveloped countries. These politico-economic developments played an important role in creating a globalizing world. However, opening up of national economies alone was not sufficient for the spread of globalization. Another essential requirement was to increase the speed of communication and transportation across the globe. This, in many ways, was made possible by technological discoveries leading to the development of information and communication technology (ICT). In course of time, ICT emerged as an indispensable platform for development of many other industries.

Entrepreneurship in the ICT Industry

Virtual merging of continents through the developments in ICT has generated scope for developed countries to outsource components of business processes to developing countries which enjoy the advantage of having a large and relatively cheap human resource (cheap, primarily due to higher conversion values of local currencies against the US $). With reference to technology-based industries, particularly ICT, it is also necessary to have a human resource which is conversant in the English language and is adept in necessary technologies. India has specifically benefited from the business process outsourcing from the USA because of suitable geographical position on the globe resulting in a large time-gap with the USA, the largest market, which makes it possible to keep office functioning for almost twenty-four hours in a day. Other than such ICT services, opportunities have also emerged for the development of software products in India for the global market (Lateef, 1997).

Opening of this floodgate of opportunity has motivated many entrepreneurs to start business ventures in this fast growing industry segment. Being essentially based on new stock of knowledge, entry into the ICT industry is open only to entrepreneurs who enjoy the advantage of possessing knowledge required for understanding the relevant technology and/or business process. It is understandable that such entrepreneurs would include both individuals who have a family background in business, and those who have no such background. Theoretically, people belonging to the first category should be in an advantageous position, as they are likely to receive family support and/or guidance in securing finance, learning business acumen, identifying human resource, building entrepreneurial team, acquiring market information, and in learning to handle various crisis situations. Notwithstanding all such advantages enjoyed by entrepreneurs hailing from business families, many entrepreneurs who have no family background in business are very much visible in the ICT industry as well-established entrepreneurs. This is apparently contradictory to the generally known pattern of entrepreneurship in India which has largely been dominated by business communities, particularly by business families. It needs to be noted here that entrepreneurs entering the ICT industry from business family background hardly enjoy the advantage of having parents who have some experience in the same industry, as the industry itself is new. As a result, entrepreneurs, irrespective of their background, have to put in extra effort to orient themselves to this industry.

The phenomenon of new entrepreneurs continuously emerging in the ICT industry may be explained by the fact that knowledge required for running a business in this industry is still in the process of development and, therefore, there is still opportunity for new players to enter. Besides, market is still expanding and has a capacity to accommodate many new players. In addition, starting a business in this industry is not essentially capital-intensive and, therefore, the entry barrier for new enterprises in terms of financial investment is relatively low. Besides, given the scope for offering high returns, financiers are often interested in bearing high risk by investing in start-up enterprises in this industry. However, this does not imply that all new entrepreneurs manage to survive in this industry. Researches testify that in any industry, not all entrepreneurs who start their business venture succeed in surviving; in fact, many leave the industry (Cooper, 2002). It may be assumed that this common rule applies to the ICT industry as well. This leads to the central research problem that I aim to address in this book: *what is the background of the entrepreneurs, who have managed to survive in the ICT industry,* and *what has helped only some entrepreneurs to survive in this industry?*

Execution of an entrepreneurial venture, like any other initiative, depends on the role played by several elements such as entrepreneur's access to necessary technical knowledge, her/his stock of business acumen, and the response received from present/prospective customers about the product/service being offered by her/him. It also depends on entrepreneur's ability to secure finance, attract capable human resource, form and lead an effective and efficient entrepreneurial team, and handle situations of crisis. Even though these elements differ drastically from each other, an entrepreneur's performance in all these elements would depend on the decisions taken by various significant economic actors like financiers, customers, employees, shareholders, and colleagues in entrepreneurial team. Any decision is an outcome of actor's negotiation with available alternatives. However, different actors negotiate differently in the same situation depending upon their interests, their socio-cultural and economic background, information available to them, their interpersonal relationship with other actors who would be influenced by the decision taken by them, and the context of decision-making. It is in this backdrop that there is a need to bring in a sensitizing concept like social capital to elucidate the current research problem regarding development of entrepreneurship in the ICT industry in India. The discussion would begin with an attempt to understand two main concepts, entrepreneurship and social capital, and then move on to relate them conceptually and in empirical contexts.

Entrepreneurship

Scholars working in the field of entrepreneurship are aware of the variation that surrounds the definition of the term. Broadly, contributors to this area have reflected on economic and psychological dimensions. 'Risk-taking' is one variable which many researchers have identified as a component of entrepreneurship. These include Richard Cantillon (entrepreneur is a *risk-taker*) (Schumpeter, 1954), Max Weber (1966) (entrepreneur is engaged in activities, which are economically rational, that is, where goals and means are decided on the basis of *precise calculation of probable risks,* and chances of profit-making), David C. McClelland (1961) (entrepreneur is a moderate *risk-taker*), and R.D. Hisrich and M.P. Peters (1995) (entrepreneurs *assume financial, psychological, and social risk* associated with the process of creating something different with value). However, Peter Drucker (1991) has criticized the importance given to risk with reference to entrepreneurship. According to him, entrepreneurs do take risk. However, risk is taken by anyone engaged in any kind of economic activity. This is because, the essence of economic activity is the commitment of present resources to future expectations, and that means uncertainty and risk. In addition to 'risk-taking', researchers have identified several other economic behaviours associated with entrepreneurship. They include *rationality* (Max Weber), *profit-orientation* (Jean Baptiste Say and Francis Walkar), *innovation* (Joseph A. Schumpeter and Peter Drucker), and *detection and exploitation of business opportunities* (Peter Drucker) (Schumpeter, 1954; McClelland, 1961; Weber, 1966; Carland et al., 1984; Bygrave and Hofer, 1991; Drucker, 1991; Hisrich and Peters, 1995; Blanchflower and Oswald, 1998).

On the other hand, the psychological traits of entrepreneurs, as identified by various researchers include *need for achievement or ambition* (David C. McClelland, J.A. Hornaday and J. Aboud, M.B. Neace, and P.R. Liles), *need for power* (J.A. Hornaday and J. Aboud, and D.G. Winter), *desire for responsibility* (F.X. Sutton), *leadership, independence* (L.E. Davids, J.A. Hornaday, J. Aboud, W.C. Dunkelberg and A.C. Cooper), *creativity* (J.A. Timmons), *originality, optimism, tenacity, result-orientation, assertiveness, tendency to trust people* (M.B. Neace), *flexibility, self-confidence* (J.A. Timmons, J.A. Welsh, and J.F. White), *aggressiveness* (J.A. Hornaday and J. Aboud), collaborative network orientation (Sorenson, Folker, and Brigham), and *inclination to use money as a measure of performance* (McClelland, 1961; Carland et al., 1984; Schein, 1994; Julien, 1998; Neace, 1999; Sorenson, Folker and Brigham, 2008).

In using psychological traits to define entrepreneurship, two aspects need to be kept in mind. First, the list of psychological traits identified by researchers is endless, and it is not necessary that each entrepreneur would possess all such traits. Psychological traits would vary from person to person depending on age, sex, socio-economic background, culture, etc. Second, the psychological traits of entrepreneurs have been identified by observing or interacting with individuals who are running their own enterprises. In a reverse way, it would be difficult to infer that an individual possessing some or all of those specific personality traits would essentially become an entrepreneur.

However, attempts at defining entrepreneurship on the basis of their economic behaviour are also not free from debates. Risk-taking, as it has been demonstrated, is one of the major points of contention in this regard. Neither entrepreneur nor financier (capitalist in

Schumpeter's terminology) may be considered as a risk-taker. They may rather be considered as economic actors, who negotiate with and thus attempt to control and reduce risk. It will also not be appropriate to use the criterion of 'profit-orientation' in defining entrepreneurship, as entrepreneurship may be found in non-profit sector as well. However, business entrepreneurship is essentially related to profit-making. What is characteristic of entrepreneurship in both profit and non-profit sectors is 'detection and exploitation of opportunity'. It is in this connection that innovation is considered as a determining criterion for defining entrepreneurship. Finally, establishment of organization is an essential element of entrepreneurship as it indicates a long-term planning. On the basis of all these considerations, for the purpose of present study, 'entrepreneurship' in business may be conceptualized as *a process of taking initiative to identify and exploit an emergent opportunity for making profit by establishing an organization and by controlling and thus reducing financial, psychological, and social risks.*

With reference to entrepreneurship, risk is assessed at the beginning of a project and attempt is made to devise appropriate strategies to reduce such risk. Developing insurance for business risks is an important element of entrepreneurial strategy. This often entails developing a package of rewards, both monetary and non-monetary, to be offered to relevant economic actors on taking a specific decision. However, the question remains what would be the procedure for identifying an economic actor who would be interested in receiving such rewards, and what would be the method of ensuring the durability of relationship between the provider and the recipient of such rewards. Mass media may have an answer to the first question. However, no one can ensure the fulfilment of second requirement, save entrepreneurs, who are aware of extensive details about the economic actors concerned through intimate social relationships. Even in the first case, knowledge emerging out of embedded social relationships may prove to be an important resource. Therefore, it is important that we attempt to understand the role that social relationships may play in insuring an entrepreneur against risk. In order to understand the resources embedded in social relationships we introduce the concept of social capital here.

Social Capital[1]

In recent years, 'social capital' has emerged as a key concept that is applied in many fields. Many researchers are engaged in understanding the conceptual framework of 'social capital' (see Woolcock, 1998; Woolcock and Narayan, 2000; Westlund and Bolton, 2003; Li, 2007a). James Coleman credits G. Loury with offering the first definition of the term 'social capital'. According to G. Loury, social capital implies 'the set of resources that inhere in family relations and in community social organization and that are useful for the cognitive or social development of a child or young person' (Coleman, 1994: 300). This definition has since experienced considerable elaboration by different theorists. Social capital involves the intangible assets residing in social networks. It is generated through mutual obligation, expectations, and norms among members of social networks (Frazier and Niehm, 2004). As a concept, social capital looks into the functional aspects of various social structural components, and thereby facilitates analysis of individual action by establishing a relationship between the structure and the agency. However, remaining within this broad framework, the definition of social capital offered by different theorists has differed significantly.

One conceptualization of social capital has visualized that a central premise behind the notion of social capital is investment in social relations with an expectation of securing returns in the market (Lin, 2003). From this standpoint, social network or social ties is considered quite critical for understanding social capital. Mark S. Granovetter (1973) is identified as one of the early contributors to the discussion on social networks. He has categorized ties depending on their strength, which is determined by the amount of time spent in maintaining a tie, emotional intensity of a relationship, and reciprocal services. According to him, whereas strong ties can be a source of support, weak ties may offer access to various external resources. R.S. Burt (1992) conceptualizes social capital as relationship with other players in a competitive arena including friends, colleagues, and more general contacts through whom one receives opportunities to use one's own financial and human capital. Opportunities here include job promotions, participation in significant projects, influential access to important decisions, and so on. Considering the fact that competition is never perfect, social capital plays an important role in deciding who gets the opportunity. Social capital concerns rate of return in the market production equation. Pierre Bourdieu has also conceptualized social capital from the point of view of its resources. He defines social capital as, 'the aggregate of the actual or potential resources, which are linked to possession of a durable network of more or less institutionalized relationships of mutual acquaintance and recognition' (1997: 51). He felt that the collective nature of this resource entitles each of the members of a network to 'credit' in different respects. According to Bourdieu (1997), social capital, in the form of networks, is essentially related to the cultural and financial capital possessed by other people in the network. He says that value of any capital lies in its convertibility. Social capital becomes valuable, because it offers access to other forms of capital.

James Coleman (1988) has also defined the term 'social capital' by its function. According to him, social capital is not a single entity; it is rather a conglomeration of diverse entities, which are composed of some dimensions of social structures, and which facilitate various actions of actors. Unlike other forms of capital, social capital lies in the structure of relations among actors. Social capital is jointly owned by parties to a relationship (Burt, 2000). No one player has exclusive ownership rights to social capital; it is a communal property (Cooke and Wills, 1999). Credit for generating a widespread discussion and debate among academicians and practitioners on social capital as a conceptual tool, particularly in the context of regional development, is often attributed to Robert Putnam's book titled *Making Democracy Work: Civic Traditions in Modern Italy* (1994). Putnam defines social capital as 'features of social organization, such as trust, norms, and networks that can improve the efficiency of society by facilitating coordinated actions' (1994: 167). Supply of social capital increases rather than decreases through use and become depleted if not used. Unlike other forms of capital, social capital is produced as a by-product of other social activities like religion, tradition, shared historical experience, and various other factors (Fukuyama, 2000). 'Social capital is an instantiated informal norm that promotes cooperation between two or more individuals' (2000: 3). Such norms can vary from reciprocity between two friends to complex and elaborately articulated religious doctrines (2000). Partha Dasgupta (2003) has considered social capital as identical with interpersonal network. Like Coleman (1988), he avers that there is no single object called social capital. It is rather a multitude of bits that may together be called social capital. Each bit reflects a set of interpersonal connections.

While talking about social capital as resources embedded in relationships, R.S. Burt brings in the concept of 'structural hole' to explain the separation between nonredundant contacts. Here, nonredundancy is significant with reference to resource value. For him,

> Nonredundant contacts are connected by a structural hole. A structural hole is a relationship of nonredundancy between two contacts … . Nonredundant contacts are disconnected in some way – either directly, in the sense that they have no direct contact with one another, or indirectly, in the sense that one has contacts that exclude the others. The respective empirical conditions that indicate a structural hole are cohesion and structural equivalence … . Under the cohesion criterion, two contacts are redundant to the extent that they are connected by a strong relationship. A strong relationship indicates the absence of a structural hole … (on the other hand) two people are structurally equivalent to the extent that they have the same contacts. Regardless of the relation between structurally equivalent people, they lead to the same sources of information and so are redundant. Cohesion concerns direct connection; structural equivalence concerns indirect connection by mutual contact (Burt, 1992: 18–19).

Structural holes are beneficial not only in terms of their resource potential, but also in terms of the opportunity they create in exercising control by utilizing information gap (Burt, 1992). However, this argument may be questioned empirically. For example, the typical collectivistic culture of China dampens the control effects of structural holes. On the other hand, in organizations that foster a clan-like high-commitment culture, a culture that emphasizes mutual investment between people, the control benefits of structural holes are dissonant with the dominant spirit of cooperation. Information benefits of structural holes cannot materialize due to the communal sharing values in such organizations (Xiao and Tsui, 2007).

An important debate has evolved around the relationship that exists between social capital and trust. According to Putnam (1994), trust is an inseparable part of social capital. It promotes cooperation and vice versa. For him, social capital emerges out of civic engagements and not trust. Whereas, a completely reverse argument has been advocated by Dasgupta (2003), who states that social capital is just a component of trust formation. According to him, trust can be developed in different ways; interpersonal network is only one among them. It is not always necessary to know people personally to develop a relationship of trust. F. Fukuyama (1996) also gives a superior status to trust. According to him, trust has to exist in order for social capital to develop. Trust, for him, emerges when members of certain community get habituated to generalized moral norms like loyalty, honesty, and dependability.

Over a period of time, trust has emerged as a phenomenon that has attracted significant attention from researchers belonging to different disciplines (see Lewis and Weigert, 1985; Li, 2007b; Kriz and Keating, 2010). Trust is part of almost each commercial transaction, especially those that are performed over time (Arrow, 1972 as cited in Dasgupta, 2003). Trust entails an individual's 'expectation about those actions of others which have a bearing on her choice of action, when that action must be chosen before she can observe the actions of those others' (2003: 312). Such expectation is based on one's knowledge about other actors' disposition, about options available to those actors, about consequences of adopting such options, about actors' ability, and so on (Dasgupta, 1988). Trust is distinct from familiarity and confidence (see Luhman, 1988). Trusting a person means believing that when offered the chance, she or he is not likely to behave in a way that is damaging to others who are trusting her/him. Trust will typically be relevant when at least one party makes itself vulnerable to the other. Higher the level of trust, higher is the likelihood for cooperation. However, cooperation does not depend on trust alone (Gambetta, 1988). Trust emerges out of reputation and reputation is an outcome of observed consistent behaviour over time. Actors invest in reputation and in doing so they give up immediate benefits to secure privileges in future (Dasgupta, 2003). Such arguments about trust and reputation may be linked to the writings of early contributors to this field like Mark Granovetter. The notion of embeddedness advocated by Granovetter (1985) emphasizes the importance of direct familiarity as opposed to trust on generalized morality or institutional arrangements. Writing about reputation system in online trading portals like ebay Bista, et al., (2010) has also observed that assigning acquaintance-based differential values to individual feedback sources on quality of past trading association leads to evolution of cooperation among the players.

Following the foregoing discussion, *social capital may provisionally be conceptualized as social networks that have resource potential.* Social networks here would imply more or less institutionalized social relationships which generate a 'we feeling' among the members. Such a definition of social capital is surely inadequate. For example, this definition of social capital does not explicate what such capital consists of. However, improvement in this definition requires empirical data. It is evident that there exists some peculiarity in various institutionalized social relationships that gives rise to resources, which may be used for purposes other than maintenance of social structure. This peculiarity is primarily observable in the pattern of such social relationship, that is, in the nature of expectations and obligations existing among the members of such social networks.

Although social network is not essential for engendering trust, quite often trust is an outcome of close-knit social networks. Therefore, *it would be improper to conclude that social capital (conceptualized as social networks having resource potential) implies only social network and not trust.* Trust (as an outcome of social networks) may function as an important resource, having its applicability in areas other than maintenance of social structure. Even social network, by itself, should not be considered as social capital; it becomes social capital only when its resource potential for application has been identified. Another aspect, which plays an important role in the formation of social capital, is norms governing the pattern of exchange within a social network, for example, the norm of reciprocal exchanges. Putnam has identified two forms of reciprocity, namely, 'balanced' (or 'specific') and 'generalized' (or 'diffuse'):

> Balanced reciprocity refers to a simultaneous exchange of items of equivalent value. Generalized reciprocity refers to a continuing relationship of exchange that is at any given time unrequited or imbalanced, but that involves mutual expectations that a benefit granted now should be repaid in the future (1994: 172).

It is this second form of reciprocity which gives rise to a trusted relationship.

Indicators for Measuring Social Capital[2]

Social capital, being a sensitizing concept, has found application in different areas of study like regional development, organization, and entrepreneurship. Studies related to social capital have, by and large, attempted to find out what role social capital plays. However, depending on the context, researchers' opinions about the role played by social capital have varied distinctly. Whereas with regard to society or organization researchers have examined the role of social capital in bringing cohesion and collaboration among people, entrepreneurship researchers have tried to explore the role of social capital in facilitating entrepreneur's effort in securing individual advantages. Therefore, indicators for measuring social capital have also varied considerably depending upon the objectives of the researcher.

For example, for studying economic development through promotion of small-scale venturing there is a need to focus on the context at large and its networks, not the individual venture (Johannisson et al., 1994). Commercial transactions in Silicon Valley in the USA rely on deep-rooted relations of trust which emerge out of reputation about the ability and character of individuals. This kind of performance-generated trust is the building block of the particular form of social capital in Silicon Valley. Unlike the form of social capital observed by Putnam (1994) in the context of socio-economic development of Italy, the one functional at Silicon Valley does not generate out of civic engagements; rather it develops out of performance (Cohen and Fields, 1999). 'All the rest (such as informal conversations in bars or bowling alleys) is, relative to many other places, somewhat underdeveloped and ancillary. It exists, it matters, but it is second in sequence and importance. It is not the defining or distinguishing element' (1999: 127). This remark, in a way, stands contrary to the conclusion reached by Neff (2005) that parties and nightlife of 'Silicon Alley', New York City's internet industry, help to constitute the production of the industry and not the other way round.

Scholars have used different indicators for measuring social capital with reference to regional development. Following collation of S. Prakash and P. Selle (2004), those indicators may be classified into three categories:

1. *Participation, networks, etc.*: This includes variables like associational milieu, group affiliation, associational membership, inter-associational linkages, participation in organizational work, membership in central bodies of one's organization, length of participation, membership in labour-sharing groups, membership in multiple organizations leading to creation of organizational networks, involvement in collective action like dealing with crop-infection or approaching the government during natural disaster, time spent in collective

action, participation in local and national voluntary associations, reading local news, voter turnout in referenda (in Italy), voter turnout in personal preference vote towards various political parties (in Italy), and one's engagement in the school of their children (see Putnam, 1994, 1995; Pai, 1999 as cited in Rudolph, 2004; Krishna, 2003; Caulkins, 2004; Dekker, 2004; Diani, 2004; Krishna, 2004; Stolle, 2004; Bandiera and Rasul, 2006; Antoci, Sacco and Vanin, 2007).

2. *Concerns, opinions, and attitudes*: This includes indicators like involvement in disciplining other's children, views about political issues, views about scope for existence of rural leadership devoid of personal interests, informal discussion of politics, newspaper readership, reading about politics, disagreement with an item of an anomie scale, attitude towards others as revealed by a scale, agreement with the statement that everyone should do voluntary work at times (considering that volunteering is something positive and not a burden), and readiness to act against injustice (see Putnam, 1994; Krishna, 2003; Dekker, 2004; Krishna, 2004; Stolle, 2004).
3. *Trust*: This includes indicators like sharing ownership of farmland, views about generalized trust, trust in various institutional actors including politicians, and trust in institutions like bank, court, police, parliament, union, business and media, Catholic institutions, and army (see Dekker, 2004; Diani, 2004; Rothstein, 2004; Stolle, 2004).

With reference to organization studies, social capital may be understood through associability, that is, willingness and ability of participants in an organization to subordinate individual goals to associated actions, trust, social network, proportion of partners and associates of a firm who have earlier worked in other industries and other agencies and are, therefore, likely to have many valuable ties with potential clients, proportion of partners and associates of a firm who have left the firm and joined its potential clients, heterogeneity in the background of firm's partners and associates, heterogeneity in destination of partners and associates of a firm who have resigned, shared codes, languages and narrative, norms, obligation and expectation, and identification (Burt, 1997; Nahapiet and Ghosal, 1998; Pennings, Lee and Witteloostuijn, 1998; Leana and Buren III, 1999).

Regarding entrepreneurship, social capital is mainly understood through social networks and their relationship with various resources. Indicators of such networks may include range (the number of external relationships to obtain resources), frequency of contact (with kins, friends, suppliers, business associates, industry contacts, and local government), intimacy, friendship, value sharing, and moral obligation (towards kins and friends), trust (on kins, friends, customers, employees, local residents, and local business owners), commitment (towards customers, employees, local residents, and local business owners), reputation (among customers, employees, local residents, business associates, non-competing businessmen in other localities, suppliers, industry contacts, and local government), longevity of social network (with customers, employees, local residents, suppliers, business associates, industry contacts, and local government), reciprocal relationship (with customers, employees, local residents, suppliers, business associates, industry contacts, and local government), goal-sharing (with local business owners), and infrequent contact (with business associates, and non-competing businessmen in other geographical localities) (Zhao and Aram, 1995; Frazier and Niehm, 2004; Tötterman and Sten, 2005; Rindova, Petkova and Kotha, 2007).

In addition, social capital in the context of entrepreneurship may be measured by exploring indicators like having parents or friends who owned businesses, membership of business networks, having experience as a member of a start-up team (Davidsson and Honig, 2003), frequency of church attendance, and marital status of the entrepreneur (Honig, 1998). In the context of rural communities Ring, Peredo, and Chrisman (2010) have argued that formation of business network is influenced by the extent to which social structure allows for constructive conflict, inclusion, and permeability. With reference to entrepreneurship among immigrant ethnic community, measurement of social capital requires certain specific indicators. These include the extent of retention of ethnic identity (absent/intermediate/strong), residence patterns (dispersed/intermediate/enclave), frequency of social events (absent/infrequent/frequent), retention of native language (assimilation/intermediate/strong), dependence on group assistance (independent/intermediate/interdependent), self-sacrifice for group success (none/intermediate/high), role differentiation based on sex (absent/intermediate/strong), class hierarchies (differential access to power roles) (absent/weak/ intermediate/strong), resistance to acculturation (open/implicit/ rigid), conflict resolution mechanism (absent/intermediate/ strong), unequal inheritance distribution (equal/intermediate/unequal), endogamous marriage (open/intermediate/rigid) (Caulkins and Peters, 2002).

The argument of this book begins by questioning the validity of certain indicators that have been used for measuring entrepreneurial social capital. Logically, it appears doubtful that we can infer about an entrepreneur's social capital by measuring the number of people known to her/him, frequency of communication with those acquaintances, length of previous conversation with them, and duration of familiarity. For example, for securing financing it may be more useful to know one influential person in the investor community, than knowing a large number of unrelated people. This is not to say that knowing more people would never amplify an individual's social capital. However, it would not inevitably be so. This means that context would play a significant role in deciding the indicators of social capital. It would rather be difficult to conceptualize universally applicable indicators for measuring entrepreneurial social capital. Parameters mentioned above for measuring social capital among ethnic entrepreneurs appears suitable for that context. However, it is definitely inapplicable in non-ethnic context. At the same time, it needs to be assessed empirically whether it is appropriate to quantify social capital measurement at all and, if so, what variables can be quantified. As an alternative, it is also necessary to understand what can be an apposite procedure for making a qualitative assessment of social capital. However, for doing that there is need for a shift in theoretical perspective. Keeping these concerns in mind, this book would base itself upon social constructionism in developing an understanding about the way in which various agencies construct meanings of the concept of social capital.

Social Capital and Entrepreneurship[3]

Social capital may be identified in social, political, and economic contexts, and is often associated with strongly integrated communities. However, not all strongly integrated communities exert the effects of social capital in respect of business activities (Cooke and Wills, 1999). In the context of business entrepreneurship, social capital is utilized for various purposes including acquiring customers, attracting employees, building reputation, and discussing the ways of solving business problems (Anderson and Jack, 2002). Salvato and Melin (2008) argue that a family firm's ability to generate financial value over generations does not result from possession of some unique resource or higher level combinative capabilities but from the ability to utilize social interaction within and without the family. Benefits of social capital are of two kinds: access to information and ability to control. Personal contacts get significant information to an individual before others receive it. It can also function as referral for future opportunities (Burt, 2000). There are primarily two ways in which social capital may influence access to various resources. First, personal relationships of the entrepreneur may allow access to resources that are not possessed internally. This rational choice perspective views social capital as a basic resource, which individuals may use only for their self-interested ends. Whereas, secondly, there exists the concept of social embeddedness, which also connotes individual freedom of action, but at the same time implies some form of reciprocity or mutuality. In embedded contexts, entrepreneurial agency would be shaped or nudged in different directions because of social obligations, expectations, trustworthiness, values, norms, and effective sanctions (Anderson and Jack, 2002).

With reference to entrepreneurship, social capital is visualized as a relational artefact. It is a by-product of the process of association whose primary purpose is to understand each other. Formation of social capital is a process of negotiating to embed the self into an appreciative relationship with another (Anderson and Jack, 2002). It is not owned, but represents a pool of goodwill residing in a social network and it can be envisaged as a revolving mutual fund of traded and un-traded interdependencies (Anderson, Park and Jack, 2007). There are many indirect ways in which social capital may influence economic action (Lin, 2003; Khan, 2006; Meccheri and Pelloni, 2006). One among them is scope for the reduction of transaction costs associated with administrative procedures (Knack and Keefer, 1997). This is because achieving a coordinated action among a group of people possessing no social capital implies additional investment for monitoring, negotiation, litigation, and enforcement of formal agreements. Preparing a contract keeping in mind every contingency that may arise in future would become an expensive affair, and, naturally, it would be inflexible and costly to enforce (Fukuyama, 2000). Informal enforcement, involving a loss of reputation and future access to the market for any party that defaults on a contract, may often be a better alternative (MacLeod, 2007).

Similarly, business processes function well if knowledge is trusted (Fukuyama, 2000; Ojha, 2002). In an emerging economy, entrepreneurs often consider it essential to trust employees, suppliers, and customers. Trust is considered as useful for facilitating learning, reducing uncertainty and thereby increasing efficiency and effectiveness (Neace, 1999). This is also supported by other researchers (see Saxenian, 2000). Interpersonal trust is critical because competition is always imperfect. Had competition been perfect, one need not have depended on interpersonal trust; one could trust the system instead. Most of the time new ventures lack access to essential resources like established products, longstanding customer relations, experienced managerial teams, sufficient capital, and strong reputation (Zhao and Aram, 1995). Social capital, particularly in the form of social network, may emerge as an important channel for accessing these resources (Svendsen and Svendsen, 2004; Hung, 2006; Ramachandran and Ray, 2006). In biotechnology start-ups, network formation and industry growth are significantly influenced by the development and maintenance of social capital. Firms that are structurally more constrained cooperate with partners who can be firmly embedded in the historical network structure. Enduring interfirm ties sustain the structure that facilitates new cooperation (Walker, Kogut, and Shan, 1997). Similarly, Kauffman, Li and Heck (2010) also argue that information technology facilitated business networks create value by combining the capabilities of multiple firms to produce and deliver demanded products and services that none of them could deliver more economically on its own.

Social capital may perform an important role in offering access to information and know-how that entrepreneurs do not have, but definitely need for better pricing, superior delivery, innovative merchandizing and accessing new products (Tötterman and Sten, 2005). Social capital building is associated with enhanced business, knowledge and innovation performance through linkage with external innovation networks (Cooke and Wills, 1999). However, the nature of information exchange and the frequency of exchange would depend on trust, commitment, reciprocal intention, and shared expectation present in the network, that is upon the strength of ties. Dense relationships with kins, close friends, employees, and customers may provide information, encouragement (or motivation) and necessary support required for initiating new business ventures. They may also provide information about customer attitudes, competitor activities, business concerns, and about financial matters. On the other hand, sparse weak ties with business acquaintances, suppliers, business associates, industry contacts and local government may provide information that serves as fuel for innovation and renewal of business strategies. Besides, they may also provide information about industry trends and market. Whereas strong ties in social network facilitate access to information that is not codified, is complex, or is rapidly changing, weak ties are often useful in tapping information about broader market and macro-environment. Access to unique information about customer needs and wants, or product availability can result in a competitive advantage over less-informed competitors (Frazier and Niehm, 2004).

However, there is growing empirical evidence that social embeddedness has negative consequences. Tightly controlled relationships reinforce social obligations and expectations that may limit the freedom of economic agents to recognize and exploit new opportunities. Previously instrumental relationships may turn into 'dark resources' or social liabilities that constrain rent-seeking activities of managers and entrepreneurs, affecting negatively their performance indicators (Batjargal, 2003; Egbert, 2009; Kuhnen, 2009). Despite their usefulness, personal relationships may have drawbacks in managing interfirm alliances. For example, strong interpersonal ties in alliances can sometimes prevent dissolution of faltering arrangements, as feelings of affection may prevent the making of difficult, yet prudent, termination decisions (Adobor, 2006). Excessive trust may as well have various negative consequences (see Goel and Karri, 2006; Zahra, Yavuz and Ucbasaran, 2006). It has also been argued that social capital or social embeddedness can be of certain analytical use as conceptual tool, but that they hardly suffice to explain human behaviour in a detailed manner (Egbert, 2006).

Social capital, conceptualized as connections, may not be sufficient for accessing various resources. For example, in cosmetics and high-technology industry in the United States Baron and Markman (2003) observed that while social capital (in the form of reputation, social network, etc.) is crucial in introducing the entrepreneurs to key players (like venture capitalists, potential customers, etc.) it is the *social competence* which then emerges as crucial in deciding their success (in obtaining finance, attracting main employees, etc.). Here, *social competence* includes skills like accuracy in perceiving others, skill at impression management, persuasiveness, etc. Zhao, Frese, and Giardini (2010) also use the concept *social competency* to understand the business growth in China. However, they understand the concept in terms of social skills, proactive and elaborate social strategies, and relational perseverance. They have argued that comprehensive social competency was consistently related to network size and business growth.

Research focusing on the relationship between social capital and entrepreneurship has given considerable emphasis on studying social networks of which entrepreneurs and enterprises are a part (see Ramachandran and Ramnarayan, 1993; Johannisson, 2000; Dodd, Jack and Anderson, 2002; Hoang and Antoncic, 2003; Täube, 2005; Roberto, 2006; Bowey and Easton, 2007; Casson and Giusta, 2007; Cope, Jack and Rose, 2007; Coviello and Cox, 2007; Elango and Pattnaik, 2007; Wu, 2007; Mainela and Puhakka, 2008; Wu, 2008). It has also highlighted how trust plays a crucial role in facilitating entrepreneurship (see Fowler, Lawrence and Morse, 2004; Brunetto and Farr-Wharton, 2007; Greiner, Ockenfels and Werner, 2007; Marcuello-Servós, 2007). In this section, we shall specifically examine the importance of both social network and trust for the development of entrepreneurial social capital.

Social Network and Entrepreneurial Social Capital

Extent of diversity of entrepreneur's social network is often considered as a variable determining business success. This is because homogeneity of social networks may lead to redundancy of information. Diversity existing in business networks facilitates business start-up process (Renzulli, Aldrich and Moody, 2000). However, such an argument may be contradicted empirically. For example, in Russia, network heterophily hinders entrepreneurial performance. The high proportion of non-industry ties in personal networks may redirect the attention, resources and time of entrepreneurs from key suppliers and customers. Relationship building and maintaining ties from industries other than one's own negatively affect firms' financial performance. This may suggest that too diversified networks are ineffective or inefficient for revenue growth, at least in Russian conditions (Batjargal, 2003). However, having social networks in industries other than one's own may actually be useful in case of an industry like ICT whose value is generated by its application in different industries.

Granovetter M. (1973) has argued that, whereas strong ties in the form of close relationships with family members and friends are source of social support, it is the weak tie which provides access to various material resources which an entrepreneur requires for making an enterprise grow. However, such an argument may be contradicted with regional observations. For example, the support that new ventures in Germany receive from strong ties is more important for business survival and growth than support from weak ties (Brüderl and Preisendörfer, 1998). Similarly, in Taiwan's network economy, the solidarity provided by family networks makes small initial business organizations possible (Luo, 1997). Based on a study conducted at New England, the USA on the Hispanic community Chang, et al., (2009) have also concluded that family social capital measured through family support contributes to venture preparedness and start-up decision. Membership in business network and earlier membership of a start-up team is significant in development of gestation activity (Davidsson and Honig, 2003). Writing about global business networks in China, Ding and Akoorie (2009) have argued that understanding and participating in business networks is significant for doing business in the country. However, based on a study conducted in Portugal Carneiro, et al., (2013) have found that although companies often cooperated the number of more formal, structured or long term networks were relatively less.

However, appropriate strong ties do act as motivating factors for development of entrepreneurship. In Sweden, having parents and/or close friends and/or neighbours with business background, as well as receiving encouragement from friends and family members, facilitates an individual's entry into entrepreneurship (Davidsson and Honig, 2003). Similar observation has been made about high-technology entrepreneurs in the USA who frequently come from families in which the father was self-employed, providing a role model that presumably stimulated his son's desire for independence (Roberts, 1991). Both broad social and interorganizational strategic networks are important for successful start-up and ongoing competitive advantage (Butler and Hansen, 1991). At the same time, in Sri Lanka, it has been observed that social network of an individual entrepreneur provides more non-material support and information, while organizational networks, especially the supporting networks, provide financial support (Premaratne, 2001). A large network is always useful for business growth. However, at the same time, increase in network size without a corresponding enhancement in diversity may cripple the network in significant ways. What matters is the number of nonredundant contacts. Contacts are redundant to the extent that they lead to the same people, and so provide the same information benefits (Burt, 2000). In biotechnology industry, firms can realize performance benefits when their members repeatedly adapt the configuration of their social capital to changing resource needs, while inertia turns a firm's social capital into a liability (Maurer and Ebers, 2006).

Trust and Entrepreneurial Social Capital

Researchers in recent times have started focusing on the role of trust in business ventures (see Soto, 2006; Welter and Smallbone, 2006; Miranda and Klement, 2009). In the context of entrepreneurship, there is a close relationship between social network and trust. However, neither trust is essentially a precondition for formation of social network, nor vice versa. Of course, presence of one often facilitates the existence of the other. Every organization is subject to uncertainty emerging out of the behaviour of both market and partner organizations. Firms can attempt to reduce the risk emerging out of partners by shielding their association with legal contracts. However, considering the difficulty of doing so, organizations may have to trust a lot on the moral integrity and goodwill of their partners. Here, trust is a social-psychological bond between two or more partners that provides mutual confidence to both to pursue a relationship in which each may be vulnerable to the other (Ojha, 2002). Personalized business trust tends to be the strongest under certain general circumstances. These include, first, conditions of fluctuating markets and consumer demand; second, a system of flexible, decentralized manufacture and distribution; and last, circumstances where avoidance of formal legal controls is necessary or desirable (Menning, 1997). Such trust, which is often visible in family firms, may at times require trust catalysts. In family businesses, different trust catalysts like high status friend, mother and wife, and outside advisor play crucial role (LaChapelle and Barnes, 1998).

Trust plays a critical role in the formation, maintenance, and transformation of interorganizational cooperative relationships (Neergaard and Ulhøi, 2006). Positive relationship exists between the level of interfirm trust and flow of incoming knowledge spillovers from business partners (Bönte, 2008). However, building interpersonal trust-based knowledge communities in industries which are dependent on innovative knowledge solution is to a large extent unrealistic (Kieser, 2001). Formation of interorganizational trust in the ICT industry is dependent on communication of trust-worthiness (Kasper-Fuehrer and Ashkanasy, 2001). Interorganizational trust also has a strong and direct relationship with organizational performance. It functions to smoothen negotiation processes and thereby reduce the transaction costs of interfirm exchange. However, high interorganizational trust does not necessarily indicate high interpersonal trust among the people in those organizations. This is because boundary-spanning individuals come and go, whereas the institutionalized structures and processes accompanying interorganizational trust are more stable and enduring. Therefore, some researchers (see Zaheer, McEvily and Perrone, 1998) opine that interpersonal trust does not have a direct relationship with organizational performance.

However, a contradictory argument is also prevalent, whereby it is argued that, without effective interpersonal trust, strategic alliances between organizations cannot sustain. Given that strategic alliances are extremely beneficial for developing and improving a firm's level of competitiveness, interpersonal trust indirectly plays a crucial role in influencing organizational performance. One crucial mechanism in managing and reducing alliance risk is reliance on personal relationships between managers in partnering firms. Personal ties are beneficial in that they can form the basis for developing trust between partners, and they aid joint decision-making and information sharing, thereby reducing some of the risks inherent in alliances (Adobor, 2006; Patzelt and Shepherd, 2008). In Turkish automotive industry, development of trust is facilitated by informal commitment (Wasti and Wasti, 2008). Trust increases accuracy and quantity of information available to organizational agents. This occurs in proportion with the level of trust between the information provider and information receiver and the actor who bridges a structural hole between the provider and receiver (Droege, Anderson and Bowler, 2003). In an industrial district in Turkey Oba and Cioz (2005) report that it is the cost of breaching trust leading to expulsion from the industrial district that makes entrepreneurs/firms depend on trust as a substitute for contracts. However, this is possible only because information about any such defection is circulated smoothly among all the actors and there is an agreement among the actors about the action to be taken in response. They also found that social factors like family/geographical origin had no role to play in trusting exchange partners. Instead they were decided by contextually rational factors like reputation, knowledge about industry, and competence.

In India, depending on the nature of the industry, the basis of trust and the role that trust plays in business vary considerably. For example, in low-end manufacturing and trading business personalized trust based on experience of collaboration, caste connection, etc. plays an important role. In contrast, higher-end business depends more on institutionalized sanctions (formal contracts and bank regulation). However, this is not to say that higher-end business does not depend on personalized trust at all. For example, among entrepreneurs in software industry in Chennai there is a striking combination of formal contract and institutionally backed sanctions and incentives, with trust built through personal connections (Harriss, 2002, 2003). John Harriss (2003) also mentioned that introduction of globalization has resulted in shift in the pattern of reliance from 'personalized relationship' to institutional innovation, abstract principles, and professional codes. However, it is doubtful whether, even after such transformation, the relationships between large and small firms in traditional industries are going to be based on trust or they are going to be based on hierarchical arm's length relationship resulting from higher power of one of the parties in the exchange (2003). Similar observation has been made in France as well (see Hancké, 1998). While firms in a local economy may derive mutual advantage from networking, which enhances the industrial strength of the whole area, individual firms compete with each other over prices charged and paid, over the ownership of technology, and over their relative share of industrial markets (Oakey, 1993). For new ventures in Germany, personal network of the founder improves the probability of survival and growth of newly founded businesses (Brüderl and Preisendörfer, 1998). Networking does not bring any significant short-term benefits for a firm in the form of growth in employment or growth in total sales. However, networking is associated with high growth in the form of geographic extension of markets which suggests that networking sustains long-term objectives of the firms (Havnes and Senneseth, 2001).

However, it has also been documented that trust may have a dark dimension as well. For example, it has been found that substituting enforcement of formal institutions like financial and legal regulations with trust emerging out of exclusive and strong network ties may breed corruption. Besides, spatial proximity, which supports face to face business contacts thereby promoting trust formation can also contribute to 'over-embeddedness' and entrenchment at the regional level. Besides, this can also lead to effective exclusion of 'others' as a result of dominance of strong ties and consequent privileging of certain groups leading to imbalanced regional development. While over-trusting can put a business at risk, fear to go beyond the trusted circle in a low-trust context can restrain business development. However, in turbulent atmosphere it definitely appears less risky for entrepreneurs to utilize the old trusted ties if their existing network is extensive and resource-rich (Welter, 2012; Goto, 2013).

The preceding discussion shows that with reference to entrepreneurship social network and trust may function as social capital. Nevertheless, the way in which they function as social capital varies regionally. As a result it was possible to observe contextual variation. One observation was that researches mentioned above have visualized social capital as relatively constant; not much attention has been given to the possible temporal variation in social capital. Secondly, another aspect which requires exploration is the reason behind any kind of contextual variation. Finally, even though the role of social network and trust in entrepreneurship is well established, there is need to understand the nature of such necessity.

Social Capital and Different Aspects of Business Operation

A wide variety of research has asserted that the level of innovation/identification of opportunity is directly proportional to the intensity of networking (see Lipparini and Sobrero, 1994; Julien,

Andriambeloson and Ramangalahy, 2004; Arenius and Clercq, 2005; Eraydin and Armatli-Köroglu, 2005). It has been discussed that social networks play diverse roles for making a business venture grow. In order to understand this diversity it would be useful to look into various aspects of business operation (including identification of business opportunity, access to customers, business growth, business financing, and development of human resource) and assess the importance of social capital for them.

Identification of Business Opportunity and Access to Customers

Fukuyama F. (1996) has argued that if people can have trust on certain generalized norms of ethical behaviour doing business would cost less. He has also argued that existence of such a relationship of trust would give rise to plethora of social relationships leading to higher organizational innovation. This argument of Francis Fukuyama clarifies that innovation is crucial to any business venture and it is innovation which, in turn, ensures the growth of an industrial economy. The question remains what facilitates development of such an environment of trust. Knowledge is essential for identifying business opportunity. Many entrepreneurs acquire such knowledge through work experience. Entrepreneurs in high-technology industry frequently initiate their business activities in spheres which are closely related to technologies and/or market segment with which they are familiar through their prior work experience (Cooper, 2002). Identification of an opportunity sets the beginning of a business venture in any industry. However, the importance of identifying business opportunity does not end there. Having an ability to identify opportunities at regular intervals is what makes an enterprise distinctive. The importance of such ability is particularly high in an industry like ICT which is based on fast changing new technology (Ramachandran and Ray, 2006).

Information about possible business opportunity is scattered unevenly among the enterprises in the market (Soh, 2003). Entrepreneurs adopt different strategies for collecting information about business opportunities. This can include asking people who may be in a position to help them in identifying an opportunity as well as finding out from purchasing agents the items for which demand exists, but supply is poor. In many corporates, departments like R&D are institutionally entrusted with the responsibility of identifying business opportunity. In addition to developing ideas on their own,

R&D departments sometimes adopt ideas suggested by individuals from other departments like marketing, purchase, etc. who play boundary-spanning roles and thus bring into the organization information about market needs and new technologies (Cooper, 2002). Considering the variation in the information acquisition process, enterprises gain differential access to external information. It is in this context that role of social capital becomes important for identifying business opportunities.

The ability to integrate a large periphery of heterogeneous weak ties and a core of strong ties is a distinctive characteristic of a lead firm's relational capability. Leveraging this dual network architecture provides fertile ground for leading firms in knowledge-intensive alliance networks to gain competitive advantages (Capaldo, 2007). Networking is an activity by which enterprises and individuals obtain potential information about untapped opportunities. However, networking may still be a time-consuming and expensive effort as information is dispersed unevenly among the enterprises in the market. Due to disparity in networking strategy, enterprises and individuals may gain differential access to external information about new technological opportunities. The firms with more efficient networking strategy, having business relationship with large number of firms and being centrally located in an industry network, will secure information before others and thus lead to better new product performance (Soh, 2003; Dyer and Hatch, 2006).

Business networking in the form of alliances is not only a protective mechanism to create benefits of scale, but also an active way of creating entrepreneurial opportunities, and organizing high technology innovation (Moensted, 2007). However, it has been observed that interorganizational networks vary in terms of nature of preference for local alliance partners and stability of alliances (Huggins, Johnston and Thompson, 2012). Influence of proximity on formation of interfirm network is one field about which researchers have made contradictory observations. 'Technology spillover'-driven innovation in high-technology industry clusters like Silicon Valley in the USA has been influenced by social networks among geographically proximate firms (Cooper, 2002; Saxenian, 2000). Whereas, in Turkey, firms with global networks have higher number of innovations than firms with dense local networks (Eraydin and Armatli-Köroglu, 2005). In Ireland, as well, networking is more likely to involve firms in the international market than firms at lower geographical levels (Andreosso-O'Callaghan and Lenihan, 2008). In Australia, only small manufacturing firms relied more heavily on external knowledge networks as an input to innovation than did large firms (Rogers, 2004). These observations may be understood in terms of the location of market for a particular industry. Criticizing the emphasis given on local networking Lorentzen (2008) has argued that firms may use different spatial scales successfully in accessing knowledge. They have even argued that geographical distance is specifically beneficial in promoting innovation.

In Belgium and Finland, individual's education as well as place of residence influences her/his access to network resources and therefore her/his capacity to recognize opportunity. Higher education qualification facilitates entrepreneur's ability to recognize opportunity through increased exposure to 'knowledgeable others' belonging to networks such as alumni organizations. Here, human capital of individual entrepreneur facilitates her/his entry into networks which provides access to information about business opportunities. At the same time, individuals residing in large urban centres are more likely to perceive opportunity compared to individuals residing in rural areas or smaller urban centres due to presence of various organizations like universities, research centres and service providers in those areas, which provide more possibilities to discover and exchange new information (Arenius and Clercq, 2005). Similar observations regarding the link between place of residence and utilization of social network was also made by other researchers (see Kristiansen et al., 2005).

Accuracy and speed of business offerings are critical factors for success in a fast-changing competitive environment. While developing business relationships no one wants to take the risk of working with enterprises whose credibility is 'unknown'. Firms look for strong brand names to be associated with. As a result, new enterprises have to struggle for getting their initial customers. In this context, networks play an extremely important role in any industry. Viewed from the perspective of enterprises in the ICT industry, networking provides access to not only valuable scarce resources, but also customers. However, membership in networks does not come automatically. Entrepreneurs have to work continuously in order to secure entry into such networks. Getting access to such networks depends upon multiple factors like quality of business idea, reputation, and entrepreneur's networking capabilities (Ramachandran and Ray, 2006). Entrepreneurial founding team members utilize different channels for accessing customers. Some use the reputation of the investors for this purpose. Some others use their own reputation developed by word of mouth reference, while networking at conferences or through publishing articles in refereed journals (Neergaard, 2005). For some, kins also play an important role as introducers to initial clients (Anderson, Jack and Dodd, 2005).

Business Growth

Relationship between networking and business growth is one area which has received considerable attention from the researchers (see Zhao and Aram, 1995; Chell and Baines, 2000). In Jamaica, social capital, in the form of marital status and church attendance, is significantly related to profitability of business for all micro enterprises excepting those in the higher tier. The reason for variation in the higher tier probably lies in the fact that this segment is addressing technologically more complex market which requires them to operate in a more bureaucratic or competitive market rather than focus on community markets and resources. The advantages provided by maintaining close associations with community groups through church participation may be lost if entrepreneurs are aiming their production at wholesale and export markets, where they have to deal with people otherwise 'unfamiliar' to them. In such cases, people who spend a lot of time in maintaining an active church life appear to be penalized financially, as the time they spend on developing community connection hardly helps them in their business (Honig, 1998).

In Italy, the outcome of industrial networks varies depending on the nature of leadership of an organization. Incremental type of contribution is dominant whenever professional management is present, while the relevance of 'architectural and radical topologies' increase when the entrepreneur is present. When the entrepreneur is leading and managing the business, more suppliers are involved in the development of new products (Lipparini and Sobrero, 1994). In Russia, possession of weak ties (acquaintances and not friends) is positively and significantly related to revenue growth. Structural autonomies found in weak relationships seem to provide greater room for flexible negotiations in buying and selling decisions, and this freedom may facilitate the revenue growth. On the contrary, strong ties do not have any significant relationship with revenue growth. Having many friends as one's business partners leaves little room for manoeuvring; financial concessions to strong ties directly harm firms' revenues and profit margins. Neither do strong ties provide the benefit of network size and network heterogeneity (Batjargal, 2003).

Social capital developed from managerial networking and social relationships with top managers at other firms, government officials (political leaders and bureaucratic officials), and community leadership enhanced organizational performance (Acquaah, 2007). Social capital impacts growth by assisting in the accumulation of human capital, by affecting financial development through its effects on collective trust and social norms, and by facilitating networking between firms that result in the creation and diffusion of business and technological innovations (Chou, 2006). Among the ICT entrepreneurs who are not located in the ICT hub, firm performance of entrepreneurs having diaspora networks is significantly better than those who do not have or do not avail of such networks. Frictions preventing entrepreneurs from locating themselves in the ICT hubs or from being able to access diaspora networks allow these differences to persist over time (Nanda and Khanna, 2007).

Business growth depends to a large extent on the ability of an enterprise to retain its existing customers and to secure new customers by remaining competitive. Therefore, firms need to collect information about their customers and competitors. In smaller firms this often becomes a responsibility of the entrepreneur, whose information and advisory network is frequently composed of family members and/or friends owning non-competing small firms (Shaw, 2006). Following Granovetter (1973), such strong ties, due to their being homophilous, have the disadvantage of information redundancy. However, empirical data contradicts such an argument; family ties need not be resource redundant. A large number of entrepreneurs receive strong support from their kin during the start-up stage in terms of business idea, finance, physical infrastructure, and advice (Anderson, Jack and Dodd, 2005). Often relationships with family members as well as friends from non-competing firms and existing clients function as multiplex relationships, which bridge the gap between personal and professional ties (Shaw, 2006).

One technique of increasing network heterogeneity is the use of personal communication network of employees. In certain firms, there are systems of encouraging and rewarding (often in kind) staff for collecting market and competitive information using their personal network (Shaw, 2006). Inter-organizational social capital has been found to be extremely beneficial for developing competitiveness among firms in the Brazilian wine industry cluster (Macke, Vallejos, Faccin and Genari, 2013). In the US wine industry, small firm entrepreneurs network even with their immediate competitors, other small firms, in order to compete with larger firms and thereby grow in business (Brown and Butler, 1995). However, this is never done by entrepreneurs studied by E. Shaw (2006).

One requirement for business growth is a strong entrepreneurial team. Strength of a team often comes from possession of diverse complimentary skills by team members. Management by a team, rather than an individual entrepreneur, is often a prerequisite in high-growth industries such as technology-based sectors, because of the wide array of skills needed to start a new technology-based venture. Sectors such as biotechnology and ICT often have high levels of team start-ups (Gartner, 1985 as cited in Neergaard, 2005; Littunen, 2000). However, heterogeneity of entrepreneurial teams, which gives competitive advantage to an enterprise and thereby facilitates its growth, does not come by default. Team members do not automatically possess dissimilar backgrounds. In fact, there is a possibility of homogeneity in the social and business network ties in which entrepreneurial team members are embedded. In many cases, entrepreneurial team members are either from the same family or they are childhood friends or classmates or work associates (Neergaard, 2005). This may result in lack of diversity in the entrepreneurial team. However, at the same time, friendship facilitates the formation of management teams for new ventures, thereby improving their early performance. It is also conducive to decision-making processes that enhances the team's effectiveness in solving critical problems and improving venture's performance. However, friendships, under different circumstances, may exert either positive or negative influences on turnover of the enterprise (Francis and Sandberg, 2000).

Successfully managing business crises helps in sustaining business growth. In the USA, owner managers of manufacturing industries depend less on building external ties when they perceive uncertainty in the market. Rather, they seek to cope with the situation by strengthening the network internal to their organization (Sawyerr, McGee and Peterson, 2003). Similar strategy is practised by entrepreneurs from metal product manufacturing firms and business service firms in Finland. Here, firms create competitive advantage, innovation and efficiency by strengthening networks internal to the firm rather than emphasizing on external networks. Emphasis is also laid on working in groups (Littunen, 2000).

In business services industry in UK, small firms depend considerably on supply and demand driven networks of informal personally-based contacts with its clients and other business service firms for various purposes including filling particular market niches and competitive pricing. Without an ability to network with other firms, many small enterprises would not be able to offer a wider range of services at a competitive price. In comparison, consultancy and research firms have very little knowledge of their competitors. Here, client's choice of external advisers is dependent on personal recommendations and on an informal selection procedure (Bryson, Wood and Keeble, 1993). Shamsuzzoha et al. (2013) have argued that in order to stay competitive small and medium-sized firms need to establish and manage dynamic and non-hierarchical collaborative networks. The nature of the network influences the way in which firms in an industry grow. In Belgium, national and international contacts are more useful for business growth than regional networks (Donckels and Lambrecht, 1995). In Turkey, small firms are governed by traditional values, sectarian affiliations, family and social environment, rather than long-term business partnerships. This character of networks acts as an inertial force over technological and managerial improvements in small firms (Özcan, 1995).

Business Financing[4]

Social capital can function as alternative collateral for those who lack access to 'ordinary credit markets'. It may also provide access to financial capital, which is not available in the 'ordinary credit markets', for example, bootstrapped/personal resources (Jones and Jayawarna, 2010). In the absence of physical assets, which may be offered as surety, people may utilize their social connections (Putnam, 1994). For instance, entrepreneurs in Taiwan depend on network finance and not on bank loan for raising start-up capital as the latter are controlled by government policies over which they have little or no control (Luo, 1997). On the contrary, Collewaert, Manigart and Aernoudt (2010) have argued that state subsidy for business angel networks enhances regional economic growth in Flanders, Belgium. They found that such networks reduce the information and financing problems that the entrepreneurial companies experience. However, Knyphausen-Aufseß and Westphal (2008) found that in Germany angels, especially serial business angels do not receive considerable benefits from networking services. Prevalence of culture advocating social obligation in Singapore and Beijing often promotes entrepreneurs to use network method. Such decisions are also influenced by absence of well developed venture capital market and an appropriate legal/regulatory framework (Zhang and Wong, 2008). Besides, at times, an entrepreneur's ability to secure finance from investors is facilitated by her/his personal relationship with the investors. For example, founders of a reputed software consulting firm in India, Mindtree, used their networks developed as a part of their professional career for securing initial financial investment (Ramachandran and Ray, 2006).

'Direct ties' (defined in terms of personal acquaintances), as well as 'indirect ties' (defined in terms of references by trusted individuals), influence a seed-stage investor's decision to invest in new ventures by providing access to non-public information in a cost-effective way (Shane and Cable, 2002). For any investor, such informants may belong to different categories. This may include other entrepreneurs whose enterprise has already received investment from the same investor. Trust plays an important role in such mediated investments (Ramachandran and Ray, 2006). Building a trust-based relationship between entrepreneur and investor is essential for facilitating a successful capital investment (see Harrison, Dibben and Mason, 1997; Lapavitsas, 2007).

In various regions in Europe, networking among organizations involved in financing business ventures (banks, Chambers of Commerce, support agencies and educational institutions) facilitates the development of greater degree of specialization. Implicit in this development is the ability to cross-refer clients between organizations for specialist support and advice. Networking facilitates exchange of information and has the potential for improvement in procedure of bank risk-assessment of propositions from small firms (Deakins and Philpott, 1995). Investment strategies of different categories of investors are not identical with one another. Investment strategies of venture capitalists (VCs) differ from that of angel investors in the United States. For collecting market information, VCs depend more heavily on their formal network with associates at other VC firms than on informal network informants. These associates are quite often co-investors who participate in risk-sharing. When it comes to risk, VCs primarily take market viability into consideration. The ability of the entrepreneur in executing a business idea is not always considered as an important issue. As one VC mentioned, 'If the people are good and the idea is good, we will do the deal and replace the entrepreneur (if found unsuitable)' (Fiet, 1995: 216).

In comparison, business angels are more concerned with evaluation of the ability of entrepreneurs. Their information is often based on the extended industry experience that they have. Like VCs, they also distinguish between the information provided by their close associates, with whom they have had extensive investment experience, and that provided by mere acquaintances. However, unlike VCs, many angel investors do not have a strong trustworthy formal network. Interestingly, despite having differences in strength of network, both VCs and angels spend significantly long time in conducting due diligence of a venture. The primary purpose of such due diligence is to assess the validity of the information already collected from various networks (Fiet, 1995). A darker side on the emphasis on trust by business angels may be that their assessment of portfolio company's performance would depend on their perception of trustworthiness of the relationship. This understanding of trustworthiness would further depend on the perception about the nature of information asymmetry existing in such a relationship. Often organizational performance as understood by the business angel and entrepreneur may not match (see Bammens and Collewaert, 2012).

Despite the growth of venture capital industry, banks continue to remain the main source of finance for smaller businesses. Provision of finance to these businesses is generally characterized by information asymmetries, which naturally lead to some amount of credit-rationing. Collateral is commonly utilized as a means for protecting the bank from any kind of unfavourable information asymmetry. An alternative mechanism is to increase the flow of information between borrower and bank. This can be achieved by development of a close working relationship. The success of such a relationship depends upon the willingness of both the parties to involve themselves with each other and work together (Binks and Ennew, 1997). Within close-knit communities, information from third parties and community involvement affects the build up of trust. The implications are that bestowing trust may increase trustworthy behaviour leading to a spiral of trust. Instead, heavy monitoring may lead to lower levels of trust in a bank and lower demand for finance and/or less trustworthy behaviour (Howorth and Moro, 2006).

In the USA, firms seeking bank financing are more likely to get loans and to receive lower interest rates on loans if their network include a mix of embedded ties and arm's-length ties with banks. This mix of ties result in network complementarity, with arm's-length ties enabling firms to scan the market for loan prices and structures and embedded ties leading to lower interest rates. Socially embedded commercial transactions between a firm and the bank it borrows from increases the expectations of trust and reciprocity among the exchange partners. It also facilitates governance of financial transaction and promotes transfer of private resources that are inaccessible otherwise through market ties. However, it has also been argued that sometimes understanding existing among in-group members may facilitate their access to credit and thereby, restrict the access of out-group members. This may happen even if discrimination is not practised in any overt way. Therefore, minority and women-managed firms are less likely to secure credit through white male relationship managers as there is often a lack of understanding of each other's restricted codes (Uzzi, 1999). Similarly, it has been observed that in Ghana women entrepreneurs had more difficulties in accessing bank finance. However, they compensated for this difficulty by cultivating social relationships and using the social capital generated from them as a resource leveraging mechanism (Kuada, 2009). Research conducted in the USA also suggests differences on the basis of gender in access and utilization of credit. It has been suggested that women seek angel financing at rates substantially lower than that of men. However, according to these researches, women have an equal probability of receiving investment. It has also been documented that women are more likely to seek, and to a lesser extent receive, financing from women angels (Becker-Blease and Sohl, 2007).

Ethnicity may facilitate an entrepreneur's access to financial capital. Immigrants to New York and Los Angeles in the USA often arrive with substantial financial capital or can obtain capital from family members back home. Ethnic groups may participate in informal credit associations or obtain loans from lending institutions (usually ethnic-owned) that consider the pre-migration finances of immigrants and the immigrant's reputation in the local ethnic community. This combination of characteristics encourages self-employment (Sanders and Nee, 1996). However, according to other researches, ethnic resources like rotating credit associations are not as crucial for business establishment as they are for business operation. It is important only through giving a competitive advantage over other ethnic or minority groups who do not utilize them (Yoo, 2000). Among the ethnic entrepreneurs in UK, Africans/Caribbeans are in the most disadvantaged position in accessing bank loans. They have a higher tendency to turn to non-bank formal sources of start-up finance (including various sources of 'last resort' lending). Although some of these difficulties are associated with certain types of business activity in which the above-mentioned entrepreneurs are concentrated, sector is not a determining influence (Smallbone, et al., 2003).

Leaving aside entrepreneurs who succeed in receiving formal investments at seed stage, for many entrepreneurs, seed capital comes from personal savings, family, and friends. Some of these funds which come through such strong ties are offered as expression of personal support, some other are made available because of personal confidence built up through past relationships (Cooper, 2002). However, according to some researchers, finance might be acquired both through friends and through regular market transactions. It is not always essential to have a strong relationship with investors in order to obtain money for a business start-up (Jenssen and Koenig, 2002). Social obligation has no role to play in the investment decisions of many seed-stage investors (Shane and Cable, 2002). However, based on data collected from the USA and Singapore Lim and Cu (2012) argue that after investment the contractual favourableness between the venture capitalist and entrepreneur is dependent on presence of direct ties leading to more advice and less disagreement. Strätling, Wijbenga and Dietz (2011) argue that in Netherlands presence of higher degree of contracts tends to reduce entrepreneurs' trust in their venture capitalist. Such distrust is not lessened by use of more informal relational contracting. However, they also found that entrepreneurs welcomed some degree of monitoring. This highlights the enduring tension between trust and control.

Human Resource

The agglomeration of labour around innovative industry clusters has been found to be beneficial for both individual and firm. While for an individual this creates employment opportunities as firms gravitate towards such clusters, movement of highly skilled individuals across the firms promotes technology transfers and fosters links across the firms. Social capital in the form of social network apparently facilitates such developments (Waters and Smith, 2008). In microbusinesses in UK the owner-managers use their weak ties for identifying prospective employees (Chell and Baines, 2000). Entrepreneurial founding team members use their networks for recruitment of human resource until these are exhausted. Then the entrepreneurs use network of the initial employees for this purpose (Neergaard, 2005). While environmental constraints are important considerations for adapting recruitment practices through networks, strategic needs and interpersonal dynamics are the key drivers behind the evolution of such practices. With transition from the start-up to the growth phase, entrepreneurial firms utilize different network pools in search of diversity, yet cling to strong ties to find talents with common values and goals (Leung, et al., 2006).

However, the nature of social network that is used for recruitment may vary depending on contexts. During situations of political instability and civil wars, social network and trust may play an important role in vetting candidates for employment. Among Algerian small and medium enterprises (SMEs), an earlier tradition of basing recruitment on extended family networks has mutated, as a result of political instability, into narrower and more confining networks based on trust. Increasingly, in Algeria, the recruitment and selection of employees depend on the ability to gain the trust of employers. To cope with an increasing lack of physical safety and institutional support, many managers narrow down the pool from which they select and recruit their employees to personal networks connected by strong trust. Personal trust is found to be more important than family connections or any other factor as a defence mechanism against threats resulting from leaking information about the performance of the business, the business partners and the political affiliations of managers (Mellahi and Wood, 2003).

It is often perceived that members of immigrant ethnic community generally seek employment in firms run by people belonging to their own community. However, unlike ethnic economies, in which co-ethnics employ co-ethnics, immigrant economies develop when immigrants hire non-co-ethic fellow immigrants. This situation usually arises when entrepreneurial immigrant groups co-exist in a labour market with working-class immigrant groups that generate few entrepreneurs of their own. This is visible in garment industry in Los Angeles where only a third of immigrant employees find jobs in a conventional ethnic economy (Light, Bernard and Kim, 1999). This implies that immigrant ethnic entrepreneurs are not always particular about employing people from their own ethnic group, especially when the institutional environment is trustworthy. At the same time, one must understand that extensive use of networks, while promoting inclusion of members results in exclusion of non-members. For example, in the film and TV industry in UK it has been observed that control established by advantaged white middle-class men has restricted the entry of professionals who were women, members of ethnic minorities, or have originated from working class (Grugulis and Stoyanova, 2012).

It is clear from the preceding discussion that two aspects which have visibly received more focus from the researchers are business growth and business finance. In comparison, other functional areas of business are in need for more empirical contributions. Specifically, research concentrating on studying business start-ups needs to focus on the role of social capital in identification of business opportunities, accessing customers (particularly initial customers), and locating human resource. There is even need for further research on the role that social capital may play in the process through which start-ups secure financing. It has also come out that the role of social capital varies contextually; there is need for further research to identify such contextual factors.

Nature and Forms of Entrepreneurial Social Network

There has been a steady increase in the number of studies in the area of entrepreneurship focusing on structures of entrepreneurial networks (see Johannisson, 1986; Paché, 1990; Birley, Cromie and Myers, 1991; Larson, 1991; Shaw, 1991; Curran, et al., 1993; Johnston, Peters and Gassenheimer, 2006; Wang and Watts, 2006; Elfring and Hulsink, 2007; Han, 2007; Virkkala, 2007; Siu and Bao, 2008). Networks may be developed artificially in an institutionalized way. This may include trade organizations, strategic alliances, and supplier-buyer networks (Frazier and Niehm, 2004). Similarly, business incubators may provide entrepreneur tenants with a wide range of contacts with consultants, financiers, advisers, lawyers, accountants, patent authorities, mentors, other tenants, post-incubated companies, and some external companies (Tötterman and Sten, 2005; Soetanto and Jack, 2011; Tello, Yang and Latham, 2011). Some of the educational institutions also facilitate the development of entrepreneurial network by linking academics and industry (see Grandi and Grimaldi, 2003; Nicolaou and Birley, 2003).

Sometimes, business network is incubated through the development of formal associations. The role of two such organizations in New Zealand, namely, Wellington Chamber of Commerce and Canterbury Business Advisory Foundation is illustrative of this. Members of both networks share a strong feeling that business growth depends on expanding personal contacts (Perry, 1996). In the USA, not-for-profit organizations are found to be excellent for setting up business networks because of their trustworthiness (Cooke, 1996). However, researchers differ on the role that government can play in development of business. Whereas Neergaard and Ulhøi (2006) argue that government agencies may unintentionally destroy existing, well-functioning, interorganizational cooperative arrangements Liu, Woywode and Xing (2012), writing about Chinese high technology clusters, observe that international *guanxi* triggers government intervention, which in turn facilitates the acquisition of local *guanxi*. They conclude that government intervention may have a positive impact on high technology start-up innovations in China.

In addition to institutionalized networks there can be informal personal connections. It is this type of network, unlike organizational network, which the small entrepreneurs often find to be more cost and time effective. Informal networks develop when members utilize ties based on social relationship, kinship, or geographic proximity (Frazier and Niehm, 2004). For example, in Finland, small coffee rooms existing in some incubators perform an important role in expanding informal social networks. At incubators, where there is a lack of physical proximity among the tenant entrepreneurs, proximity is a generally felt need (Tötterman and Sten, 2005). Physical proximity though often viewed as a precondition for development of informal networks is not always beneficial for business. For example, in business incubators where tenants are fierce competitors, physical closeness may actually increase mental distance (Tötterman and Sten, 2005). While knowledge flow along informal networks has been broadly acknowledged by many researchers Egeraat and Curran (2013) have brought a new dimension to this based on their study of the Irish biotechnology industry. They have concluded that the flow of technical knowledge across these networks is restricted to a maximum of one or two steps in the network structure. The nature of knowledge that is primarily shared across these networks is 'know-who/market type' kind of knowledge.

It has been observed that entrepreneurial network may be local, regional, national, or international. There are various factors which influence the geographical location of entrepreneurial networks. According to some researchers, entrepreneurs who live in the ICT hubs in India, where the local institutional environment is strong, are able to avail these benefits and do not necessarily gain significantly from relying more on diaspora networks (Nanda and Khanna, 2007). However, this argument can be contradicted by stating that in the ICT industry in Bangalore, a large city in India with strong institutional environment, transnational diasporic networks play an important role for development of entrepreneurship (Upadhya, 2004; Upadhya and Vasavi, 2008). Entrepreneurs based in smaller cities, however, are faced with a weaker institutional environment, where information asymmetries create barriers to trade. Entrepreneurs who have lived abroad and are currently located in smaller cities are much more likely to tap into diaspora networks for help with their business (Nanda and Khanna, 2007).

Many a time, this variation in the nature of networks is an outcome of the nature of activity in which the enterprise is engaged. For example, many technology-intensive small firms need to internationalize their activities, and especially sales, at a very early stage of their development because of the limited and global nature of the technological market niche which they are attempting to exploit. Such firms in UK are engaged in a range of international networks and internationalization processes, including internationalization of markets, research collaboration, labour recruitment, ownership and facilities' location. However, this does not mean that for these firms local networks were substituted by international networks; the firms are instead embedded in strong local networks in research collaboration and intra-industry links (Keeble, et al., 1998). It has been found that inter-firm trust between geographically close partners exceeds that between distant partners (Bönte, 2008). For small firms in traditional industries in the USA, proximity did not seem to be an important factor shaping the structure of inter-firm informal networks (Kingsley and Malecki, 2004). Whereas, for wineries in the same country, transnational and transregional networks, even with modern forms of communication available, are not as effective as networks that exist locally (Brown and Butler, 1993). Similar is the case of SMEs in Aberdeen oil complex in UK, for which extra-local networks play a crucial role in providing access to wider sources of information and knowledge. However, at the same time, an Aberdeen location still matters to oil-related firms as it offers access to crucial forms of industry-specific information and expertise (Mackinnon, Chapman and Cumbers, 2004).

In the discourse over role of social networks in entrepreneurship, discussion over inter-firm alliances has occupied a critical position. Alliances have often been defined as voluntary arrangements that two or more firms get into for the purpose of sharing or co-development of products, technologies, or services. Formation of alliances is often dependent on various forms of social networks. For example, among small manufacturing firms in the USA, formation of inter-firm alliances depends on the social network of executives (BarNir and Smith, 2002). Often initial relationships between business partners lack social relationships. However, with time, some of these business relationships develop into close ties. In an embedded relationship, firms may invest in specialized assets, develop specific knowledge of their partner's plans and problems, and do more than required by the letter of the contract. Such alliance partners may be identified through stakeholders like suppliers (particularly in small firms) and members of board of directors (Cooper, 2002). In Norway and Sweden, personal networking involvement of specific directors was often found to be of greater importance than that of others. Therefore, the number of directors on board was not directly connected to the access to network-based resources. However, it was observed that level of networking by board members differed depending on the incentives received by them (Borch and Huse, 1993).

Formation of alliance for developing cooperative outsourcing, a major means of downscaling, is found to be of special relevance for small firms (Suarez-Villa, 1998). For small independent firms, the creation of alliances across national boundaries is a social event that relies upon the building and nurturing of a series of entrepreneurial networks. Such networks may be realized through the use of gatekeepers who facilitate the creation of a 'network-of-networks', that is, a global network of local networks. Social events, such as international symposia, exchange programmes, or conventions are important mechanisms for identifying potential partners (Hara and Kanai, 1994). To be an effective competitor in today's global marketplace one needs to be an effective cooperator in some network of organization. Such cooperative networks are characterized by relationship commitment and trust. Commitment and trust develop when firms attend to relationship by (i) providing resources, opportunities and benefits that are superior to the offerings of alternative partners; (ii) maintaining high standards of corporate values and allying oneself with exchange partners having similar values; (iii) communicating valuable information, including expectations, market intelligence, and evaluation of the partner's performance; and (iv) avoiding malevolently taking advantage of their exchange partners (Morgan and Hunt, 1994).

Over a period of time, existence of trust in entrepreneurial networks has emerged as an important area of research (see Lane and Bachmann, 1998; Dibben, 2000). Inter-firm cooperation is strongly influenced by various forms of network (Håkansson and Johanson, 1988; Walker, 1988). Based on a study conducted in East German and Czech border regions Leick (2011) has argued that business cooperation and networks support the creation of competitive advantage. Based on a study of cooperative enterprises in Italy Menzani and Zamagni (2010) have argued that cooperative networks are useful in achieving a 'critical mass' in the market through a coordinated presence and by exploiting a common brand. In becoming immersed in a network, the crucial step seems to be establishing the initial intensive linkages, or finding the right niche in the network (Yli-Renko and Autio, 1998). Silicon Valley in the

USA is characterized by long-term trust-based alliances between system firms and interdependent but autonomous supplier firms, which emerged out of longstanding tradition of informal information exchange, inter-firm mobility and networking. Collaboration with suppliers is seen as a long-term investment (than a short-term procurement relationship) which is needed for pacing up new product introductions and improving product quality and performance. This is more of a reciprocal relationship where both sides are committed not to take advantage of one another when market conditions change. It involves supporting suppliers through tough time – by extending credit, providing technical assistance or manpower, or helping them find new customers (Saxenian, 2000).

Entrepreneurship necessitates networks of various forms. Young (2010) has argued that in Port Hardy, Canada local and extra-local business networks tend to have little direct overlap. However, at times, locality and extra-locality interact, although indirectly and sometimes in unexpected ways. According to Frazier and Niehm (2004) five different forms of networks are utilized by small rural retailers in the United States of America. 'Advisor' network comprises of few localized dense ties with kins and friends. 'Grapevine' network is composed of large localized dense ties with employees, customers, and community residents. 'Merchant' network consists of large localized dense ties with local business owners. In advisor, grapevine, and merchant networks, the rural retailers hold a central position. 'Inspiration' network consists of sparse weak ties with business acquaintances who are situated outside the geographical locality. Finally, 'expert' network involves sparse weak ties with suppliers, business associates, industry contacts and local government. Both 'inspiration' and 'expert' networks are based on weak ties with people who are not located in nearby geographical area. Here, the rural retailers are located at the periphery of the network. These relationships are purposefully initiated and sustained. Finally, the same individual may be a part of more than one type of network. The distinction between social and business network in such cases is quite often blurred.

According to Renzulli, Aldrich and Moody (2000), actors in the social network of entrepreneurs may be broadly divided into six categories, namely, kins, friends, co-workers, business associates, consultants, and fellow group or association members. This categorization is based on the premise that resources received from them would differ. However, there is a possibility for existence of heterogeneity of resources from similar types of relationships. At the same time, there is also a possibility of resource homogeneity across diverse relationships. In this context, it would be relevant to bring in the term 'multiplex relationships', where the same actor may perform more than one role with reference to entrepreneurship (Greve and Salaff, 2003). It has been observed that in the US nascent entrepreneurs emphasize a lot on multiplex relationships. They develop homophilous relationship in terms of age and gender only when there is a possibility of multiplexity (Grossman, Yli-Renko and Janakiraman, 2012). Structure of entrepreneurial social network varies depending on the industry and the scale of business operation (Tötterman and Sten, 2005). For example, in Sweden, in comparison to traditional entrepreneurs, those in knowledge-based firms invest more time in networking and also build more focused networks. Entrepreneurs in science parks establish less dense local networks than traditional entrepreneurs in the industrial districts. However, differences between knowledge-based and traditional firms with respect to personal networking are reduced over time (Johannisson, 1998).

It is erroneous to perceive that entrepreneurial networks are constant. Their structure as well as functioning changes with time. In Netherlands, it was observed that outsourcing, supplier, and cooperative relationships shift from social to business contacts over time, whereas sales relationships shift from business to social contacts (Schutjens and Stam, 2003). It has been found that, in Russia, greater the initial network size, the lesser is the increase in network size, strong and weak ties, and resources over time (Batjargal, 2006). Entrepreneurial networks change as the venture grows. Following Greve and Salaff (2003) growth of entrepreneurship may be divided into three different stages. In *the motivation phase*, entrepreneurs discuss the initial idea and develop their business concept. In *the planning phase*, entrepreneurs prepare to set up a firm. Getting the necessary knowledge and resources in this phase entails quite diverse activities. In *the establishment phase*, when entrepreneurs establish and run a firm, they focus more narrowly on daily activities, or exchanges, and on problem solving. The stage of entrepreneurial growth plays an important role in determining the size of network discussion partners of entrepreneurs. Network size is the largest in the planning phase and smallest in the motivation phase. There is a significant difference in the size of network between motivation phase and establishment phase. Similarly, there prevails a significant difference between network size at motivation phase and planning phase, on the one hand, and between motivation phase and establishment phase, on the other. However, there is no significant difference in network size between the planning phase and establishment phase. Like network size, the time spent on developing and maintaining the network also varies depending on the entrepreneurial stage. Entrepreneurs spend the least time behind network development and maintenance in the motivation phase and most time in the planning phase.

As regards the effect of having family members in entrepreneurial networks, researchers have come up with contradictory conclusions. One conclusion is that entrepreneurs with a high percentage of family members in their networks spend significantly less time in maintaining their contacts than others (Greve and Salaff, 2003). Another argument is that entrepreneurs having strong family relations as network participants take energy and focus away from the external aspects of strategic management (Borch and Huse, 1993). It appears that the effect of the presence of family members in entrepreneurial networks may vary contextually. Similarly, various other factors related to entrepreneurial networks vary depending on context. Keeping the importance of context in mind, the present section would highlight different contextual factors like entrepreneur's educational qualification, gender, ethnicity, and region. This section would also highlight the geographical expanse of entrepreneurial network as well as inter-firm alliances as entrepreneurial networks.

Education and Entrepreneurial Network

It was observed that in the USA education and previous work history did not significantly affect the likelihood of business start-up (Renzulli, Aldrich and Moody, 2000). In Sweden as well, general formal education was found to have no measurable effect on entrepreneur's success in business gestation activity. However, attending a course on business education as well as having previous experience of start-up as a team member was found to be useful in executing a business idea (Davidsson and Honig, 2003). Even though formal education as human capital did not directly influence entrepreneurial performance, indirectly it did influence business by structuring the nature of business network formed by them. In Netherlands, the level of education of entrepreneurs influenced the location of business relationships developed by them: highly educated entrepreneurs were more strongly oriented outside their own region for all business relationships except supplier relationships (Schutjens and Stam, 2003).

Education was also found to be indirectly useful for the Korean immigrants in Atlanta, Canada. It was observed that those with higher educational backgrounds often started business sooner. This phenomenon could be explained by the existence of more dedicated and robust social networks among higher educated people. It was such networks that provided access to crucial business information. As a result of all these factors, it was possible to visualize a class formation around education (Yoo, 2000). Carbonell, Hernandez and Gracía (2011) have also reached similar conclusion based on a study conducted on the immigrant entrepreneurs in the Valencian community in Spain. Effect of education is also visible in the networking strategies practised by the ICT entrepreneurs in Bangalore, India. Many of these entrepreneurs are involved in transnational networks with alumni and/or ex-colleagues. Educational qualification is a prerequisite for participating in these networks (Upadhya, 2004; Upadhya and Vasavi, 2008). Chirwa (2008) also found that education is a critical factor for the success of female-owned businesses in Malawi. This has also been found to be valid in Kenya and Ghana (Gathenya, Bwisa and Kihoro, 2011; Bowles, 2013).

Gender and Entrepreneurial Network

It has been observed that women and men were equally likely to start a business in the USA. Entrepreneur's age, sex, marital status, and number of children had no direct correlation with business start-up (Renzulli, Aldrich and Moody, 2000). However, gender did have an effect on the structure and functioning of entrepreneurial network (Loscocco, et al., 2009; Robinson and Stubberud, 2009). In Italy, Norway, Sweden, and the USA, women often had more kins in their networks than men (Renzulli, Aldrich and Moody, 2000; Greve and Salaff, 2003), which, for many, acted against business start-ups. The reason for this may lie in the valuable time consumed in maintenance of kin ties. The number of family members in entrepreneur's discussion networks varied from country to country. In general, in all the countries mentioned above, female entrepreneurs had more network partners than males (Greve and Salaff, 2003). In both Italy and the USA, personal networks of women still included few men (Aldrich, Reese and Dubini, 1989). However, not all researches agreed about the differences in entrepreneurial network based on gender. In Ireland, for example, it has been observed that the level of heterogeneity of business networks remained the same for both male and female entrepreneurs. Women were as active in their networking as men and they were no more likely to consult family and friends than were men (Cromie and Birley, 1992). On the contrary, it has been observed that in Ghana women depended more on their social relationships for moral and emotional support during the initial stages of their enterprise development (Kuada, 2009).

It has also been asserted by other researchers that entrepreneur's gender does not bring any difference in structure and performance of a firm (Smeltzer and Fann, 1989). However, such an observation is context-dependent. For example, using confidential micro data from US Census Bureau Fairlie and Robb (2009) argue that female-owned businesses are less successful than male-owned businesses because they have less start-up capital, less business human capital acquired through prior work experience in a similar business, and less prior work experience in a family business. They (and also Robinson and Stubberud, 2011) also found that female owners worked for fewer hours and at times had different preferences for the goal of their businesses that could have implications on their business outcomes. Roomi (2013), on the other hand, argues that in the discriminatory social set-up of Pakistan women entrepreneurs do not enjoy the same privileges that are enjoyed by men. Only a handful women entrepreneurs received encouragement from immediate male family members resulting in restricted social mobility and limited development of relevant social capital. In a similar line, based on a study conducted on the Arab, immigrant, and Israeli born Jewish women in Israel Heilbrunn and Davidovitch (2011) have concluded that work-family balance remains a major issue for self-employed women. Interestingly, it has been observed that in Malawi female-owned businesses grew faster in terms of employment than male-owned ones although there were no significant differences in profit margins (Chirwa, 2008).

Ethnic Iranian women entrepreneurs in Los Angeles in the USA were found to be active participants in ethnic economy. Gender was an important factor in determining one's access to ethnic resource utilization at these work sites. Women's business in the ethnic economy, similar to men's, made use of family labour and was highly labour intensive. Through their businesses, Iranian women entrepreneurs diversified and expanded their range of social contacts beyond their own religio-ethnic networks in the Iranian community. Iranian women entrepreneurs in Los Angeles made use of their gender resources and the distinct ethnic component that they embodied to create small businesses in settings where work and social activity converged, such as in case of home-operated businesses. In home-operated businesses, the social visit and networking that occurred was essential to the economic transaction that followed. In such work environment information regarding happenings in the community, new friends, as well as employment and purchasing possibilities occurred simultaneously (Dallalfar, 1994).

Ethnicity and Entrepreneurial Network

Ethnicity often played an important role in the development of business networks among immigrant entrepreneurs (Yetim, 2008). While at times being a part of an ethnic minority implies access to various restricted resources it also involves investment of additional energies to develop a business. For example, it has been observed that entrepreneurs belonging to ethnic minorities need to consider their own culture as well as that of the 'mainstream' to develop their business (see Klyver and Foley, 2012). Social capital facilitated the growth of business initiatives undertaken by ethnic minority communities in Scotland (Deakins, et al., 2007). Different kinds of networks were visible among Israeli immigrants in Los Angeles. While they collaborated with American Jews and revealed solidarity on a community-wide basis, those sharing commonalities based on premigration ties appeared to have developed especially active networks (Gold, 1994). It has been observed that Manangi trade communities in South and Southeast Asia use kinship and religious practices to sanction a system of social and economic cooperation in their community. By pooling labour, information, material and financial resources, ensured by trust and mutual obligation, they could lower their operating costs. By extending kinship relations to societies abroad through various means, such as through marriages with local women, they could secure access to both local and 'translocal' trade networks, as well as, reduce protection costs (Ratanapruck, 2007).

Social networks comprising the 'community' and the 'family' play a central role in the operation of an ethnic enterprise. However, reliance on these networks is frequently shaped by racism in the wider environment; and the network itself is not an unqualified resource (Ram, 1994). Social capital located in immigrant ethnic groups does not necessarily play an important role in the development of self-employed people, particularly in the first generation. Instead, family-based social capital may be more supportive of immigrant entrepreneurship (Caulkins and Peters, 2002). At the same time, not all members of ethnic groups would require community or family-based social capital. In Canada, immigrants entering the host society with pre-migration intentions of business ownership possess sufficient human capital to enable them to disregard the formation and utilization of ethnic social capital in their economic adaptation (Marger, 2001).

Commonly, it is perceived that family-based homogeneous ties play a significant role in traditional businesses. However, this need not essentially be so. Gold traders in West Africa have established intricate webs of relations based on personal dyadic affiliations. These extended networks are very heterogeneous, involving a multitude of actors, spanning regional, ethnic and social categories. It is not a business carried out by members of a single ethnic group. Despite this heterogeneity, confidence between all actors is created, particularly in this case, where there is no legal recourse when informal contracts are broken. A patron-client system of risk-sharing at various economic levels is the basis both for economic rationale and cohesion among all actors (Grätz, 2004).

Region and Entrepreneurial Network

Entrepreneurial networks vary depending on geographical location of the entrepreneurs or the political system within which they have to function. For example, entrepreneurial networks in China take a specific form as a result of the existence of a Communist political system. Traditional patron-client relationship is functional in a different way in the market economy in China. Under a Communist political system it is essential for entrepreneurs to maintain a close network with the state (Chan, 2008). It has been observed that size of government network was related to business growth since start-up (Zhao, Frese and Giardini, 2010). Entrepreneurs refer to their ties with officialdom in Government as *guanxi* capital and classify their *guanxi* capital by the principles of efficacy. Efficacy refers to the degree of benefits that an entrepreneur hopes to receive from a tie relative to the cost of developing it. One tool for measuring the efficacy of *guanxi* is 'connectivity' which refers to the extent that a patron links an entrepreneur to others in the bureaucracy. Connectivity is efficacious because a tie with a cadre can give an entrepreneur an access to the cadre's ties with others, reducing the probable cost of the entrepreneur of developing each tie from the scratch. Similarly, another way of judging efficacy of *guanxi* is 'obligation', which stems from consanguinity. The strongest obligation is 'endowed' *guanxi* capital that is ascriptive and produced by birth. Somewhat weaker ties accumulated through life experiences are called *guanxi* savings. Savings are personal ties formed prior to the business career that has been 'pulled over' for commercial purposes. They involve 'emotional' attachments created by shared experiences. Affect is stronger if the shared experience was in childhood or youth. The weakest obligations are found in *guanxi* investments. These are personal ties forged after inception of business for commercial ends (Wank, 1996). *Guanxi* networks can explain well members' effectiveness as work team member. Effects of members' *guanxi* networks on individual effectiveness as work team member are mediated by member's centrality in trust networks (Chou, et al., 2006). It has also been observed that effects of *guanxi* varies depending on the types of entrepreneurship (for example, sole proprietorship, entrepreneurs with employees, micro firms, larger new firms) and types of *guanxi* (for example, Chinese Communist Party membership by entrepreneur or by parents/family members of entrepreneurs) (Troilo and Zhang, 2012).

The political system emerging out of socialism also tended to influence the pattern of institutional trust existing in a country. Performance of SMEs in the ICT industry in post-socialist eastern Germany was negatively affected by entrepreneur's perception of a general lack of market power (Nuissl, 2005). The nature of entrepreneurial networks may differ regionally. For example, professional networks of the Chinese software entrepreneurs are smaller, denser and more homogeneous in educational specializations, compared with the networks of Russian entrepreneurs. Furthermore, both ties and interpersonal trust in the referral tie are stronger in China than in Russia (Batjargal, 2007). In the USA, weak-tie networking among entrepreneurs was less than those among the managers (Katz and Williams, 1997). In comparison, in UK social networking pattern of self-employed persons was found to be similar to that of salary/wage earners (Dodd, 1997).

Comparative data collected from Italy, Norway, Sweden, and the USA shows that the number of the network discussion partners varies depending on entrepreneur's country of residence (Greve and Salaff, 2003). Another study supported by comparative data collected from Ireland, Greece, Italy, Japan, Scotland, Sweden, and the USA concludes that the number of both strong and weak ties is smaller for Scottish entrepreneurs in comparison to their counterparts from other countries mentioned above. It is presumed to be a consequence of the geographic isolation of the region used for the study. However, network size is not influenced by the number of years an entrepreneur has run a business. Similarly, having self-employed parents does not have any effect on the size of network of an entrepreneur (Dodd, Jack and Anderson, 2002). Even within one region, entrepreneurs may differ from one another. For example, entrepreneurs in England differ in their networking activities according to the competitive strategy pursued by the firm (Ostgaard and Birley, 1994).

A survey of small and medium size firms in Slovenia and Bosnia-Herzegovina shows that the institutional environment in Slovenia gives rise to more trust, which facilitates actors to base their business relationships on trust rather than on contract. In addition, when actors rely on trust, it is usually institutional trust, not interpersonal trust. In contrast, Bosnia, with a weaker institutional environment, generates less trust, leading actors to base their economic relationships on contract. Even when trust is used in Bosnia as a basis of business relationships, it is likely to be centred on interpersonal trust (Rus and Iglič, 2005). In Italy, Percoco (2012) argues, it is institutional history of a particular region including size of not-for-profit sector, presence of a university, and experience of being an independent city-state in the early middle ages that determines the development of an entrepreneurial culture in a particular region.

From the discussion it is visible that the binary opposition between strong/dense ties and weak ties that Granovetter had proposed in his article published in 1973 still continues to have a significant influence on social network literature. However, the validity of this binary opposition appears questionable. As both the terms are subjective, comparison becomes difficult. There is need for better terminology. Some researchers (see Neace, 1999; Anderson and Jack, 2002) have argued that formation of social capital is not necessarily related to its utility. For some entrepreneurs, formation of social capital is an end in itself; establishing social networks is more important than utilizing them. However, the validity of this observation appears questionable as no entrepreneur would get involved in formation of social capital if there is no potential for value.

Mapping the Territory

Various dimensions of concepts like entrepreneurship and social capital and the relationship that exists between them reveal that social network and trust are crucial for different aspects of business like identification of business opportunity, business growth, and access to customers, business finance, and human resource. This justifies the decision to use 'social capital' as a sensitizing concept for understanding the development of business venture, as it is found to be intimately associated with social network and trust needed for business. It was discussed earlier that with its dependence on new technology, entrepreneurship in the ICT industry differs from that found in various traditional industries. Therefore, it may be presumed that the entrepreneurial social capital in the ICT industry would also have its own uniqueness. For example, the existence of a large number of first generation entrepreneurs in the ICT industry suggests that hailing from business family/community, which is significant for development of entrepreneurship in traditional industries, may not be that important for development of entrepreneurship in the ICT industry. However, there is need for empirical exploration in order to assess the validity of such a logical argument.

ICT is one industry where it is possible to find a large number of entrepreneurs who lack business background in their family/community. It is quite different from the traditional industries where support from community members, particularly family, plays an important role in development of a business venture. Given this uniqueness, exploring the background of ICT entrepreneurs necessitates studying not only their family/community background but also looking into their geographical location, educational qualification, professional career, demographic details, gender, and the factors motivating them to become entrepreneurs. Such a strategy is necessary to facilitate examination of alternative channels of support for entrepreneurs lacking family/community background in business. At the same time, it is also beneficial in understanding the utility of having a family/community background in business for developing a business venture in a new technology-based industry like ICT.

Having decided to use social capital as a sensitizing concept it is felt necessary to develop an empirical understanding about the concept. The need for such an understanding is crucial considering the diverse interpretation of the concept not only across fields like regional development, organization, and entrepreneurship, but also within each of these fields. Considerable vacuum exists in operationalization and measurement of this concept. Analysis of existing literature shows that social capital facilitates the development of business venture by influencing different aspects of business. However, it is difficult to ascertain from the literature how essential social capital is in ensuring that an enterprise sustains in the market. Empirical data may be of help in understanding the importance of social capital in different aspects related to business operation like identification of business opportunity, getting customers, retaining customers, getting finance, getting office accommodation, getting human resource, and building collaboration so as to explain why only some entrepreneurs in the ICT industry sustain in market. Logically, it is understandable that as relationships keep changing through time their resource value would naturally change. However, existing literature has hardly focused on the temporality of social capital utilization, thus creating an impression that social capital is static in nature. In order to understand the importance of social capital in the development of ICT entrepreneurship, it is necessary to explore the changes in the utilization of social capital.

This book focuses on the ICT industry in India. Considering the reason for selecting the ICT industry, as mentioned earlier, the conclusions may also be extended to other new technology-based industries, which share similarity with the ICT industry regarding the process of business development, for example, certain segments of biotechnology and information technology enabled services industry. It must be said, however, that what is applicable in the case of the ICT industry is not necessarily applicable in traditional industries. Considering the interest in using social capital as a sensitizing tool for understanding the development of ICT entrepreneurship, the book highlights the importance of relationship in various areas of business operation. However, while highlighting the influence of relationship on business, it also points out how, at times, business develops without the intervention of relationship. Looking at business development in this way helps in assessing the relative importance of social capital for development of business. For understanding the influence of social capital on business development, the primary focus is on social network and trust. Having narrowed down to individual entrepreneurs I choose to focus on founder-driven entrepreneurship as opposed to employee-driven entrepreneurship. For similar reasons, I avoid looking much into interfirm alliances where enterprise becomes more important than individual entrepreneurs.

The Pathways: Methodological Decisions

In view of the broad research problem it is quite understandable that the current research requires interaction with entrepreneurs in the ICT industry. It has been decided to operationalize entrepreneurs as individuals who have founded a business organization, either a firm or a company, in the ICT industry and are running it at present as its executive head. By such an operationalization, the current study equates entrepreneur with founder of a company or a firm. Our decision to interact with the founder rules out the possibility of considering other individuals as entrepreneurs, for example, those who have inherited a family business or those who have acquired an existing business. The current study also excludes large-scale corporate entrepreneurship where employees play an important entrepreneurial role to the extent that the role of the founder is not pervasive in organizational decision-making. This indirectly limits the study to Small and Medium Enterprises (SMEs). However, concentration on SMEs alone facilitates enrichment of the body of knowledge. As more detailed secondary data is available on the large enterprises research on entrepreneurship has often gravitated towards that direction, thereby, creating a vacuum in the body of knowledge on SMEs which are numerically the majority in any industry.

Interacting with founders of organizations who are executive heads at present has been found to be crucial. Being involved with all strategic decisions of the organization they are the best persons to talk about the process of development of their enterprises since inception. Besides, the decision to converse with founders has also been guided by my interest in exploring the relationship between social capital and entrepreneurship. As founders play a key role in the formation and utilization of social capital relevant for the development of an enterprise, they are the most appropriate persons to speak about the development of entrepreneurial social capital over a period of time. Interacting with executive heads of enterprises who inherited or acquired the business cannot naturally provide first-hand information about the process of establishment of a business.

After discussing with several experts at the Entrepreneurship Development Institute, Ahmedabad and many entrepreneurs involved in different industries, it was gathered that, on an average, any business organization which survived for three years after its establishment or inception of operation (whichever is later) may be considered as successful in surviving in an industry by facing various business start-up challenges. Given the fast changing nature of the ICT industry, experts felt that an organization which has survived in this industry for three years has a higher probability of not going to go out of business soon. Therefore, it can be categorized as an organization which has survived in the ICT industry. This argument is also validated by looking into the standards accepted by various venture capital firms in this regard. They consider that on an average it takes three to seven years for any company to generate substantial returns (India Infoline, n.d.). Therefore, any organization which has survived in the ICT industry for three years or more after registration/inception of operation (whichever is later) has a higher possibility of sustaining in business. However, to be on the safer side, it was decided that preferably those entrepreneurs would be selected for the present research, whose venture has been functioning for five years or more.

Primary data for this research was collected from four cities in India where many ICT enterprises are located, namely, Bangalore,

Chennai, Mumbai, and Pune. The decision to collect data from four different cities was guided by an interest in exploring whether location was important for shaping the nature of ICT entrepreneurship in India. Such a decision emerged from our familiarity with observations made by past researchers that location has proved to be vital in the rise of ICT clusters in Silicon Valley in the USA (see Saxenian, 2000). The cities were selected keeping in mind their history of entrepreneurship: while Bangalore and Pune represented cities that have entered the world economic map with the rise of ICT entrepreneurship there, Chennai and Mumbai represented old business centres which also encouraged the development of new industries like ICT. In fact, Mumbai was the initial centre for the development of ICT industry in India (Heeks, 1996).

Identification of entrepreneurs to become participants for this study was a challenging endeavour. Initially, the idea was to prepare a sampling frame containing a comprehensive list of enterprises in the ICT industry which was to be used for drawing sample entrepreneurs. Keeping that in mind, it appeared pertinent to look for such a list with the Registrar of Companies, Department of Company Affairs, Government of India, as all companies in India irrespective of industry have to register with them. The Department of Company Affairs in association with the National Informatics Centre has published a database of companies registered with them in the form of a CD ROM. This database provides an industry-wise classification of 640 thousand companies registered under Indian Companies Act and provides basic contact details of those companies. In this database there were details of about 23,000 companies which were involved in software services. However, in view of the difficulty of accessing information from this database and considering the missing data, it was finally decided not to use it for constructing a comprehensive database. This database was not useful in any case for developing a comprehensive list of enterprises as it did not include companies operating in India which were registered abroad. The database also naturally did not include the firms (both partnership and sole proprietorship). Although, on the advice of experts at the Indira Gandhi Institute of Development Research, Mumbai and the Indian Institute of Technology (Bombay), Mumbai, I looked for alternative lists like Company Watch and databases developed by Centre for Monitoring Indian Economy, namely, Prowess and First Source, none were comprehensive in nature. I also looked into relevant news magazines like *IT Direct*, *Dataquest*, and *PC Express* for knowing about the enterprises in the ICT industry. However, I found that these magazines were primarily focused on corporate entrepreneurship, which was outside the scope of this research.

In the absence of availability of any comprehensive list of all ICT enterprises functioning in India, it was decided to collect contact details and enterprise details of as many organizations as possible from multiple sources and draw the sample from them. One source of data was a database called COMPASS. This database provided details of about 1,945 ICT enterprises located in different parts of India. Another database that was used for this research was maintained by <BangaloreIT.in> in their website (www.bangaloreitevent.in). <BangaloreIT.in> is hosted by the Department of Information Technology, Biotechnology and Science and Technology, Government of Karnataka, and Software Technology Parks of India (STPI) (BangaloreIT, n.d.). From this database I collected details of 1,017 ICT enterprises located in Bangalore. A third database that was used for the study was the list of members available from the website of STPI Chennai, which began its operations in 1995 (STPI, n.d.). From this database I collected details of 1,048 member enterprises located in Chennai. The last database that was looked into for this research was the list of members of the Mumbai Chapter of The Indus Entrepreneurs (TiE). Using TiE Mumbai database of Associated Members I drew up a list of 45 ICT entrepreneurs. In addition, I also looked into the list of Charter Members of TiE Mumbai which had details of 61 entrepreneurs from different industries. However, I did not use either of the TiE lists for directly contacting the entrepreneurs for the current research, as that was the kind of understanding that I got into with TiE Mumbai. Instead, it was agreed upon that, if I find an entrepreneur in the list whom I would like to interview, the request would be routed through TiE. In a way it was beneficial for the research, as reference from TiE was valuable for contacting its members.

Considering that the association with TiE Mumbai was much more than using its membership database for the purpose of current research, it would be pertinent to mention further details about it. TiE, a not-for-profit network of entrepreneurs and professionals, was founded in 1992 in Silicon Valley by a group of successful entrepreneurs, corporate executives, and senior professionals with roots in the Indian subcontinent. Currently, TiE's mission is to foster entrepreneurship globally through mentoring, networking, and education. At present, TiE has 60 chapters across 17 countries. Each of the TiE offices is called a chapter. TiE has more than 8,500 Associated Members and over 2,500 Charter Members all over the world. Charter Members are the backbone of TiE. A typical profile of a Charter Member is a highly successful entrepreneur and high achiever in an industry, who is ready, able, and willing to invest time and energy in mentoring and sharing knowledge with the TiE ecosystem. Associated Members, on the other hand, are either entrepreneurs or aspiring entrepreneurs and professionals with an interest in entrepreneurship. At the same time, TiE also strongly encourages participation of entrepreneurship enthusiasts as volunteers in activities organized by it (TiE, n.d. b; TiE, n.d. c).

Mumbai chapter of TiE has been in existence since 1999 (TiE, n.d. a). For the purpose of current research, I associated myself with the activities of this chapter of TiE as a volunteer. In addition to volunteering for the regular activities of TiE Mumbai, I also participated in TiE Entrepreneurial Conference organized by TiE Mumbai during 17–19 December 2006. One purpose of volunteering was to listen to speakers and participants at various events organized by TiE Mumbai to understand the various issues of concern for the entrepreneurs. Another purpose of volunteering was to build a relationship with participant entrepreneurs in order to explore the possibility of interviewing them for the purpose of the current research. In addition to events organized by TiE Mumbai, another forum in which I participated frequently for the purpose of identifying prospective research participants was the gatherings organized by the Mumbai Entrepreneurship Meetup Group <http://entrepreneur.meetup.com/656/>. Leaving aside all the sources mentioned above, there was one entrepreneur whom I contacted through reference from another entrepreneur whom I interviewed.

For the purpose of collection of primary data, entrepreneurs were identified from the different sources mentioned above. Out of the total 30 entrepreneurs sampled for current research, eight were contacted personally at different gatherings: six at various TiE events, and two at gatherings organized by the Mumbai Entrepreneurship Meetup Group. While conversing with them we orally enquired about their interest in participating in the current research. Leaving aside these eight entrepreneurs, who were contacted verbally, there was one entrepreneur who was contacted over the phone through reference from another entrepreneur whom I had interviewed. There were two other entrepreneurs for whom reference was used. They were identified from membership database of TiE Mumbai, but were contacted through TiE Mumbai executives. The remaining 19 entrepreneurs were contacted through unreferenced personalized emails which enquired about their interest in participating in the current study. Different sources were used for contacting these entrepreneurs, five through COMPASS database, 10 through database maintained by <BangaloreIT.in>, and four through STPI Chennai membership database. The emails informed them about the source through which I got to know about them and about their enterprise. Along with the email an attachment containing an overview of the study was sent to enable them to make a decision about participation in the study. In case the entrepreneurs responded to the email, I followed it up either through email or through telephone whichever they preferred. If they agreed to participate in the current research and if they were found suitable for the same, information about the entrepreneur and the enterprise was collected from the website of their enterprise. Later on, while meeting them, brochures containing enterprise profile were collected from the entrepreneurs, wherever available.

Considering the interest in addressing certain conceptual gaps in a specific empirical context, grounded theory (see Glaser and Strauss, 1970; Corbin and Strauss, 2008; Bryant and Charmaz, 2010) appeared to be the most suitable methodology for the current research. Keeping this methodology in mind, theoretical sampling technique was utilized for collection of data where the aim of sampling was to incorporate extensive diversity in data till saturation was reached. In order to bring such diversity it was ensured that selected entrepreneurs were unique in some or other way. Various criteria that were used for bringing in diversity included age, gender, nature of business activities, and geographical location of the entrepreneur. Variations in the above-mentioned criteria brought corresponding diversity in other areas like entrepreneur's educational qualification, employment career, family support, friends circle, and motivating factors in becoming an entrepreneur. Details about these variations can be found in Chapters Two and Three.

Entrepreneur is the sampling unit for this research. Data about entrepreneurship was collected through the method of case study supported by in-depth personal interview of the entrepreneurs. The interviews were supported by an interview guide and an interview schedule. Both the interview guide and the interview schedule were kept flexible; this permitted me to bring any necessary modification as necessitated by the situation. The interview guide was used for collecting data about the various aspects related to the process of business development as experienced by the entrepreneur. The interview schedule was utilized for collecting data about the socio-cultural background and family background of the entrepreneurs, and about the profile of their enterprises.

The data that was collected for current research was not in any way sensitive in nature. However, it was felt that maintaining confidentiality would improve the quality of the data. With this consideration in mind, entrepreneurs were informed during the interview that their names, names of their enterprises as well as names of other organizations or individuals mentioned by them would not be disclosed. Having made this commitment, pseudonyms were created for all the names available in the data. Only these pseudonyms have been used while writing the book. Processing and analysis of data took place immediately after collecting data. After conducting the interview, the voice recording of the interview was transcribed verbatim as early as possible. Data collected with the help of the interview guide was processed using ATLASti software. Data collected using the interview schedule was processed using Microsoft Access software. In Microsoft Access, data about entrepreneurs' educational qualification, employment career, and family background was organized separately. Similarly, data about clients of enterprises and their office locations were arranged. All the data were interconnected by generating a unique number for each entrepreneur and the enterprise founded by her/him. For analysing data processed through ATLASti, thematic codes were generated keeping the research objectives in mind and quotation of entrepreneurs were classified under these codes. For the purpose of reaching precision in analysis, same quotations were often classified under multiple codes. Other than conducting within-case analysis, cross-case analysis was conducted by using the thematic codes. For writing on each topic, quotations under multiple codes were utilized.

This book has been thematically organized into six chapters. The current chapter titled 'Introduction: Business Venture and Social Capital' develops the research problem by exploring the literature in various relevant areas and discusses the methodology that has been adopted for addressing it. Chapter Two titled 'The Industry and its Enterprises' attempts to understand the nature and development of information and communication technology industry. It also reflects on the business operation of different enterprises included in this study. Chapter Three titled 'The ICT Entrepreneurs' attempts to capture the nature of entrepreneurship in information and communication technology industry. In doing so, the chapter attempts to identify the poster boys (there aren't any poster girls in this industry in India!) among the ICT entrepreneurs by analysing the media reports about them. The chapter uses the media reports about the luminaries and my dialogues with the 'lesser known' to understand the range that exists in the profile of ICT entrepreneurs in India. Chapter Four titled 'Customers, Business Development, and Social Capital' explores the process of business development and the role of social capital in it. Chapter Five titled ' "Business Ecosystem" and Social Capital' examines the various necessities of business development with special reference to social capital. Sixth and the last chapter titled 'Relationships as Resource' attempts to assess and conclude how significant social capital is as an entrepreneurial resource.

Notes

1. Content of this section was published earlier in Sengupta (2010).
2. Content of this section was published earlier in Sengupta (2010).
3. Content of this section was published earlier in Sengupta (2010).
4. Content of this section was published earlier in Sengupta (2011).

References

Acquaah, M. (2007). Managerial social capital, strategic orientation, and organizational performance in an emerging economy. *Strategic Management Journal*, 28(12), 1235–1255.

Adobor, H. (2006). The role of personal relationships in inter-firm alliances: Benefits, dysfunctions, and some suggestions. *Business Horizons*, 49(6), 473–486.

Aldrich, H., Reese, P.R. and Dubini, P. (1989). Women on the verge of a breakthrough: Networking among entrepreneurs in the United States and Italy. *Entrepreneurship and Regional Development*, 1(4), 339–356.

Anderson, A., Park, J. and Jack, S. (2007). Entrepreneurial social capital: Conceptualizing social capital in new high-tech firms. *International Small Business Journal*, 25(3), 245–272.

Anderson, A.R. and Jack, S.L. (2002). The articulation of social capital in entrepreneurial networks: A glue or a lubricant. *Entrepreneurship and Regional Development*, 14(3), 193–210.

Anderson, A.R., Jack, S.L. and Dodd, S.D. (2005). The role of family members in entrepreneurial networks: Beyond the boundaries of the family firm. *Family Business Review*, XVIII(2), 135–154.

Andreosso-O'Callaghan, B. and Lenihan, H. (2008). Networking: a question of firm characteristics? The case of the Shannon region in Ireland. *Entrepreneurship and Regional Development*, 20(6), 561–580.

Antoci, A., Sacco, P.L. and Vanin, P. (2007). Social capital accumulation and the evolution of social participation. *Journal of Socio-Economics*, 36(1), 128–143.

Arenius, P. and Clercq, D.D. (2005). A network-based approach on opportunity recognition. *Small Business Economics*, 24(3), 249–265.

Bammens, Y. and Collewaert, V. (2012). Trust between entrepreneurs and angel investors: Exploring positive and negative implications for venture performance assessments. *Journal of Management*. Retrieved 17 August 2013, from http://jom.sagepub.com/content/early/2012/11/06/0149 206312463937.full.pdf+html.

Bandiera, O. and Rasul, I. (2006). Social networks and technology adoption in northern Mozambique. *The Economic Journal*, 116(514), 869–902.

BangaloreIT. (n.d.). Index of BangaloreIT. *BangaloreIT*. <http://www.bangaloreitevent.in/index.php? option=com_content&task=view&id =76&Itemid=81> retrieved 31 December 2008.

BarNir, A. and Smith, K.A. (2002). Interfirm alliances in the small business: The role of social networks. *Journal of Small Business Management*, 40(3), 219–232.

Baron, R.A. and Markman, G.D. (2003). Beyond social capital: The role of entrepreneurs' social competence in their financial success. *Journal of Business Venturing*, 18(1), 41–60.

Batjargal, B. (2003). Social capital and entrepreneurial performance in Russia: A longitudinal study. *Organization Studies*, 24 (4), 535–556.

Batjargal, B. (2006). The dynamics of entrepreneurs' networks in a transitioning economy: The case of Russia. *Entrepreneurship and Regional Development*, 18 (4), 305–320.

Batjargal, B. (2007). Comparative social capital: Networks of entrepreneurs and venture capitalists in China and Russia. *Management and Organization Review*, 3(3), 397–419.

Becker-Blease, J.R. and Sohl, J.E. (2007). Do women-owned businesses have equal access to angel capital? *Journal of Business Venturing*, 22(4), 503–521.

Binks, M.R. and Ennew, C.T. (1997). Smaller businesses and relationship banking: The impact of participative behaviour. *Entrepreneurship Theory and Practice*, 21(4), 83–92.

Birley, S., Cromie, S. and Myers, A. (1991). Entrepreneurial networks: Their emergence in Ireland and overseas. *International Small Business Journal*, 9(4), 56–74.

Bista, S.K., Dahal, K., Cowling, P., and Tuladhar, B.M. (2010). Acquaintance-based trust model for the evolution of cooperation in business games. *Service Oriented Computing and Applications*, 4(3), 181–189.

Blanchflower, D.G. and Oswald, A.J. (1998). What makes an entrepreneur? *Journal of Labour Economics*, 16(1), 26–60.

Bönte, W. (2008). Inter-firm trust in buyer-supplier relations: Are knowledge spillovers and geographical proximity relevant? *Journal of Economic Behavior and Organization*, 67(3–4), 855–870.

Borch, O.J. and Huse, M. (1993). Informal strategic networks and the board of directors. *Entrepreneurship Theory and Practice*, 18(1), 23–36.

Bourdieu, P. (1997). The forms of capital. In A.H. Halsey, H. Lauder, P. Brown, and A.S. Wells (eds), *Education: Culture, economy and society*. Oxford: Oxford University Press, 46–58.

Bowey, J.L. and Easton, G. (2007). Entrepreneurial social capital unplugged: An activity-based analysis. *International Small Business Journal*, 25(3), 273–306.

Bowles, L.R. (2013). Transnational mobility, social capital, and cosmopolitan women traders in Ghana. *African and Black Diaspora: An International Journal*, 6(2), 208–2017.

Brown, B. and Butler, J.E. (1993). Networks and entrepreneurial development: the shadow of borders. *Entrepreneurship and Regional Development*, 5(2), 101–116.

Brown, B. and Butler, J.E. (1995). Competitors as allies: A study of entrepreneurial networks in the US wine industry. *Journal of Small Business Management*, 33(3), 57–66.

Brüderl, J. and Preisendörfer, P. (1998). Network support and the success of newly founded businesses. *Small Business Economics*, 10(3), 213–225.

Brunetto, Y. and Farr-Wharton, R. (2007). The moderating role of trust in SME owner/managers' decision-making about collaboration. *Journal of Small Business Management*, 45(3), 362–387.

Bryant, A. and Charmaz, K. (2010). *The Sage handbook of grounded theory*. London: Sage Publications.

Bryson, J., Wood, P. and Keeble, D. (1993). Business networks, small firm flexibility and regional development in UK business services. *Entrepreneurship and Regional Development*, 5(3), 265–277.

Burt, R.S. (1992). *Structural holes: the social structure of competition*. Cambridge, Mass: Harvard University Press.

Burt, R.S. (1997). The contingent value of social capital. *Administrative Science Quarterly*, 42(2), 339–365.

Burt, R.S. (2000). The network entrepreneur. In R. Swedberg (ed.), *Entrepreneurship: The Social Science View*. New Delhi: Oxford University Press, 281–307.

Butler, J.E. and Hansen, G.S. (1991). Network evolution, entrepreneurial success, and regional development. *Entrepreneurship and Regional Development*, 3(1), 1–15.

Bygrave, W.D. and Hofer, C.W. (1991). Theorizing about entrepreneurship. *Entrepreneurship: Theory and Practice*, 16(2), 13–22.

Capaldo, A. (2007). Network structure and innovation: The leveraging of a dual network as a distinctive relational capability. *Strategic Management Journal*, 28(6), 585–608.

Carbonell, J.R., Hernandez, J.C.P., and Gracía, F.J.L. (2011). Business creation by immigrant entrepreneurs in the Valencian community: The influence of education. *International Entrepreneurship and Management Journal* (online first). <http://link.springer.com/ article/ 10.1007/s11365-011-0211-2#> retrieved on 19 July 2013.

Carland, J.W., Hoy, F., Boulton, W.R. and Carland, J.A.C. (1984). Differentiating entrepreneurs from small business owners: A conceptualization. *Academy of Management Review*, 9 (2), 354–359.

Carneiro, L.M., Soares, A.L., Patricio, R., Azevedo, A.L., and Sousa, J.P.D. (2013). Case studies on collaboration, technology, and performance factors in business networks. *International Journal of Computer Integrated Manufacturing*, 26(1 and 2), 101–116.

Casson, M. and Giusta, M.D. (2007). Entrepreneurship and social capital: Analysing the impact of social networks on entrepreneurial activity from a rational action perspective. *International Small Business Journal*, 25(3), 220–244.

Caulkins, D.D. (2004). Organizational memberships and crosscutting ties: Bonding or bridging social capital? In S. Prakash, and P. Selle (eds),

Investigating social capital: comparative perspectives on civil society participation and governance, New Delhi: Sage, 162–183.

Caulkins, D.D. and Peters, C. (2002). Grid-group analysis, social capital, and entrepreneurship among North American ethnic groups. *Cross-Cultural Research*, 36(1), 48–72.

Chan, B. (2008). Demystifying Chinese *guanxi* networks: Cultivating and sharing of knowledge for business benefit. *Business Information Review*, 25(3), 183–189.

Chang, E.P.C., Memili, E., Chrisman, J.J., Kellermanns, F.W., and Chua, J.H. (2009). Family social capital, venture preparedness, and start-up decisions: A study of Hispanic entrepreneurs in New England. *Family Business Review*, 22(3), 279–292.

Chell, E. and Baines, S. (2000). Networking, entrepreneurship and micro-business behaviour. *Entrepreneurship and Regional Development*, 12(3), 195–215.

Chirwa, E.W. (2008). Effects of gender on the performance of micro and small enterprises in Malawi. *Development Southern Africa*, 25(3), 347–362.

Chou, L-F., Cheng, B-S., Huang, M-P. and Cheng, H-Y. (2006). *Guanxi* networks and members effectiveness in Chinese work teams: Mediating effects of trust networks. *Asian Journal of Social Psychology*, 9(2), 79–95.

Chou, Y.K. (2006). Three simple models of social capital and economic growth. *The Journal of Socio-Economics*, 35 (5), 889–912.

Cohen, S.S. and Fields, G. (1999). Social capital and capital gains in Silicon Valley. *California Management Review*, 41(2), 108–130.

Coleman, J.S. (1988). Social capital in the creation of human capital. *American Journal of Sociology*, 94 (Supplement), S95-S120.

Coleman, J.S. (1994). *Foundations of social theory*. Cambridge: The Belknap Press of Harvard University Press.

Collewaert, V., Manigart, S., and Aernoudt, R. (2010). Assessment of government funding of business angel networks in Flanders. *Regional Studies*, 44(1), 119–130.

Cooke, P. (1996). The new wave of regional innovation networks: Analysis, characteristics and strategy. *Small Business Economics*, 8(2), 159–171.

Cooke, P. and Wills, D. (1999). Small firms, social capital and the enhancement of business performance through innovation programmes. *Small Business Economics*, 13(3), 219–234.

Cooper, A.C. (2002). Networks, alliances, and entrepreneurship. In A.M. Hitt, R.D. Ireland, S.M. Camp, and D. Sexton (eds), *Strategic enterprise: Creating a new mindset*. UK: Blackwell Publishers, 203–222.

Cope, J., Jack, S. and Rose, M.B. (2007). Social capital and entrepreneurship: An introduction. *International Small Business Journal*, 25(3), 213–219.

Corbin, J. and Strauss, A. (2008). *Basics of qualitative research: techniques and procedures of developing grounded theory*. Thousand Oaks, California: Sage Publications.

Coviello, N.E. and Cox, M.P. (2007). The resource dynamics of international new venture networks. *Journal of International Entrepreneurship*, 4(2–3), 113–132.

Cromie, S. and Birley, S. (1992). Networking by female business owners in Northern Ireland. *Journal of Business Venturing*, 7(3), 237–251.

Curran, J., Jarvis, R., Blackburn, R.A. and Black, S. (1993). Networks and small firms: Constructs, methodological strategies and some findings. *International Small Business Journal*, 11(2), 13–25.

Dallalfar, A. (1994). Iranian women as immigrant entrepreneurs. *Gender and Society*, 8(4), 541–561.

Dasgupta, P. (1988). Trust as a commodity. In D. Gambetta (ed.), *Trust: Making and breaking cooperative relations* (pp. 49–72). New York, USA: Basil Blackwell Inc.

Dasgupta, P. (2003). Social capital and economic performance: Analytics. In E. Ostrom, and T.K. Ahn (eds), *Foundations of social capital* (pp. 309–339). Cheltenham: Edward Elgar Publishing Limited/Inc.

Davidsson, P. and Honig, B. (2003). The role of social and human capital among nascent entrepreneurs. *Journal of Business Venturing*, 18(3), 301–331.

Deakins, D. and Philpott, T. (1995). Networking by external support agencies and financial institutions: Evidence from different financing arrangements in two European regions: West Midlands, UK and Baden-Württemberg, Germany. *International Small Business Journal*, 13(2), 47–58.

Deakins, D., Ishaq, M., Smallbone, D., Whittam, G. and Wyper, J. (2007). Ethnic minority businesses in Scotland and the role of social capital. *International Small Business Journal*, 25(3), 307–326.

Dekker, P. (2004). Social capital of individuals: Relational asset or personal quality? In S. Prakash, and P. Selle (eds) (pp. 88–110).

Diani, M. (2004). How associations matter: An empirical assessment of the social capital-trust-voluntary action link. In S. Prakash, and P. Selle (eds) (pp. 137–161).

Dibben, M.R. (2000). *Exploring interpersonal trust in the entrepreneurial venture*. Hampshire: Macmillan Press Ltd.

Dicken, P. (2000). A new geo-economy. In D. Held and A. McGrew (eds), *The global transformations reader: An introduction to the globalization debate*. Cambridge: Polity Press, 251–258.

Ding, Q. and Akoorie, M.E.M. (2009). Constructing global business networks in China. *Journal of East-West Business*, 15(3 and 4), 295–315.

Dodd, S.D. (1997). Social network membership and activity rates: Some comparative data. *International Small Business Journal*, 15(4), 80–87.

Dodd, S.D., Jack, S. and Anderson, A.R. (2002). Scottish entrepreneurial networks in the international context. *International Small Business Journal*, 20(2), 213–219.

Donckels, R. and Lambrecht, J. (1995). Networks and small business growth: An explanatory model. *Small Business Economics*, 7(4), 273–289.

Droege, S.B., Anderson, J.R. and Bowler, M. (2003). Trust and organizational information flow. *Journal of Business and Management*, 9(1), 45–59.

Drucker, P. F. (1991). *Innovation and entrepreneurship: Practice and principles*. New Delhi: Affiliated East West Press Pvt. Ltd.

Dyer, J.H. and Hatch, N.W. (2006). Relation-specific capabilities and barriers to knowledge transfers: Creating advantage through network relationships. *Strategic Management Journal*, 27(8), 701–719.

Egbert, H. (2006). Cross-border small-scale trading in south-eastern Europe: Do embeddedness and social capital explain enough? *International Journal of Urban and Regional Research*, 30(2), 346–361.

Egbert, H. (2009). Business success through social networks? A comment on social networks and business success. *American Journal of Economics and Sociology*, 68(3), 665–677.

Egeraat, C.V. and Curran, D. (2013). Social networks and actual knowledge flow in the Irish biotech industry. *European Planning Studies*. <http://www.tandfonline.com/doi/pdf/10.1080/09654313.2012.761746> 7 October 2013.

Elango, B. and Pattnaik, C. (2007). Building capabilities for international operations through networks: A study of Indian firms. *Journal of International Business Studies*, 38(4), 541–555.

Elfring, T. and Hulsink, W. (2007). Networking by entrepreneurs: patterns of tie-formation in emerging organizations. *Organization Studies*, 28(12), 1849–1872.

Eraydin, A. and Armatli-Köroglu, B. (2005). Innovation, networking and the new industrial clusters: The characteristics of networks and local innovation capabilities in the Turkish industrial clusters. *Entrepreneurship and Regional Development*, 17(4), 237–266.

Fairlie, R.W. and Robb, A.M. (2009). Gender differences in business performance: Evidence from the characteristics of business owners survey. *Small Business Economics*, 33(4), 375–395.

Fiet, J.O. (1995). Reliance upon informants in the venture capital industry. *Journal of Business Venturing*, 10(3), 195–223.

Fowler, S.W., Lawrence, T.B. and Morse, E.A. (2004). Virtually embedded ties. *Journal of Management*, 30(5), 647–666.

Francis, D.H. and Sandberg, W.R. (2000). Friendship within entrepreneurial teams and its association with team and venture performance. *Entrepreneurship Theory and Practice*, 25(2), 5–25.

Frazier, B.J. and Niehm, L.S. (2004). Exploring business information networks of small retailers in rural communities. *Journal of Development Entrepreneurship*, 9(1), 23–42.

Fukuyama, F. (1996). *Trust: The social virtues and the creation of prosperity*. London: Penguin Books.

Fukuyama, F. (2000). *Social capital and civil society*. International Monetary Fund Working Paper, WP/00/74, 1–18.

Gambetta, D. (1988). Can we trust trust? In D. Gambetta (ed.), *Trust: Making breaking cooperative relations* (pp. 213–237). New York: Basil Blackwell.

Gathenya, J.W., Bwisa, H.M. and Kihoro, J.M. (2011). Interaction between women entrepreneur's age and education on business dynamics in small and medium enterprises in Kenya. *International Journal of Business and Social Science*, 2(15), 265–272.

Glaser, B.G. and Strauss, A.L. (1970). The discovery of grounded theory (Excerpts from a book of the same title written by the authors). In P. Worsley (ed.), *Modern sociology: Introductory readings*. Harmond sworth, England: Penguin, 34–37.

Goel, S. and Karri, R. (2006). Entrepreneurs, effectual logic, and over-trust. *Entrepreneurship Theory and Practice*, 30(4), 477–493.

Gold, S.J. (1994). Patterns of economic cooperation among Israeli immigrants in Los Angeles. *International Migration Review*, 28(1), 114–135.

Goto, K. (2013). Social networks, informal trade credit and its effects on business growth: Evidence from the local garment trade in Vietnam. *Journal of the Asia Pacific Economy*, 18(3), 382–395.

Grandi, A. and Grimaldi, R. (2003). Exploring the networking characteristics of new venture founding teams. *Small Business Economics*, 21(4), 329–341.

Granovetter, M. (1985). Economic action and social structure: The problem of embeddedness. *American Journal of Sociology*, 91(3), 481–510.

Granovetter, M.S. (1973). The strength of weak ties. *American Journal of Sociology*, 78(6), 1360–1380.

Grätz, T. (2004). Gold trading networks and the creation of trust: A case study from northern Benin. *Africa*, 74(2), 146–172.

Greiner, B., Ockenfels, A. and Werner, P. (2007). The dynamic interplay of inequality and trust—An experimental study. *HBS Working Knowledge*. <http://hbswk.hbs.edu/item/ 5807.html.> retrieved 7 October 2013.

Greve, A. and Salaff, J.W. (2003). Social networks and entrepreneurship. *Entrepreneurship: Theory and Practice*, 28(1), 1–22.

Grossman, E.B., Yli-Renko, H. and Janakiraman, R. (2012). Resource search, interpersonal similarity, and network tie valuation in nascent entrepreneurs' emerging networks. *Journal of Management*, 38(6), 1760–87.

Grugulis, I. and Stoyanova, D. (2012). Social capital and networks in film and TV: Jobs for the boys? *Organization Studies*, 33(10), 1311–1331.

Håkansson, H. and Johanson, J. (1988). Formal and informal cooperation strategies in international industrial networks. In F.J. Contractor and P. Lorange (eds), *Cooperative strategies in international business: Joint ventures and technology partnership between firms.* Toronto: D.C. Heath and Company, 369–379.

Han, M. (2007). Developing social capital to achieve superior internationalization: A conceptual model. *Journal of International Entrepreneurship*, 4(2–3), 99–112.

Hancké, B. (1998). Trust or hierarchy? Changing relationships between large and small firms in France. *Small Business Economics*, 11(3), 237–252.

Hara, G. and Kanai, T. (1994). Entrepreneurial networks across oceans to promote international strategic alliances for small businesses. *Journal of Business Venturing*, 9(6), 489–507.

Harrison, R.T., Dibben, M.R. and Mason, C.M. (1997). The role of trust in the informal investor's investment decision: An exploratory analysis. *Entrepreneurship Theory and Practice*, 21(4), 63–81.

Harriss, J. (2002). *On trust, and trust in Indian business: Ethnographic explorations*. Development Studies Institute Working Paper Series, No. 02–35. London: Development Studies Institute, London School of Economics and Political Science.

Harriss, J. (2003). Widening the radius of trust: Ethnographic explorations of trust and Indian business. *Journal of the Royal Anthropological Society*, 9(4), 755–773.

Havnes, P-A. and Senneseth, K. (2001). A panel study of firm growth among SMEs in networks. *Small Business Economics*, 16(4), 293–302.

Heeks, R. (1996). *India's Software Industry: State Policy, Liberalisation and Industrial Development*. New Delhi: Sage Publications.

Heilbrunn, S. and Davidovitch, L. (2011). Juggling family and business: Work-family conflict of women entrepreneurs in Israel. *Journal of Entreprenuership*, 20(1), 127–141.

Held, D., McGrew, A., Goldblatt, D. and Perraton, J. (1999). *Global transformations: Politics, economics and culture*. Cambridge: Polity Press.

Hisrich, R.D. and Peters, M.P. (1995). Entrepreneurship: Starting, developing and managing a new enterprise. Chicago: Irwin.

Hoang, H. and Antoncic, B. (2003). Network-based research in entrepreneurship: A critical review. *Journal of Business Venturing*, 18(2), 165–187.

Honig, B. (1998). What determines success? Examining the human, financial, and social capital of Jamaican microentrepreneurs. *Journal of Business Venturing*, 13(5), 371–394.

Howorth, C. and Moro, A. (2006). Trust within entrepreneur bank relationships: Insights from Italy. *Entrepreneurship Theory and Practice*, 30(4), 495–517.

Huggins, R., Johnston, A. and Thompson, P. (2012). Network capital, social capital, and knowledge flow: How the nature of interorganizational networks impacts on innovation. *Industry and Innovation*, 19(3), 203–232.

Hung, H. (2006). Formation and survival of new ventures: A path from interpersonal to interorganizational networks. *International Small Business Journal*, 24(4), 359–378.

India Infoline. (n.d.). Venture Capital. *India Infoline*. <http://www.indiainfoline.com/bisc/veca/ch01.html.> retrieved 12 May 2006.

Jenssen, J.I. and Koenig, H.F. (2002). The effect of social networks on resource access and business start-ups. *European Planning Studies*, 10(8), 1039–1046.

Johannisson, B. (1986). Network strategies: Management technology for entrepreneurship and change. *International Small Business Journal*, 5(1), 19–30.

Johannisson, B. (1998). Personal networks in emerging knowledge-based firms: Spatial and functional patterns. *Entrepreneurship and Regional Development*, 10(4), 297–312.

Johannisson, B. (2000). Networking and entrepreneurial growth. In D.L. Sexton and H. Landström (eds), *The Blackwell handbook of entrepreneurship*. Oxford, UK: Blackwell Publishers Ltd., 368–386.

Johannisson, B., Alexanderson, O., Nowicki, K. and Senneseth, K. (1994). Beyond anarchy and organization: Entrepreneurs in contextual networks. *Entrepreneurship and Regional Development*, 6(4), 329–356.

Johnston, W.J., Peters, L.D. and Gassenheimer, J. (2006). Questions about network dynamics: Characteristics, structures, and interactions. *Journal of Business Research*, 59(8), 945–954.

Jones, O. and Jayawarna, D. (2010). Resourcing new businesses: Social networks, bootstrapping and firm performance. *Venture Capital*, 12(2), 127–152.

Julien, P. (1998). *The state of art in small business and entrepreneurship*. Hampshire: Ashgate Publishing Company.

Julien, P., Andriambeloson, E. and Ramangalahy, C. (2004). Networks, weak signals and technological innovations among SMEs in the land-based transportation equipment sector. *Entrepreneurship and Regional Development*, 16(4), 251–269.

Kasper-Fuehrer, E.C. and Ashkanasy, N.M. (2001). Communicating trustworthiness and building trust in interorganizational virtual organizations. *Journal of Management*, 27(3), 235–254.

Katz, J.A. and Williams, P.M. (1997). Gender, self-employment and weak-tie networking through formal organizations. *Entrepreneurship and Regional Development*, 9(3), 183–197.

Kauffman, R.J., Li, T. and Heck, E.V. (2010). Business network-based value creation in electronic commerce. *International Journal of Electronic Commerce*, 15(1), 113–143.

Keeble, D., Lawson, C., Smith, H.L., Moore, B. and Wilkinson, F. (1998). Internationalization processes, networking and local embeddedness in technology-intensive small firms. *Small Business Economics*, 11(4), 327–342.

Khan, S.R. (2006). Learning from South Asian 'successes': Tapping social capital. *South Asia Economic Journal*, 7(2), 157–178.

Kieser, A. (2001). Trust as a change agent for capitalism or as ideology? A commentary. *Organization Science*, 12(2), 241–246.

Kingsley, G. and Malecki, E.J. (2004). Networking for competitiveness. *Small Business Economics*, 23(1), 71–84.

Klyver, K. and Foley, D. (2012). Networking and culture in entrepreneurship. *Entrepreneurship and Regional Development*, 24(7–8), 561–588.

Knack, S. and Keefer, P. (1997). Does social capital have an economic payoff? A cross-country investigation. *Quarterly Journal of Economics*, 112(4), 1251–88.

Knyphausen-Aufseß, D.Z. and Westphal, R. (2008). Do business angel networks deliver value to business angels? *Venture Capital*, 10(2), 149–169.

Krishna, A. (2003). *Active social capital: Tracing the roots of development and democracy*. New Delhi: Oxford University Press.

Krishna, A. (2004). Putting social capital to work: Agency and development. In S. Prakash, and P. Selle (eds) *Investigating social capital.* London: Sage, 207–231.

Kristiansen, S., Kimeme, J., Mbwambo, A. and Wahid F. (2005). Information flows and adaptation in Tanzanian cottage industries. *Entrepreneurship and Regional Development*, 17(5), 365–388.

Kriz, A. and Keating, B. (2010). Business relationships in China: Lessons about deep trust. *Asia Pacific Business Review*, 16(3), 299–318.

Kuada, J. (2009). Gender, social networks, and entrepreneurship in Ghana. *Journal of African Business*, 10(1), 85–103.

Kuhnen, C.M. (2009). Business networks, corporate governance, and contracting in the mutual fund industry. *The Journal of Finance*, LXIV(5), 2185–2220.

LaChapelle, K. and Barnes, L.B. (1998). The trust catalyst in family-owned businesses. *Family Business Review*, XI(1), 1–17.

Lane, C. and Bachmann, R. (Eds) (1998). *Trust within and between organizations: Conceptual issues and empirical applications*. Oxford: Oxford University Press.

Lapavitsas, C. (2007). Information and trust as social aspects of credit. *Economy and Society*, 36(3), 416–436.

Larson, A. (1991). Partner networks: Leveraging external ties to improve entrepreneurial performance. *Journal of Business Venturing*, 6(3), 173–188.

Lateef, A. (1997). Linking up with the global economy: A case study of the Bangalore software industry (Discussion Paper). Geneva: International Institute for Labour Studies.

Leana, C.R., and Buren III, H.J. (1999). Organizational social capital and employment practices. *The Academy of Management Review*, 24(3), 538–555.

Leick, B. (2011). Barriers to cooperation and competitive advantage: Cross-border business networks of Saxon and Northern Bohemian firms. *Journal of East European Management Studies*, 16(2), 162–184.

Leung, A., Zhang, J., Wong, P.K. and Foo, M.D. (2006). The use of networks in human resource acquisition for entrepreneurial firms: Multiple 'fit' considerations. *Journal of Business Venturing*, 21(5), 664–686.

Lewis, J.D. and Weigert, A. (1985). Trust as a social reality. *Social Forces*, 63(4), 967–985.

Li, P.P. (2007a). Social tie, social capital, and social behavior: Toward an integrative model of informal exchange. *Asia Pacific Journal of Management*, 24(2), 227–246.

Li, P.P. (2007b). Towards an interdisciplinary conceptualization of trust: A typological approach. *Management and Organization Review*, 3(3), 421–445.

Light, I., Bernard, R.B. and Kim, R. (1999). Immigrant incorporation in the garment industry of Los Angeles. *International Migration Review*, 33(1), 5–25.

Lim, K. and Cu, B. (2012). The effects of social networks and contractual characteristics on the relationship between venture capitalists and entrepreneurs. *Asia Pacific Journal of Management*, 29(3), 573–596.

Lin, N. (2003). *Social capital: A theory of social structure and action*. Cambridge: University of Cambridge.

Lipparini, A. and Sobrero, M. (1994). The glue and the pieces: Entrepreneurship and innovation in small-firm networks.

Littunen, H. (2000). Networks and local environmental characteristics in the survival of new firms. *Small Business Economics*, 15(1), 59–71.

Liu, Y., Woywode, M., and Xing, Y. (2012). High technology start-up innovation and the role of *guanxi*: An explorative study in China from an institutional perspective. *Prometheus*, 30(2), 211–229.

Lorentzen, A. (2008). Knowledge networks in local and global space. *Entrepreneurship and Regional Development*, 20(6), 533–545.

Loscocco, K., Monnat, S.M., Moore, G. and Lauber, K.B. (2009). Enterprising women: A comparison of women's and men's small business networks. *Gender and Society*, 23(3), 388–411.

Luhman, N. (1988). Familiarity, confidence, trust: Problems, and alternatives. In D. Gambetta (ed.), *Trust: Making breaking cooperative relations* (pp. 94–107). New York: Basil Blackwell.

Luo, J.D. (1997). The significance of networks in the initiation of small businesses in Taiwan. *Sociological Forum*, 12(2), 297–317.

Macke, J., Vallejos, R.V., Faccin, K. and Genari, D. (2013). Social capital in collaborative networks competitiveness: The case of the Brazilian wine industry cluster. *International Journal of Computer Integrated Manufacturing*, 26 (1–2), 117–124.

Mackinnon, D., Chapman, K. and Cumbers, A. (2004). Networking, trust and embeddedness amongst SMEs in the Aberdeen oil complex. *Entrepreneurship and Regional Development*, 16(2), 87–106.

MacLeod, W.B. (2007). Reputations, relationships, and contract enforcement. *Journal of Economic Literature*, 45(3), 595–628.

Mainela, T. and Puhakka, V. (2008). Embeddedness and networking as drivers in developing an international joint venture. *Scandinavian Journal of Management*, 24(1), 17–32.

Marcuello-Servós, C. 2007. Networks, trust and social capital: Theoretical and empirical investigations from Europe. *International Sociology*, 22(2), 200–202.

Marger, M.N. (2001). The use of social and human capital among Canadian business immigrants. *Journal of Ethnic and Migration Studies*, 27(3), 439–453.

Maurer, I. and Ebers, M. (2006). Dynamics of social capital and their performance implications: Lessons from Biotechnology start-ups. *Administrative Science Quarterly*, 51(2), 262–292.

McClelland, D.C. (1961). *The achieving society*. New York: D. Van Nostrand Company.

Meccheri, N. and Pelloni, G. (2006). Rural entrepreneurs and institutional assistance: An empirical study from mountainous Italy. *Entrepreneurship and Regional Development*, 18(5), 371–392.

Mellahi, K. and Wood, G.T. (2003). From kinship to trust: Changing recruitment practices in unstable political contexts. *International Journal of Cross Cultural Management*, 3(3), 369–381.

Menning, G. (1997). Trust, entrepreneurship and development in Surat city, India. *Ethnos*, 62(1–2), 59–90.

Menzani, T. and Zamagni, V. (2010). Cooperative networks in the Italian economy. *Enterprise and Society*, 11(1), 98–127.

Miranda, R. And Klement, J. (2009). Authentic trust in modern business. *Journal of Wealth Management*, 11(4), 29–47.

Moensted, M. (2007). Strategic networking in small high tech firms. *International Entrepreneurship and Management Journal*, 3(1), 15–27.

Morgan, R.M. and Hunt, S.D. (1994). The commitment-trust theory of relationship marketing. *Journal of Marketing*, 58(3), 20–38.

Nahapiet, J. and Ghosal, S. (1998). Social capital, intellectual capital, and the organizational advantage. *The Academy of Management Review*, 23(2), 242–266.

Nanda, R. and Khanna, T. (2007). *Diasporas and domestic entrepreneurs: Evidence from the Indian software industry* (Working paper No. 08–003). Harvard: Harvard University Press.

Neace, M.B. (1999). Entrepreneurs in emerging economies: Creating trust, social capital and civil society. *Annals of American Academy of Political and Social Science*, Vol. 565 (September) (Civil Society and Democratization), 148–161.

Neergaard, H. (2005). Networking activities in technology-based entrepreneurial teams. *International Small Business Journal*, 23(3), 257–276.

Neergaard, H. and Ulhøi, J.P. (2006). Government agency and trust in the formation and transformation of interorganizational entrepreneurial networks. *Entrepreneurship Theory and Practice*, 30(4), 519–539.

Neff, G. (2005). The changing place of cultural production: The location of social networks in a digital media industry. *Annals of American Academy of Political and Social Science*, 597, 134–152.

Nicolaou, N. and Birley, S. (2003). Academic networks in a trichotomous categorisation of university spinouts. *Journal of Business Venturing*, 18(3), 333–359.

Nuissl, H. (2005). Trust in a 'post-socialist region': A study of east German ICT entrepreneurs' willingness to trust each other. *European Urban and Regional Studies*, 12(1), 65–81.

Oakey, R.P. (1993). Predatory networking: The role of small firms in the development of the British biotechnology industry. *International Small Business Journal*, 11(4), 9–22.

Oba, B. and Cioz, F.S. (2005). Antecedents of trust in industrial districts: An empirical analysis of inter-firm relations in a Turkish industrial district. *Entrepreneurship and Regional Development*, 17(3), 163–182.

Ojha, A.K. (2002). 'Trust' as a foundation for strategic alliances in global software outsourcing. *Vikalpa*, 27(2), 3–12.

Ostgaard, T.A. and Birley, S. (1994). Personal networks and firms competitive strategy – A strategic or coincidental match? *Journal of Business Venturing*, 9(4), 281–305.

Özcan, G.B. (1995) Small business networks and local ties in Turkey. *Entreprenuership and Regional Development*, 7(3), 265–282.

Paché, G. (1990). The role of small business in the development of network organization: The case of France. *International Small Business Journal*, 8(4), 71–76.

Patzelt, H. and Shepherd, D.A. (2008). The decision to persist with underperforming alliances: The role of trust and control. *Journal of Management Studies*, 45(7), 1217–1243.

Pennings, J.M., Lee, K. and Witteloostuijn, A. (1998). Human capital, social capital, and firm dissolution. *The Academy of Management Journal*, 41(4), 425–440.

Percoco, M. (2012). Entrepreneurship, social capital, and institutions: Evidence from Italy. *Spatial Economic Analysis*, 7(3), 339–355.

Perry, M. (1996). Network intermediaries and their effectiveness. *International Small Business Journal*, 14(4), 72–80.

Prakash, S. and Selle, P. (eds). (2004). *Investigating social capital: Comparative perspectives on civil society, participation and governance*. New Delhi: Sage Publications.

Premaratne, S.P. (2001). Networks, resources, and small business growth: The experience in Sri Lanka. *Journal of Small Business Management*, 39(4), 363–371.

Putnam, R. (1994). *Making democracy work: Civic traditions in modern Italy*. Princeton: Princeton University Press.

Putnam, R.D. (1995). Bowling alone: America's declining social capital. *Journal of Democracy*, 6(1), 65–78.

Ram, M. (1994). Unravelling social networks in ethnic minority firms. *International Small Business Journal*, 12(3), 42–53.

Ramachandran, K. and Ramnarayan, S. (1993). Entrepreneurial orientation and networking: Some Indian evidence. *Journal of Business Venturing*, 8(6), 513–524.

Ramachandran, K. and Ray, S. (2006). Networking and new venture resource strategies: A study of information technology start-ups. *The Journal of Entrepreneurship*, 15(2), 145–168.

Ratanapruck, P. (2007). Kinship and religious practices as institutionalization of trade networks: Manangi trade communities in South and Southeast Asia. *Journal of the Economic and Social History of the Orient*, 50(2), 325–346.

Renzulli, L.A., Aldrich, H. and Moody, J. (2000). Family matters: Gender, network, and entrepreneurial outcomes. *Social Forces*, 79(2), 523–546.

Rindova, V.P., Petkova, A.P. and Kotha, S. (2007). Standing out: How new firms in emerging markets build reputation. *Strategic Organization*, 5(1), 31–70.

Ring, J.K., Peredo, A.M. and Chrisman, J.J. (2010). Business networks and economic development in rural communities in the United States. *Entrepreneurship: Theory and Practice*, 34(1), 171–195.

Roberto, R. (2006). The relationship between economics and sociology: The contribution of economic sociology, setting out from the problem of embeddedness, *International Review of Sociology*, 16(1), 31–48.

Roberts, E.B. (1991). *Entrepreneurs in high technology: Lessons from MIT and beyond*. Oxford: Oxford University Press.

Robinson, S. and Stubberud, H.A. (2009). Sources of advice in entrepreneurship: Gender differences in business owners' social networks. *International Journal of Entrepreneurship*, 13, 83–101.

Robinson, S. and Stubberud, H.A. (2011). Gender differences in entrepreneurs' perceived problems, profits, and plans. *International Journal of Entrepreneurship*,15, 25–44.

Rogers, M. (2004). Networks, firm size and innovation. *Small Business Economics*, 22(2), 141–153.

Roomi, M.A. (2013). Entrepreneurial capital, social values and Islamic traditions: Exploring the growth of women owned enterprises in Pakistan. *International Small Business Journal*, 31(2), 175–191.

Rothstein, B. (2004). Social capital and institutional legitimacy: The Corleone connection. In S. Prakash, and P. Selle (eds) *Investigating social capital*. New Delhi: Sage, 113–136.

Rudolph, S.H. (2004). Is civil society the answer? In S. Prakash and P. Selle (eds) (pp. 64–87).

Rus, A. and Igliè, H. (2005). Trust, governance and performance: The role of institutional and interpersonal trust in SME development. *International Sociology*, 20(3), 371–391.

Salvato, C. and Melin, L. (2008). Creating value across generations in family-controlled businesses: The role of family social capital. *Family Business Review*, XXI(3), 259–276.

Sanders, J.M. and Nee, V. (1996). Immigrant self-employment: The family as social capital and the value of human capital. *American Sociological Review*, 61(2), 231–249.

Sawyerr, O.O., McGee, J. and Peterson, M. (2003). Perceived uncertainty and firm performance in SMEs: The role of personal networking activities. *International Small Business Journal*, 21(3), 269–290.

Saxenian, A.L. (2000). The origins and dynamics of production networks in Silicon Valley. In R. Swedberg (ed.), *Entrepreneurship: The social science view*. New Delhi: Oxford University Press, 308–331.

Schein, E.H.W. (1994). Commentary: What is an entrepreneur. *Entrepreneurship: Theory and Practice*, 19(2), 87–88.

Schumpeter, J. A. (1954). *History of economic analysis*. New York: Oxford University Press.

Schutjens, V. and Stam, E. (2003). The evolution and nature of young firm networks: A longitudinal perspective. *Small Business Economics*, 21(2), 115–134.

Sengupta, A. (2010). Social capital and entrepreneurship: An analysis of methodological issues. *Sociological Bulletin*, 59(3), 323–344.

Sengupta, A. (2011). Network strategy and access to business finance: Indian entrepreneurs in the information and communication technology industry. *Journal of Entrepreneurship*, 20(1), 103–126.

Shamsuzzoha, A., Kankaanpaa, T., Carneiro, L.M., Almeida, R., Chiodi, A. and Fornasiero, R. (2013). Dynamic and collaborative business networks in the fashion industry. *International Journal of Computer Integrated Manufacturing*, 26(1–2), 125–139.

Shane, S. and Cable, D. (2002). Network ties, reputation, and the financing of new ventures. *Management Science*, 48(3), 364–381.

Shaw, B. (1991). Developing technological innovations within networks. *Entrepreneurship and Regional Development*, 3(2), 111–128.

Shaw, E. (2006). Small firm networking: An insight into contents and motivating factors. *International Small Business Journal*, 24(1), 5–27.

Siu, W. and Bao, Q. (2008). Network strategies of small Chinese high-technology firms: A qualitative study. *Journal of Product Innovation Management*, 25(1), 79–102.

Smallbone, D., Ram, M., Deakins, D. and Baldock, R. (2003). Access to finance by ethnic minority businesses in the UK. *International Small Business Journal*, 21(3), 291–312.

Smeltzer, L.R. and Fann, G.L. (1989). Gender differences in external networks of small business owner/managers. *Journal of Small Business Management*, 27(2), 25-32.

Soetanto, D.P. and Jack, S.L. (2013). Business incubators and the networks of technology-based firms. *The Journal of Technology Transfer*, 38(4), 432–453.

Soh, P.H. (2003). The Role of networking alliances in information acquisition and its implications for new product performance. *Journal of Business Venturing*, 18(6), 727–744.

Sorenson, R.L., Folker, C.A. and Brigham, K.H. (2008). The collaborative network orientation: Achieving business success through collaborative relationships. *Entrepreneurship: Theory and Practice*, 32(4), 615–634.

Soto, H.D. (2006). Trust, institutions and entrepreneurship. *International Research in the Business Disciplines*, Vol. 5, 3–19.

Stolle, D. (2004). Communities, social capital and local government: Generalized trust in regional settings. In S. Prakash, and P. Selle (eds) *Investigating social capital*. New Delhi: Sage, 184–206.

STPI Chennai. (n.d.). About STPI Chennai. *STPI Chennai*. Retrieved 18 July 2013, from http://www.chennai.stpi.in/aboutus.htm.

Strätling, R., Wijbenga, F.H. and Dietz, G. (2011). The impact of contracts on trust in entrepreneur–venture capitalist relationships. *International Small Business Journal*, 30(8), 811–831.

Suarez-Villa, L. (1998). The structures of cooperation: Downscaling, outsourcing and the networked alliance. *Small Business Economics*, 10(1), 5–16.

Svendsen, G.L.H. and Svendsen, G.T. (2004). Social capital and entreprneuership. In *The creation and destruction of social capital: Entrepreneurship, cooperative movements and institutions* (pp. 10–45.). Northampton, Mass. Edward Elgar.

Täube, F.A. (2005). Social capital, diversity and (economic) development: Evidence from the Indian IT industry, Bangalore (Paper presented to ISEC/Cornell Conference on Social Science and Development in Karnataka: A Vision for Public Action, Bangalore, June 10–12 2005). <http://www.isec.ac.in/Taeube_ Social_Capital_and_Diversity.pdf.> Retrieved 29 June 2006.

Tello, S., Yang, Y. and Latham, S. (2012) Nascent entrepreneurs access and use of network resources in a technology incubator. *Journal of Small Business and Entrepreneurship*, 25(3), 375–397.

TiE. (n.d. a). About TiE. *TiE*. <http://mumbai.tie.org/chapterHome/about_tie/AboutTiENewMumbai20070730545453 5724/viewOrganizationPagePT.> retrieved 31 December 2008.

TiE. (n.d. b). About TiE Global. *TiE.* <https://www. tie.org/about-tie-global.> Retrieved 18 July 2013.

TiE. (n.d. c). Our Network. *TiE.* <https://www.tie. org/our-network.> Retrieved 18 July 2013.

Tötterman, H. and Sten, J. (2005). Start-ups: Business incubation and social capital. *International Small Business Journal*, 23(5), 487–511.

Troilo, M. and Zhang, J. (2012). *Guanxi* and entrepreneurship in urban China. *Journal of the Asia Pacific Economy*, 17(2), 315–331.

Upadhya, C. (2004). A new transnational capitalist class? Capital flows, business networks and entrepreneurs in the Indian software industry. *Economic and Political Weekly*, 39(48), 5141–5151.

Upadhya, C. and Vasavi, A.R. (2008). Outposts of the global information economy: Work and workers in India's outsourcing industry. In C. Upadhya, and A.R. Vasavi (eds), *In an outpost of the global economy: Work and workers in India's information technology industry.* New Delhi: Routledge, 9–49.

Uzzi, B. (1999). Embeddedness in the making of financial capital: How social relations and networks benefit firms seeking financing. *American Sociological Review*, 64(4), 481–505.

Virkkala, S. (2007). Innovation and networking in peripheral areas: A case study of emergence and change in rural manufacturing. *European Planning Studies*, 15(4), 511–529.

Walker, G. (1988). Network analysis for cooperative interfirm relationships. In F.J. Contractor and P. Lorange (eds), *Cooperative strategies in international business: Joint ventures and technology partnership between firms.* Toronto: D.C. Heath and Company, 227–240.

Walker, G., Kogut, B. and Shan, W. (1997). Social capital, structural holes and the formation of an industry network. *Organization Science*, 8(2), 109–125.

Wang, P. and Watts, A. (2006). Formation of buyer-seller trade networks in a quality-differentiated product market. *Canadian Journal of Economics*, 39(3), 971–1004.

Wank, D.L. (1996). The institutional processes of market clientelism: *Gunaxi* and private business in a South China city. *The China Quarterly*, No. 147, 820–838.

Wasti, S.N. and Wasti, S.A. (2008). Trust in buyer–supplier relations: the case of the Turkish automotive industry. *Journal of International Business Studies*, 39(1), 118–131.

Waters, R. and Smith, H.L. (2008). Social networks in high-technology local economies: The cases of Oxfordshire and Cambridgeshire. *European Urban and Regional Studies*, 15(1), 21–37.

Weber, M. (1966). *The theory of social and economic organization*. tr. A.M. Henderson and T. Parsons. New York: The Free Press, and London: Collier-Macmillan Limited.

Welter, F. (2012). All you need is trust? A critical review of the trust and entrepreneurship literature. *International Small Business Journal*, 30(3), 193–212.

Welter, F. and Smallbone, D. (2006). Exploring the role of trust in entrepreneurial activity. *Entrepreneurship Theory and Practice*, 30(4), 465–475.

Westlund, H. and Bolton, R. (2003). Local social capital and entrepreneurship. *Small Business Economics*, 21(2), 77–113.

Woolcock, M. (1998). Social capital and economic development: Towards a theoretical synthesis and policy framework. *Theory and Society*, 27(2), 151–208.

Woolcock, M. and Narayan, D. (2000). Social capital: Implications for development theory, research, and policy. *The World Bank Research Observer*, 15(2), 225–249.

Wu, L-Y. (2007). Entrepreneurial resources, dynamic capabilities and start-up performance of Taiwan's high-tech firms. *Journal of Business Research*, 60(5), 549–555.

Wu, W. (2008). Dimensions of social capital and firm competitiveness improvement: The mediating role of information sharing. *Journal of Management Studies*, 45(1), 122–146.

Xiao, Z. and Tsui, A.S. (2007). When brokers may not work: The cultural contingency of social capital in Chinese high-tech firms. *Administrative Science Quarterly*, 52(1), 1–31.

Yetim, N. (2008). Social capital in female entrepreneurship. *International Sociology*, 23(6), 864–885.

Yli-Renko, H. and Autio, E. (1998). The network embeddedness of new, technology-based firms: Developing a systemic evolution model. *Small Business Economics*, 11(3), 253–267.

Yoo, J-K. (2000). Utilization of social networks for immigrant entrepreneurship: A case study of Korean immigrants in the Atlanta area. *International Review of Sociology—Revue Internationale de Sociologie*, 10(3), 347–363.

Young, N. (2010). Business networks, collaboration and embeddedness in local and extra-local spaces: The case of Port Hardy, Canada. *Sociologia Ruralis*, 50(4), 392–408.

Zaheer, A., McEvily, B. and Perrone, V. (1998). Does trust matter: Exploring the effect of interorganizational and interpersonal trust on performance. *Organization Science*, 9(2), 141–159.

Zahra, S.A., Yavuz, R.I. and Ucbasaran, D. (2006). How much do you trust me? The dark side of relational trust in new business creation in established companies. *Entrepreneurship Theory and Practice*, 30(4), 541–559.

Zhang, J. and Wong, P-K. (2008). Networks vs. market methods in high-tech venture fundraising: The impact of institutional environment. *Entrepreneurship and Regional Development,* 20(5), 409–430.

Zhao, L. and Aram, J.D. (1995). Networking and growth of young technology-intensive ventures in China. *Journal of Business Venturing,* 10(5), 349–370.

Zhao, X, Frese, M., and Giardini, A. (2010). Business owner's network size and business growth in China: The role of comprehensive social competency. *Entrepreneurship and Regional Development,* 22(7 and 8), 675–705.

2

The Industry and its Enterprises

ICT, as an industry is, in many ways, distinct from other industries existing in India. To some extent this uniqueness is because of the virtual nature of software products and services (ICT hardware industry is almost non-existent in India). The uniqueness is also because of sheer newness of this industry in India (both in terms of technology and business model) that has resulted in the rise of a completely new set of people as entrepreneurs. Given the historical point of time when this industry developed in India necessary fillip also came from the paradigm shifts taking place in policy environment. Given all these dimensions, the relationship that exists between social capital and business in this industry is also in many ways different from that in other industries. Therefore, to comprehend this relationship it is important to understand the history, structure, and operation of ICT industry. While relevant literature is used to understand the development of ICT industry in India, I attempt to understand functioning of this industry by looking into the enterprises purposively selected for this research. These enterprises vary depending on their areas of business operation, nature of clientele, location of business operation, size of the enterprise, and duration of business operation. They also vary depending on the way in which enterprises attempt to build confidence about them in the minds of relevant economic actors like customers, financiers, etc. These variations among the enterprises help us understand their experience in relating social capital to their business.

Genesis and Growth of the ICT Industry in India

After independence, Indian economists and policy-makers emphasized the need for industrialization as an avenue for bringing development in the country. Given the requirement for setting up basic heavy industries and considering the large capital investment that was required for the same, it was decided to promote industrialization by establishing public sector companies. At the same time, emphasis was also laid on import substitution and export promotion, thinking that this would support the development of skill and competitiveness of domestic producers. With the same intention, restriction was imposed upon foreign investment. In order to support the small enterprises, the government had also restricted the development of monopoly by controlling the size of private firms and by offering protection and subsidies in various forms to small enterprises (Brunner, 1995; Heeks, 1996). Initial development of the ICT industry in India began under such protectionism. However, the phenomenal growth that the ICT industry has witnessed in recent years is primarily an outcome of the Government of India's policy liberalization since the 1990s (Lal, 2001).

Rise of ICT Hardware Industry

Until the mid–1960s, India's electronics industry was very small and unsophisticated. Therefore, the requirement for computer in India was basically met by foreign suppliers like IBM and ICL. The Industrial Policy Resolution of 1956 had not included the then budding computer industry in the list of basic and strategically important sectors. However, since the mid–1960s, India recognized the strategic importance of electronics industry and did not want to leave it completely in the hands of multinationals. In 1965, Dr Homi Bhaba Committee stated in its technical report on computers that India should become self-sufficient in computer technology within the next 10 years. However, considering India's technological capability at that point of time, this was an over-expectation. Such an extreme position went through modification during the 1970s. The Department of Electronics was established in 1970. Shortly thereafter, the Electronics Commission was formed for regulating the activities of private and public companies in the electronics industry. Following the recommendation of Bhaba Committee, The

Electronics Corporation of India (ECIL) began producing small and medium-sized computer systems in 1971 (Brunner, 1995).

In 1973, the government recognized the strategic importance of the computer industry and in its computer policy emphasis was laid on developing complete self-sufficiency in computers. Computer Mainframe Corporation (CMC), established in 1975, was given the monopoly right to service all foreign systems installed in the country. These steps towards developing self-sufficiency were further buttressed by governmental strategy of restricted import and tariff control for imported goods under the supervision of Department of Electronics, Directorate General of Technical Development and Chief Controller of Imports and Exports (Brunner, 1995).

Rise of ICT Software Industry

Until the mid-1960s, software was also provided by multinational hardware providing companies like IBM and ICL. In the West, software development outside multinational hardware providers began to flourish in the late 1970s, as it became increasingly difficult for hardware producing companies to provide the full range of software applications required to make efficient use of their hardware products. This was also facilitated by the standardization of job activities, programming languages, and hardware environments. However, initially such software development was primarily restricted to the effort of in-house developers writing programs for their own organizations. Software development began to be outsourced to external organizations as the number of commercial organizations using computers increased. This created a domestic market for software services. With the growth in India's hardware industry, indigenous hardware manufacturers began developing an increasing range of operating systems, compilers, and application packages. For some companies, software export was one avenue for securing governmental permission to import hardware (Heeks, 1996; Lateef, 1997).

The first firm in India which agreed to export software in return for permission to import hardware was Tata Consultancy Services (TCS); it was in 1974. This year, therefore, symbolically marks the birth of Indian software industry. After TCS, a number of other companies which imported computer hardware began their half-hearted efforts in the realm of software export. However, some of them gave up once their export obligations were fulfilled. At the same time, data-processing departments of some large companies and the software groups of some Indian hardware manufacturers started attempting to sell their in-house software. Initially, these companies were targeting the domestic market. However, after recognizing the revenue-potential of software, some of them made their software division more export-oriented, sometimes even hiving them off as a separate company within their overall business. The departure of IBM from India in 1978 gave the software industry an added impetus, with several of the 1,200 ex-IBM employees setting up small software companies (Heeks, 1996).

Policy Liberalization and ICT Entrepreneurship

Although the growth of the ICT industry was slow and inconsistent, exports particularly began to grow after 1981. Small and medium-sized domestic-oriented companies tried to get into export, looking into the opportunities for making higher profit. Between the mid–1970s and mid–1980s, Government of India re-evaluated its economic policies in order to find solutions to various problems faced by the economy. For this purpose, a number of expert panels were formed. These panels suggested the policy of liberalization as an avenue for improving the economic condition. These recommendations significantly influenced Government's decision to gradually move towards liberalization of economy by reducing its control over international trade, by encouraging foreign investment, and by opening up areas hitherto reserved for public sector (Heeks, 1996). The Government's move towards liberalization of international trade resulted in the rapid rise in the volume of imports since 1978 and particularly since 1982. This rise was partly due to the fast growth of the computer industry at that time (Brunner, 1995). Sign of change was visible in the Technology Policy Statement (1983), which stressed self-reliance but also emphasized on international competitiveness and on exports (Heeks, 1996).

When Rajiv Gandhi became the prime minister of India, science and technology received a further boost. This significantly facilitated the development of the ICT industry (Heeks, 1996) through introduction of selective deregulation, relaxed controls, and lowered tariffs for the electronics industry as a whole consistent with the liberalized trade regime introduced in other sectors of the economy (Mahalingam, 1989). After the introduction of 1984 hardware policy, thousands of PCs came into India and this led to the creation of a large number of software companies, especially small ones, seeking to meet the service and product needs of the new computer owners (Heeks, 1996). Companies like Wipro Infotech, which was started by Azim Premji in Bangalore in 1981, benefited from the new policy to establish production and marketing agreements with a variety of foreign computer companies. Wipro became the first of the ICT success stories in Bangalore. However, most of the domestic market for computer hardware relied heavily on imported components (Heitzman, 2004).

It was software which allowed India and particularly Bangalore to earn an international reputation in ICT (Heitzman, 2004). Government's commitment to software development was stated in its policy document of November 1986 which sought to promote software industry by emphasizing on exports, simplifying the governmental procedure, and by increasing the use of computers in decision-making and enhancing efficiency (Lakha, 1990). Till the late 1970s, software export was primarily dominated by two companies, namely, Tata Consultancy Services and Tata Burroughs Limited (later changed to Tata Unisys). In the early 1980s, a number of other companies, such as Infosys, were established in Bangalore. The typical arrangements were variations on 'body shopping' agreements, where Indian programmers would travel to overseas locations and work for several weeks or months (Lakha, 1994; Heitzman, 2004). From the late 1980s, there was a considerable rise in local and multinational interest in exports alone with a number of large Indian firms spinning off software divisions (Heeks, 1996).

From the late 1980s, the pattern of public deficits was increasing in India. As a result, growth in 1990–91 dropped to 1.2 per cent. The central fiscal deficit became 8.4 per cent of GDP, and foreign exchange reserves dropped to levels below one month of imports. All these coincided with the collapse of India's most powerful international ally, the Soviet Union. At the same time, the Gulf War began resulting in the increase in cost of oil imports and fall in remittances received from Indian workers in the gulf. As a result of all these, the Government of India was compelled to borrow from International Monetary Fund (IMF). The Government was forced by IMF to bring in structural adjustment as a condition for advancing loans. The Government of India brought in structural adjustment by introducing what it called New Economic Policy in 1991. As a part of this policy, the government relaxed the then existing restrictions on import of foreign technology and on developing tie-ups with foreign corporations. All these facilitated the development of the ICT industry, particularly software industry in India (Heitzman, 2004). By the mid–1990s, even those firms, which had initially focused on hardware, were pushing into software exports (Heeks, 1996).

Initially, the ICT industry, like any other industry, began developing in the traditional business centres like Mumbai and to some extent in Chennai. Gradually over a period of time, due to the growth of various necessary infrastructure facilities, new centres started emerging in the ICT industry. Bangalore was the premiere among them. One factor which presumably facilitated the growth of the ICT entrepreneurship in Bangalore was the establishment of a new industrial estate called Electronics City (also called Electronic City) near Bangalore as early as in 1977. After 1987, the Department of Electronics developed the Software Technology Parks of India (STPI) scheme in order to attract offshore software production houses and 100 per cent export-oriented units by offering broadband communication networks, reliable infrastructure, tax relief, etc. The Department of Electronics decided to establish one of its initial six STPIs on the campus of Electronics City. The STPI's broadband communication system named SoftNET, first established in Bangalore, offered international lease lines, emails, videoconferencing, and shared internet service (Heitzman, 2004).

Electronics and computer industry being closely related, Bangalore was a natural location for the development of the ICT industry. Clustering of electronics-related industries and large public sector enterprises in Bangalore brought people from all over India, thereby energizing the city's already existing cosmopolitan character and culture. In addition, relatively low cost of living in Bangalore, when compared with Mumbai and Delhi, made it attractive from a cost point of view. Besides, the ICT industry comprised of young, highly educated workforce. This bred a particular lifestyle, which could grow only in culturally open locations. Bangalore was much less conservative in comparison to many other Indian cities. Furthermore, Bangalore was in an advantageous position in terms of having a strong technically skilled workforce due to the presence of academic community at institutions like the Indian Institute of Science and due to the existence of many high-tech industries (Lateef, 1997). Other factors which presumably promoted the growth of ICT industry in Bangalore included a fairly stable relationship between the state government and the private sector and an international promotional campaign on the part of the state government trying to project Bangalore as the 'Silicon Valley of India' (Lateef, 1997; Heitzman, 2004).

Recent Scenario

Bangalore's success in promoting the growth of ICT entrepreneurship encouraged other states to think on similar lines. As a result, centres for the development of ICT industry emerged in cities like Hyderabad, New Delhi/Gurgaon/Noida, and Pune, and started spreading even further. Leaving aside Bangalore, claiming 26.64 per cent of the ICT exports during the financial year (FY) 2000–2001, other locations claiming a share in export included New Delhi/Gurgaon/Noida (15.34%), Chennai (10.42%), Hyderabad (7.02%), Mumbai/Navi Mumbai (5.68%), Pune (3.39%), Kolkata (0.88%), Ahmedabad/Gandhinagar (0.36%), Thiruvananthapuram (0.03%), and Chandigarh/Mohali (0.01%) (Parthasarathy, 2004).

Over the years, the ICT industry, also referred as the IT industry, including hardware, software product, software services, and related business services, increased its contributions to India's GDP from 1.2 per cent in FY 1997–98 to 4.8 per cent in FY 2004–2005. This industry, with its strong export orientation, emerged as a key contributor to India's foreign exchange earnings. In FY 2004–2005, only 36 per cent of the business for this industry came from the domestic market, whereas 64 per cent of the business came from international market. In the same financial year, the Indian ICT exports touched US$ 18.2 billion, which was a significant increase over the corresponding figure for FY 2000–2001, that was, US$ 6.2 billion. The United States, from the beginning, remained the key export market for the Indian ICT industry. In FY 2004–2005, the destination for more than 68.4 per cent of the Indian ICT exports was the USA. Next export destination was Europe, accounting for 23.1 per cent of the total exports. The industry verticals, which accounted for the larger share in ICT export in FY 2004–2005, include financial services (39%), telecommunications (13%), and retail (9%) (NASSCOM, 2006).

In parity with the previous years, the ICT services and software continued to dominate this industry by contributing over 47 per cent of the total industry revenue in FY 2004–2005. In the same year, the hardware, the IT enabled services (ITES) – Business Process Outsourcing (BPO) and engineering and Research and

Development (R&D) services segments accounted for 21 per cent, 18 per cent, and 14 per cent of the industry revenue respectively (NASSCOM, 2006). Reputation about quality has been an issue of important concern for companies in the Indian ICT industry (Banerjee and Duflo, 2000). As a result, many Indian companies have been active in securing quality certification offered by International Standards Organization (ISO) as well as Software Engineering Institute's five-level Capability Maturity Model (SEI-CMM) (Parthasarathy, 2004).

In the ICT industry, India specifically benefited because of suitable geographical position on the globe resulting in a large time-gap with the USA, the largest market, which made it possible to keep office functioning for almost twenty-four hours in a day (Lateef, 1997). Development of the ICT industry in India was also largely facilitated by the rise of Indian entrepreneurs in the Silicon Valley in the USA. These US educated Indian-origin 'technopreneurs' extended their business activities to India initially by tapping the low-cost skill, and over and time by contributing to highly localized processes of entrepreneurial experimentation and upgrading, while maintaining close ties with the technology and markets in the Silicon Valley (Saxenian, 2005).

In addition to having a workforce of 1.3 million directly employed in the ICT industry, 3 million indirect and induced employment have been generated by this industry. Indirect employment includes expenditure on vendors related to telecom, power, construction, facility management, transportation, catering, and other services. Induced employment is driven by consumption expenditure of employees on food, clothing, utilities, recreation, health, and other services (NASSCOM, 2006). However, one concern is that the boom in the software industry may have negatively affected the growth of other industries.

The boom in the software export sector, on account of exogenous increase in world demand, resulted in an increase in the demand for labour in that sector. This caused a rise in the wage rate in that sector (note that the wage rate in the software grew by 25–30% during the 1990s). The higher wage rate naturally attracted labour, which was mobile, to the software export sector from the other sectors, which were competing with the software sector for technical manpower. Either they (the other sectors) had to pay salaries on par with the software firms, or be satisfied with the second best by paying lower wages (Joseph and Harilal, 2001). At the same time, challenges were observed within the structure of human resource in the ICT industry itself. Relatively low remuneration offered to employees in developing countries, to which the ICT jobs were being transferred from the industrialized countries, prevented them from getting the benefits that workers in industrialized countries lost as a result of investment abroad (Prasad, 1998).

The disparity of growth across segments in the ICT industry, with the dominating role of low-revenue earning software services, was pointed out as a crisis faced by the industry (Radhakrishnan, 2003). This was an outcome of the poor performance of pre-packaged software segment, which had the highest profit potential. Low development of this segment in India implied lower growth in industry revenue (Chakraborty and Jayachandran, 2001). Lack of initiative in the embedded software sector resulted in a crippling effect on the Indian software industry. With the revenue of software service industry depending on high conversion value of the local currency against US Dollar/Euro/Pound Sterling, orientation towards export increased. Too much of dependence on the export market at the cost of domestic market was identified as an issue worth consideration for ensuring sustainable development of the Industry (Kumar, 2001). However, as a result of export orientation, entry into this sector opened up to anyone who had developed contacts with overseas clients (especially in the US market). Easy entry into this industry, therefore, created opportunity for small and tiny firms to enter this business, thus creating a long-tailed structure of the industry (Kumar, 2000; Nath and Hazra, 2002). This facilitated the rise of first-generation entrepreneurship, a focus of this book.

The Enterprises

While the industry pictures tend towards generalization based on observation of dominant patterns, like any other sector ICT industry is also characterized by considerable diversity. And it is important to understand this diversity in order to make sense of the significance of business experiences of ICT entrepreneurs. For example, while social capital relevant for business in ICT industry varies considerably depending on life experiences of the entrepreneur, diversity among enterprises also plays a significant role in it. Different parameters may be identified to capture the variation that exists among enterprises in ICT industry. Here we look into areas of business operation, nature of clientele, location of business operation, size of the enterprises, and duration of business operation to capture the variation that existed among the enterprises that came directly under the purview of this research.

Areas of Business Operation

Based on the business focus of an enterprise, we could identify considerable differences in the way in which business was conducted in the ICT industry. One broad differentiation was based on the involvement of an enterprise in developing ICT products as opposed to its involvement in offering ICT services or in trading ICT products. For organizations involved in developing products, the focus was on identifying business areas for which some product could be developed, be it hardware or software. At the same time, organizations offering a particular product needed to invent additional features and identify new uses of the product on a continuous basis. The functioning of product organizations was based on standardization of their business offering so as to develop something which catered to the requirements of more than one person and/or organization. On the other hand, the functioning of organizations offering services was based on customization of the offering to satisfy the requirement of each customer. At times, enterprises developing products also offered services for their own products. The trading organizations also needed to understand the requirements of each customer in order to offer the right product.

Figure 2.1

Business Areas of Enterprises

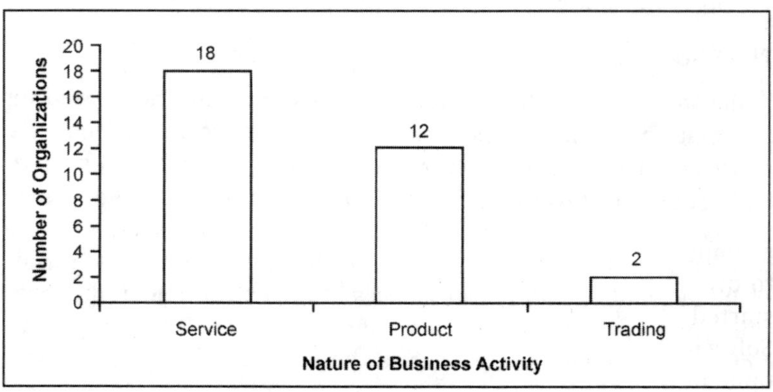

Figure 2.1 confirmed the broad trend of Indian ICT companies being skewed in favour of services. Various services offered by the studied companies included customized software solutions for various industries, data recovery, ICT infrastructure management, technical writing, e-learning, Very Large System Integration (VLSI) designing, Business Process Outsourcing (BPO), internet services, data migration services, design and user interface consultancy, branding and multimedia, business research, usability and Human-Computer Interaction consultancy, services in website development, website hosting, networking, and Linux. Products developed by the enterprises studied were targeted towards financial market, export businesses, entertainment industry, knowledge management, and healthcare industry. Finally, trading involved software as well as hardware products.

It was observed that many enterprises were involved in more than one business activity. Diversification of business was one of the strategies followed by all these enterprises to face competition. Some of the enterprises offered multiple services, or multiple products, or combination of products and services or combination of services and trading. Entrepreneurs diversified business for different reasons. For O.P. Nayar, founder of Accent Tech Solutions, diversification was part of the strategy to foster the growth of the existing business. He mentioned,

> When we started, we had a training division. The original idea was to run training for two years; then discontinue that. But then I realized that this training is always required, because trained people are always required. So I could not discontinue that. So the training division remained. Then after some time we realized that okay we need to get into (developing software) solutions. Infrastructure management (with which the business began) alone will not facilitate growth. You need to provide (software) applications also. Then only you become a true system integrator. So we started a software division.

There can be other reasons for diversification as well. For example, Amit Sharma, founder of Sindh Infotech Pvt. Ltd. decided to diversify and enter the ICT industry when his family business started facing tremendous crisis. Pankaj Sen, founder of Advanced Software Systems Pvt. Ltd. decided to diversify into product development in order to avoid competition from large companies in his original area of operation that is consultancy for resolving Y2K crisis, a problem with the year 2000 resulting out of the practice of abbreviating a four-digit year into two digits. Like Pankaj Sen, Arjun Desai, founder of Win Infotech Ltd. also diversified to avoid competition from larger companies, and moved from ICT training to ICT infrastructure management. However, later on, when he diversified from ICT infrastructure management to BPO services, serendipity played an important role. Arjun Desai mentioned,

> This happened somewhere in end of 1998 .... We got a small project related to BPO from a local customer, a MNC. Those days we didn't know that BPO would grow so well .... But then we were in touch with the market and suddenly things changed and this project became extremely important.

Although the reason for business diversification varied, it was obvious that an enterprise chose a new business area on the basis of its connection with its existing areas of business operation. Choosing a business area to venture into was mostly based on entrepreneur's familiarity with that area. For example, Tech Writers Inc. founded by Anil Despande diversified from offering technical writing services to a related area, offering a training programme in technical writing. Hitesh Patel wanted to diversify considering the challenges that his family business was going through. He recalled that, when he was looking for a new line of business in which he could diversify, he interacted with one of his friends who was running a business in the ICT industry. Hitesh Patel's friend advised him that he should get into an area which he was familiar with. One option here was that Hitesh Patel could develop something based on the ERP and CRM solutions that he had prepared for the textile company owned by his family. He could sell those solutions to other textile companies. However, he felt that there was a possibility of having a large competition from companies which were already doing the same. Instead, Hitesh Patel thought that he would be able to develop a unique product if he worked on the question-answer building software which he had created for his wife.

Nature of Clientele

With ICT emerging as a basic infrastructure for business operations, the ICT companies attracted clients from diverse industries. Therefore, it was necessary for both founders and employees from

ICT companies to learn the operation procedures of their clients. Each company specialized in multiple industry verticals. This was referred to as 'domain specialization'. This happened with reference to both product and services. Many a time, such specialization developed over a period through exposure to industry. And such exposure could sometimes help in the development of social capital.

A large number of clients that the selected companies had were from industries like ICT, manufacturing, banking and finance, education, telecommunication, government administration, and healthcare. These enterprises also served clients from industries like real estate, automobile, biotechnology, pharmaceutical, hospitality, entertainment, apparel, logistics, trading, ITES, retail, floriculture, electronics, electrical, research, media, publishing and printing, travel and accommodation, and security and training. In addition, clients of these companies included various associations, organizers of events like conferences, and independent professionals like consultants and attorneys.

Given the need for diversification of business activities, every enterprise wanted to portray itself as having specialized knowledge to contribute towards multiple industries. Therefore, while documenting the industries of the clients on the website, enterprises presented as diverse a picture as possible. One way of portraying such diversity was by highlighting that the enterprise served clients from different industries. Even though all enterprises attempted to portray such diversity, it was possible to categorize the enterprises in terms of the industry of their clients. For example, at Tech Writers Inc., a large number of clients were from ICT, telecommunications, banking and finance, and electrical industry. Whereas, for Software Consultants Pvt. Ltd., clients were visible in industries like banking and finance, education, electronics, entertainment, healthcare, hospitality, manufacturing, and logistics.

Location of Business Operation

ICT industry was often highlighted as prioritizing virtual space over geographical location (Dicken, 2000). It was a popular impression that neither in software product sector nor in software service sector a company essentially needed to be located close to its clients. However, geography was not completely unimportant in the ICT industry. In fact, the initial development of the ICT industry in India was characterized by the companies hiring people from India and sending them abroad to work on-site for their client's projects. This phenomenon was popularly known as 'body shopping'. This trend continues even today. At the same time, geographical clustering of ICT companies continued to play an important role in attracting suitable human resource. Besides, being located at a geographical location relatively close to the client also helped in developing trust as well as in understanding the client's requirements. The largest number of clients of these enterprises were from India. However, some other countries where significant number of clients were located included Australia, France, Malaysia, Singapore, UK, and the USA. Other than that, the enterprises had clients from Brazil, China, Denmark, Germany, Greece, Indonesia, Japan, Philippines, and Sweden. When it came to clients from abroad, a clustering of clients was often observed. For example, Tech Writers Inc. and Software Consultants Pvt. Ltd. had many clients from the USA, whereas, Soft Solutions Pvt. Ltd. had many clients from Singapore.

Out of the 30 enterprises which were intensely studied for this research, 16 had only one office establishment. Whereas, Accent Tech Solutions had as many as 33 offices and Ahead Technologies Pvt. Ltd. had nine offices. Enterprises which had more than one office establishment, often had one or more of their offices located outside India. For example, Magnatech Inc. had one of its offices in the USA, whereas Tech Writers Inc. had one of its offices in the USA and another in Singapore. The other locations where enterprises had offices included France, Germany, Singapore, The Netherlands, Taiwan, and the UAE. Enterprises established offices abroad for catering to the requirements of existing clients in those regions as well as for expanding business activities. However, office establishments needed to be maintained cost effectively. This was specifically important with reference to offices abroad, as the operation cost of such offices was quite high. Therefore, many enterprises established business partnerships with enterprises in different countries, so that they did not need to maintain offices in all regions where they did business. For example, Netware Pvt. Ltd. had partnership with a company abroad. At the same time, Datainformatics Pvt. Ltd. functioned as a business partner in India for companies located abroad.

Size of the Enterprise

Enterprise culture often varied depending on the size of the enterprise measured in terms of the number of employees. Accent Tech Solutions was the largest among the enterprises studied in terms of employee strength. Their group which consisted of two companies had altogether around 3,000 employees. There were two other enterprises which also had relatively high number of employees: Integrated Software Solutions had around 900 employees and Ryze Softech Pvt. Ltd. had around 490 employees. All these three enterprises were involved in more than one business activity. The only other organization which had similar number of employees despite being involved in a single business activity was Ahead Technologies Pvt. Ltd. Their employee strength was 800. If the number of consultants was taken into consideration while calculating employee strength, Ahead Technologies would have been one of the largest employers; around 3,200 people were working as consultants for this enterprise.

In comparison to these relatively large enterprises in the SME category Raj Software and Communications had only two employees. At the same time, there were two start-up enterprises which were completely freelancer-driven. They did not have any employees at all. Leaving aside these two poles, other enterprises were spread out in between. Figure 2.2 shows that a larger number of enterprises had employees either between 11 and 25 (8 enterprises) or between 26 and 50 (6 enterprises).

Figure 2.2

Number of Employees in Enterprises

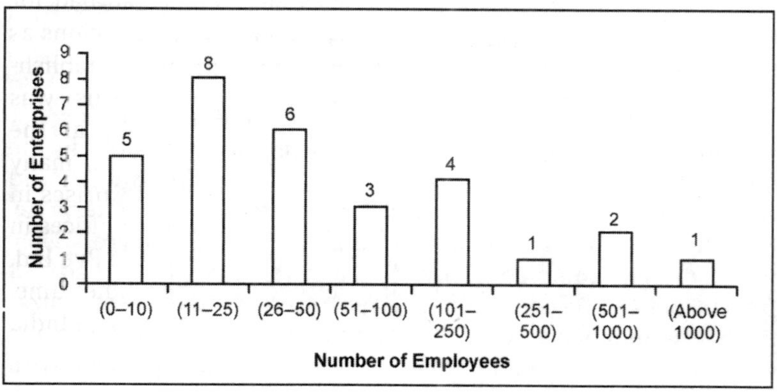

Given the dependence on technology, it was quite natural to find that most employees in all these enterprises were technical personnel. Only a small part of the workforce was administrative or managerial staff. Except for one, in no enterprise the number of administrative staff was more than that of the technical personnel. This organization, Datainformatics Pvt. Ltd., was primarily involved in trading, which probably explained why it had more non-technical than technical staff. In all other organizations, more than 60 per cent of the employees were technical personnel. In six organizations, all the employees were technical personnel. Leaving aside one of these six organizations, which had 40 employees, in rest five the number of employees was below 15. This indicated the trend that smaller organizations expected their employees to perform multiple tasks. Instead of appointing separate employees for administrative work, they expected their technical employees to perform non-technical tasks as well.

Figure 2.3

Technical Employees of Enterprises

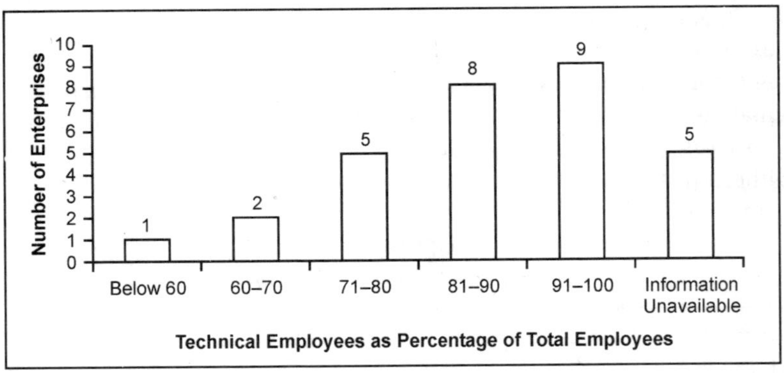

Given the nature of work in the ICT industry, it was not essential for an employee to be always physically located in the office. We found enterprises employing many freelancers and consultants who were not physically located at the enterprise. Knowhow and Design Lab had no 'employee' on their payroll. They were driven completely by freelancers. Knowhow had 35 freelancers and Design Lab had 5 freelancers. Both these organizations were founded and run by women entrepreneurs. As these two enterprises were still in their seed stage, running them with freelancers was part of the business strategy to keep provision for scaling down costs when there was a decline in the flow of business.

Duration of Business Operation

The style of functioning of an enterprise underwent changes with time. For understanding these changes, it was necessary to classify the enterprises in terms of the number of years for which their business had been operating. For most of the enterprises, the year of registration and the year of initiation of business operations were the same. However, there were enterprises which were either registered first, but initiated business operations later on, or began their business operations first, but got themselves registered later on. In the second category, often registration took place when it was necessary for getting business, or for securing finance. At the same time, there were enterprises like Netware Pvt. Ltd., Infonet Pvt. Ltd., and Datainformatics Pvt. Ltd. which were initially registered as 'firm', but later on were re-registered as a 'company'. The need to transform a firm into a company was to facilitate external financial investment into the enterprise.

One interesting observation from Figure 2.4 is that, out of the 30 enterprises, only one was registered before 1985. All the other enterprises were registered between 1985 and 2005. This, in a way, matched with the trends in the growth of ICT industry in India. The impetus to growth for the ICT industry had come with the gradual liberalization of industry regulations which began around 1985. However, initiatives towards liberalization became stronger with

Figure 2.4

Duration of Operation of Enterprises

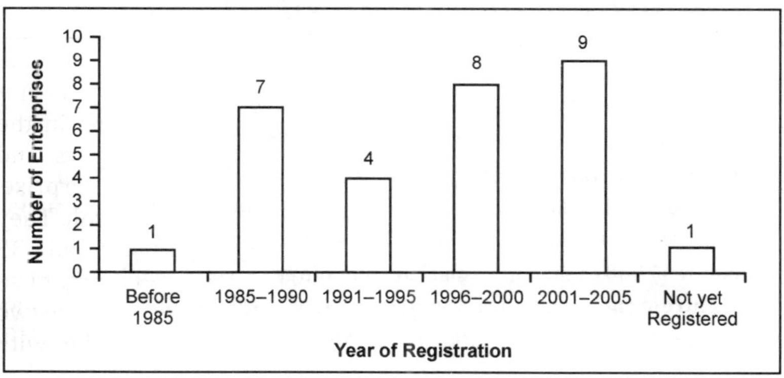

the implementation of the New Economic Policy in 1991. Therefore, probably it was no coincidence that majority of the enterprises were established after 1991.

Irrespective of the diversity that existed among enterprises in ICT industry we found frequent references being made by entrepreneurs about the importance of trust, reputation, and goodwill for the development of business. Although conceptually we segregated the three terms, empirically, at times, the distinction between them got blurred. Often, it was found that different entrepreneurs perceived these terms differently. For example, whereas some entrepreneurs understood customer reference as reputation, others considered it as goodwill. In view of the importance given by entrepreneurs to trust, reputation, and goodwill in relation to various aspects of business operation, it appeared necessary to elucidate these terms. Chapter Four and Five would attempt such an elucidation while looking into various facets of business.

References

Banerjee, A.V. and Duflo, E. (2000). Reputation effect and the limits of contracting: A study of the Indian software industry. *The Quarterly Journal of Economics*, 115(3), 989–1017.

Brunner, H. (1995). *Closing the technology gap: Technological change in India's computer industry*. New Delhi: Sage Publications.

Chakraborty, C. and Jayachandran, C. (2001). Software sector: Trends and constraints. *Economic and Political Weekly*, XXXVI (34), 3255–3261.

Dicken, P. (2000). A new geo-economy. In D. Held and A. McGrew (eds), *The global transformations reader: An introduction to the globalization debate*. Cambridge: Polity Press, 251–258.

Heeks, R. (1996). *India's software industry: State policy, liberalisation and industrial development*. New Delhi: Sage Publications.

Heitzman, J. (2004). *Network City: Planning the information society in Bangalore*. New Delhi: Oxford University Press.

Joseph, K.J. and Harilal, K.N. (2001). Structure and growth of India's IT exports: Implications of an export-oriented growth strategy. *Economic and Political Weekly*, XXXVI(34), 3263–3270.

Kumar, N. (2000). Small information technology services, employment and entrepreneurship development: Some explorations into Indian experience. *The Indian Journal of Labour Economics*, 43(4), 935–948.

Kumar, N. (2001). Indian software industry development: International and national perspective. *Economic and Political Weekly*, XXXVI(45), 4278–4290.

Lakha, S. (1990). Growth of computer software industry in India. *Economic and Political Weekly*, XXV(1), 49–56.

Lakha, S. (1994). The new international division of labour and the Indian computer software industry. *Modern Asian Studies*, 28(2), 381–408.

Lal, K. (2001). Institutional environment and the development of information and communication technology in India. *The Information Society*, 17(2), 105–117.

Lateef, A. (1997). *Linking up with the global economy: A case study of the Bangalore software industry* (Discussion Paper). Geneva: International Institute for Labour Studies.

Mahalingam, S. (1989). Computer industry in India: Strategies for late-comer entry. *Economic and Political Weekly*, XXIV(42), 2375–2384.

NASSCOM (National Association of Software and Services Companies). (2006). *Strategic review 2006: The IT industry in India*. New Delhi: NASSCOM.

Nath, P. and Hazra, A. (2002). Configuration of Indian software industry. *Economic and Political Weekly*, XXXVII(8), 737–742.

Parthasarathy, B. (2004). India's Silicon Valley or Silicon Valley's India? Socially embedding the computer software industry in Bangalore. *International Journal of Urban and Regional Research*, 28(3), 664–685.

Prasad, M. (1998). International capital on 'Silicon Plateau': Work and control in India's computer industry. *Social Forces*, 77(2), 429–452.

Radhakrishnan, K.G. (2003). India's software industry: A structural break-up. *Journal of Indian School of Political Economy*, XV(3), 689–704.

Saxenian, A. (2005). From brain drain to brain circulation: Transnational communities and regional upgrading in India and China. *Studies in Comparative International Development*, 40(2), pp. 35–61.

3

The ICT Entrepreneurs

Success of an enterprise, to a large extent, depends upon the ability of the entrepreneur to identify the right business opportunity, secure necessary financial investment, get and retain customers, build up a competent team of professionals to work for her/him, and effectively handle situations of crisis. Success attained by different entrepreneurs in all these aspects varied considerably from one another. Diversity in entrepreneur's background could be considered as one framework for explaining this variation. Background may be understood in diverse ways. Here we use parameters like entrepreneur's geographical location, educational qualification, professional experience, family background, demographics, and gender. We also looked into the diverse factors which motivated individuals to become entrepreneurs.

Geographical Location

Information and Communication Technology (ICT) industry considerably undermined the importance of geography in the development of business operations. With the advancement in this technology, space presumably became more important than place. Forces of globalization resulted in the functional integration of internationally dispersed economic activities, leading to the creation of global production chains and reconstruction of existing distribution chains (Dicken, 2000). For example, although Dell Computers had its manufacturing plant located in Austin, Texas in the USA, it used components produced in different parts of the world: power supply components from China, soundcards from France, video cards and microprocessors from Hong Kong, RAM chips and CD ROM drives from Japan, floppy drives from Malaysia, keyboards from Mexico, SCSI cards and disk devices from Singapore, and network cards, monitors and cooling fans from Taiwan (College of Business, San José State University, n.d.).

However, the real revolution has come in the ICT service sector particularly with the development of internet. For example, Wipro, an Indian ICT company has set up its Global Command Centre (GCC) in 2002 to offer its clients online service of managing and monitoring their ICT infrastructure from a remote location. This facility brings down the service cost by reducing the need for onsite maintenance and thereby making it possible to offer ICT infrastructure services from offshore locations. This facility also gives the clients an opportunity to know the real time health status of their ICT infrastructure. Theoretically, introduction of such a high-end online service makes it possible for Wipro GCC to run the entire New York Stock Exchange and all the computerized water dams and electricity supply units across the world from Bangalore (Wipro, n.d. and Marico Innovation Foundation, n.d.).

Such developments may be one reason for further growth of localized ICT industrial clusters (Parthasarathy, 2004). Internationally, the name of Silicon Valley in the USA is well known. In India also, there are equivalents of Silicon Valley located in various cities like Bangalore, Gurgaon, Hyderabad, and Pune. Other than these newly developed business centres, the presence of ICT industry is also visible in older economic centres like Chennai (Madras), Kolkata (Calcutta), and Mumbai (Bombay). Out of the 30 entrepreneurs with whom we interacted as a part of the study which forms the basis for this book, 13 were from Bangalore, nine were from Mumbai, seven were from Chennai, and one was from Pune.

Educational Qualification

Being based on technology, running an organization in the ICT industry required certain technical knowledge. Most of the entrepreneurs with whom we interacted acquired at least part of such knowledge through their educational pursuit: 22 had some or other degree or diploma or certificate in the area of technology. Out of these 22 entrepreneurs, 18 were educationally qualified specifically in computer and allied fields like computer applications and programming, computer science, computer systems engineering, electrical and communication engineering, electronics and electrical engineering, industrial electronics, radiophysics, usability, and web. Of these 18 entrepreneurs, 14 had completed BE or BTech in relevant fields. The rest included people who had completed Diploma in Industrial Electronics or had Master's Degree in computer sciences or electronic communication. They also included two persons who were Certified Usability Analysts, Certified Web Masters, Microsoft Certified Systems Engineers, or Microsoft Certified Software Developers. Both of them were women, and had obtained these certifications after graduating in social science subjects, like economics and sociology. Our sample also included a person who was a PhD in computer sciences. Findings of the current research regarding number of high-technology entrepreneurs with Master's Degree differed from that of E.B. Roberts (1991). Whereas, Roberts found that median education of high technology entrepreneurs in the USA was a Master's Degree, in the current study it was people without a Master's Degree. The distribution of entrepreneurs in terms of their educational qualification is shown in Table 3.1.

Table 3.1

Educational Qualification of Entrepreneurs

Under Graduation Degrees/Diplomas/ Certificates		*No PG Degree*	*Post Graduation Degrees (Including PhD)*			
			Computer and Related Fields	*Non-applied Science*	*Management*	*Total*
Technology and related fields	Computer and related fields	8	8	Nil	2	18
	Others	3	Nil	Nil	1	4
Other fields	Non-applied sciences	Nil	1	1	2	4
	Commerce	4	Nil	Nil	Nil	4
Total		15	9	1	5	30

However, it was found that having an educational background in computer or related fields was not indispensable for becoming an entrepreneur in the ICT industry. Not all engineers whom we interviewed had specialized in fields related to computer. There were four entrepreneurs who had specialized in fields like Chemical Engineering and Mechanical Engineering. Other than that, there were four entrepreneurs who only had a graduation degree in commerce. There were also other entrepreneurs who either had degrees in management or in disciplines like physics. These people learnt about technology either through their professional life or by reading relevant literature. However, people having engineering degree stood out among all. This finding however matched with that of E.B. Roberts (1991).

As it can be observed in Table 3.2 most of the entrepreneurs had completed their education from state level institutions and universities. Some of the relatively well-known state level institutions from which these entrepreneurs had graduated included Andhra University, Annamalai University, Bangalore University, Calcutta University, Jaihind College (Mumbai), Madras Christian College, Mithibai College of Arts (Mumbai), St. Xavier's College (Mumbai), St. Xavier's College (Kolkata), University of Mysore, University Visvesvaraya College of Engineering (Bangalore), and Veermata Jeejabai Technological Institute (Mumbai). Various national level institutions from which some of the entrepreneurs completed their education included Indian Institute of Science (Bangalore), Indian Institute of Technology Bombay (Mumbai), Indian Institute of Technology Madras (Chennai), Birla Institute of Technology (Pilani), Narsee Monjee College (Mumbai), and Bharti Vidyapith Polytechnic (Pune). The institutions in the USA from where some of the entrepreneurs graduated included Cornell University (New York), North-Eastern University (Boston), Steven's Institute of Technology (New Jersey), Syracuse University (New York), University of Dallas (Texas), and University of Nebraska (Lincoln). None of the entrepreneurs had acquired foreign degrees from any country other than the USA.

Table 3.2

*Place of Study**

Courses Studied	*Place of Study*			
	State Level Institution in India	*National Level Institution in India*	*Institutions in the United States of America*	*Total*
Under Graduation (including Certificates/ Diplomas)	27	8	Nil	35
Post Graduation	5	5	5	15
PhD	Nil	Nil	1	1
Total	32	13	6	51

* Cumulative total in the 'Total' column/row is more than the number of sample entrepreneurs, as many entrepreneurs have obtained more than one degree/diploma/certificate.

Professional Career

Many glorious success stories of Indian ICT industry showcased professionals with or without business family background leaving their secure employments to set up companies. In case of companies set up by group of individuals professional background of the founders at same workplace was often, though not always, the case. Hindustan Computers Limited (HCL), for example, was founded by a group of six engineers working at the calculator division of Delhi Cotton Mills (DCM) (Rediff, 2007). Likewise, before starting Infosys N.R. Narayana Murthy was an employee of Patni Computer Systems (Murthy, n.d.) and before starting Microland Pradeep Kar worked for different companies including Wipro, Computer Point, and Sonata Software (Kar, 2010).

Out of the sample of 30 entrepreneurs, only three had never worked as an employee. Two among them started their career by joining family business. The third entrepreneur, who did not hail from business family, became successful in his first business venture itself which he started right after completing studies. Hence, the question of joining an organization as an employee did not arise for him. The remaining 27 entrepreneurs had taken up some kind of employment before starting off as entrepreneurs. Often, having experience of working as an employee proved to be beneficial for these entrepreneurs. As Alok Dutta, founder of Silicon Networks Pvt. Ltd.[1] mentioned, 'I understand the minds of people who work ... coming from the entrepreneur's side if you have never worked with your colleagues, you don't know how the others are thinking'. Besides, there were other benefits of having a strong professional career, for example, learning business acumen, developing professional network, etc.

The number of years participants of this study worked as an employee before becoming an entrepreneur varied considerably. From Table 3.3, one trend that we can observe is that relatively less number of interviewees had become entrepreneurs after working for two years or less. Those who became entrepreneurs after working for 2.1–5[2] years formed the single largest group. This was quite different from the findings of Roberts (1991). He found that, in the USA, the typical technical entrepreneur had 13 years of work experience. In the current study, the number of individuals who had become entrepreneurs after working for 5.1–10 years, or 10.1–15 years, or 15.1–20 years was also considerably high. However, the number of persons who worked for more than 20 years as employees before becoming entrepreneurs was quite low. It was also interesting to observe that the largest group of entrepreneurs worked as employees in not more than two organizations before becoming entrepreneurs. At the same time, few entrepreneurs within this group had worked for more than 10 years as employees.

Table 3.3

*Employment Prior to Starting Present Business**

*Length of Employment (in Years)***	*Employed in Organizations (Number)*				*Total*
	1–2	*3–5*	*6–10*	*11+*	
0.1–2	2	Nil	Nil	Nil	2
2.1–5	6	1	1	Nil	8
5.1–10	3	Nil	2	1	6
10.1–15	Nil	4	1	Nil	5
15.1–20	2	2	1	Nil	5
20.1+	Nil	1	Nil	Nil	1
Total	13	8	5	1	27

* The table excludes three entrepreneurs who did not ever work as employees prior to starting their present businesses. Therefore, the total number of entrepreneurs in the table is 27, and not 30.

** The number before decimal implies year and the number after decimal implies month. For example, 2.1 means two years and one month.

At times, the decision to become entrepreneur could get guided by dissatisfaction with employment career. Anil Despande, founder of Tech Writers Inc. said, 'I am not suitable for a (salaried) job. So I changed something like six or seven (salaried) jobs in two years'. However, in many other cases, entrepreneurs felt that their professional background facilitated their performance as entrepreneurs. For example, Alok Dutta, founder of Silicon Networks Pvt. Ltd., who worked with ZCT (name changed; originally it was a large Indian ICT company) before starting his business venture, mentioned.

> ... when I graduated I had no clue as to how to start business. At ... ZCT, I think, nothing they did in that sense (which helped me in building entrepreneurial skill), but observing their operation as a young executive gave me the ideas as to how possibly one can take a foot out, you know, within a low cost environment. So I would say ... ZCT to that extent gave me the ideas (about) how to start.

This was also mentioned by well-known ICT entrepreneur Pradeep Kar, founder of Microland, in an interview. He said, 'When I saw my experience with Wipro and Sonata Software I clearly felt that if I can do this for someone else why not try and do this for myself' (Kar, n.d.). Same was true for O.P. Nayar, founder of Accent Tech Solutions. He said,

> (I was working for a) company at Okhla. But then ... CCT (name changed; originally it was a large Indian ICT company) started. I joined ... CCT. Then ... CCT itself was an entrepreneur-driven company. So I was one of those early engineers to work in that company. So then I realized how enterprising these people are, and how they are trying to build their business ... but still you don't have the kind of courage to really start something. Because you need an experience ... and you need some financial stability before you can get into something.

Often, individuals planned out their professional life keeping in mind their interest in becoming an entrepreneur. Rupa Datta, founder of Infonet Pvt. Ltd. said,

> I was actually (working as) a networking consultant as a single person all my life. And at that point, I suddenly realized that as one person I couldn't really make any difference. And that's when I started to think do I want to be a single person or do I want to be an organization. And I saw lot of limitations of being a single person. Then I first went to a trust ... I started working with the trust. That was ITVI (name changed; originally it was an association for visually handicapped persons). There I was a trustee.

Same was true for Dinesh Marwari, founder of Ryze Softech Pvt. Ltd. Coming from a business family background, he was aware of his entrepreneurial future from the very beginning. Therefore, after completing his MS in Computer Science, instead of looking for a job as a software engineer, he sought and finally got himself a business role in a software services company.

Listening to entrepreneurs at various events organized by TiE clarified that, at times, having a successful professional career as an employee could deter an individual from becoming an entrepreneur. Entrepreneurs expressed concern about the ease with which young people got jobs which provided them lucrative salary! It was a concern, because a lucrative salary often dissuades many young people from taking the risk of becoming an entrepreneur. In the initial phase, entrepreneurship was not only risky, it was also less rewarding. Most entrepreneurs agreed that economic rewards during the initial phase of their business were lower in comparison to their salary in the last job. Also there was no promise that a business would necessarily become more profitable in the long run. In reality, very few organizations managed to sustain profitably in the industry![3] Given these challenges, it is no surprise that most of the entrepreneurs stated that they needed time in deciding to start a business venture. During that time, they worked as employees in different organizations.

With time, ICT has penetrated more and more into diverse industries. Therefore, having exposure in industries other than ICT often facilitated the ICT entrepreneurs in identifying business opportunities. It was interesting to note from Table 3.4 that, out of the total number of employments taken up by the sample entrepreneurs in India, more were in industries other than ICT. These industries included aeronautics, automobile, ceramic, diamond, education, electronics, financial services, hospitality, pharmaceutical, placement services, research, steel casting, television, and textiles. It would be worth mentioning here that, in Israel, median high-technology entrepreneurs had prior work experience in army as officers in either combat or technical position (Malach-Pines, Dvir and Sadeh, 2004).

Table 3.4

*Industry Exposure**

Worked in	*Industry Exposure through Professional Career Prior to Becoming Entrepreneur (Number of Employments)*		*Total*
	In ICT Industry	*In Other Industries*	
India	37	40	77
Abroad	16	Nil	16
Total	53	40	93

* Cumulative total in the 'Total' column/row is more than the number of sample entrepreneurs as many entrepreneurs had held more than one employment.

The ICT industry generated considerable opportunities for Indians to work abroad. As it is visible in Table 3.4, all the entrepreneurs who worked abroad did so in the ICT industry. Majority of them worked in the USA, and some in countries like France, Singapore, and UK. Exposure from working abroad was not only beneficial for understanding the expectations of foreign clients, it was also advantageous in developing professional network required for business. However, working abroad was not the only path through which entrepreneurs developed business contacts abroad. There were entrepreneurs who developed such business contacts through friends, family members, ex-colleagues, or classmates located abroad.

It would be worth pointing out that business families often groomed individuals, particularly boys, for a career in business within the family itself. Before starting a full-fledged entrepreneurial career, Ajay Aggarwal, founder of Netware Pvt. Ltd. worked as an apprentice in different professions. Often it was his family that facilitated his opportunity to become an apprentice. Some of the entrepreneurs who did not have a family background in business tried out their hand in business on their own. After retirement from employment, father of Ullas Gowda, founder of Knowledge Solutions Pvt. Ltd. started a business in typing, photocopying, etc. Ullas Gowda, that time an engineering student, used to help his father in that business. His first business initiative began using his father's infrastructure. However, later on he moved out of it. Entrepreneurs thus sought to build their professional expertise either by working as employees or by trying out their hand in business before entering a full-fledged entrepreneurial career.

Family Background and Demographic Details

There was a complete mismatch between the profession of the entrepreneurs in our sample and that of their parents. Given the fact that ICT was a new industry in India, it was quite natural that none of these entrepreneurs had parents who were part of the same industry. That implied that none of the entrepreneurs had the advantage of learning about their industry from their parents. However, in comparison with others, entrepreneurs originating from traditional business family background naturally had the opportunity to learn general ground rules of business from their parents and/or from other family members. For example, Sudha Sharma, founder of Design Lab said that she learnt the basics of management at home as her father was into the business of film production. Alok Dutta, founder of Silicon Networks Pvt. Ltd., on the other hand, felt that culture of business was never there at his home as he was not from a business family. Entrepreneurs originating from business family also received better moral support from their family members, as they understood business process and, therefore, knew what to expect from an entrepreneur.

Quite often, entrepreneurs, who did not hail from business family, faced opposition from some family members while entering business. The root of such an attitude lied in non-comprehension of entrepreneurship emerging out of lack of familiarity. Such was the experience of entrepreneurs like Anil Despande, founder of Tech Writers Inc., Alok Dutta, founder of Silicon Networks Pvt. Ltd., Pankaj Sen, founder of Advanced Software Systems Pvt. Ltd., and Vishnu Krishnaswamy, founder of Techvision. It, however, didn't mean that entrepreneurs hailing from families lacking business background received no moral support from any of their family members. Some family members were at times sympathetic towards one's decision to become an entrepreneur. For example, mother of Akhtar Hussain, founder of Communication Networks was empathetic, while his father was not. Similarly, mother-in-law of Anil Despande, founder of Tech Writers Inc. was supportive, while his father was not. For entrepreneurs like Pankaj Sen, founder of Advanced Software Systems Pvt. Ltd., Chandan Sivaram, founder of Soft Solutions Pvt. Ltd., and S. Ram, Integrated Software Solutions wives were strong sources of support. Not all entrepreneurs who had a family background in business found support from their family. At times, there was insufficient support from family members due to their lack of awareness about the style of operation of ICT industry. For example, Kirti Harlalka, founder of Knowhow said, 'My father-in-law ... lives in a small town in Bihar ... he trades in ... small items ... . For him (it is difficult) to understand how I make money'.

It was found that opposition came from family members especially when an individual was leaving a well-paying job to get into business. Opposition was much less when an entrepreneur was a student (for example, Jayant Srinivas, founder of Ahead Technologies Pvt. Ltd.) or was not formally employed (for example, S. Ram of Integrated Software Solutions) or was a consultant (for example, Ranjan Raghavan, founder of Bangalore Technologies) immediately prior to becoming an entrepreneur. Opposition was also less if parents of entrepreneurs did not have too high expectations from their children (for example, Kunal Raman, founder of Sharp Technologies Pvt. Ltd.).

Keeping concerns of family members in mind, some entrepreneurs who lacked family background in business chose to get into business before they got married. For example, Rajat Apte, founder of Magnatech Inc., who did not have any family background in business, said,

> ... if you have a career and get to late 30s and late 40s before you start your business, by that time you are likely to have family, children so on and so forth. So the decision becomes lot more complicated. (While) ... you would have better skill-set (at that age), in some way it is much more complex because you are carrying along lots of responsibilities.

Table 3.5 clearly indicates that family background in business was not indispensable for becoming an entrepreneur, at least in the ICT industry. Out of the sample of 30 entrepreneurs, 17 did not have any family member involved in business. Even among other entrepreneurs who had family member(s) engaged in business, for two, those family members were from their own generation, their brothers. These findings were quite different from that of Roberts (1991), who found that two-thirds of the high-technology entrepreneurs in the USA had self-employed fathers.

Table 3.5

Family Background

*Regional Roots**	*At Least One Family Member is Involved in Business*		*No Family Member is Involved in Business*	*Total*
	From a Traditional Business Community	*Not from a Traditional Business Community*		
Andhra Pradesh	Nil	Nil	3	3
Gujarat	2	Nil	Nil	2
Karnataka	Nil	1	4	5
Kerala	Nil	Nil	1	1
Maharashtra	Nil	1	3	4
North India	Nil	1	Nil	1
Punjab	3	Nil	Nil	3
Rajasthan	2	Nil	Nil	2
Tamil Nadu	Nil	2	5	7
West Bengal	Nil	1	1	2
Total	7	6	17	30

* Understood according to father's regional background.

In order to understand the entrepreneurs' socio-cultural background, I collected information about their religion and caste/sect/denomination background. Getting information about their caste turned out to be a difficult endeavour. For example, when I asked Ranjan Raghavan, founder of Bangalore Technologies whether he belongs to any backward caste, his response was, 'I prefer not to answer'. K. Padmakumar, founder of Frontech Ltd. was so unhappy about my interest in knowing about his caste background that he spoke for almost next twenty minutes to convince me why caste background did not matter at all in a high-technology industry like ICT. The experience was quite similar with many other entrepreneurs. Probably, the reason for the displeasure of entrepreneurs about any question related to caste lied in the nature of the industry. ICT industry, being based on technology, became a symbol of modernity for its proponents. These proponents related socio-cultural background with tradition and probably, therefore, most of the entrepreneurs found it politically correct to distance themselves from anything to do with caste.

In course of the research, the caste question had to be rephrased. Instead of trying to find out about specific caste background of an entrepreneur, we found that it was relatively easy to indirectly ask entrepreneurs whether they belonged to any backward communities or not. Even this question was also met with resentment from some entrepreneurs. Out of the seven entrepreneurs who mentioned the name of their caste, interestingly five were Brahmins. Of the other two, one was from a weaver community and the other was from a fisherman community. Out of the 19 entrepreneurs from whom we could find information about religion, one was a Sunni Muslim, another was a Jain; rest all were Hindus.

Table 3.6 shows a clear concentration of sample entrepreneurs in the age groups of 31–40 and 41–50 years. In the USA as well, mid-thirties was the dominant age range of technical enterprise founders (Roberts, 1991). In Israel, median successful high-technology entrepreneurs were in mid-forties (Malach-Pines, Dvir and Sadeh, 2004). One probable explanation behind the presence of less number of entrepreneurs beyond 50 years of age, particularly beyond 60 years of age, was the recent emergence of the ICT industry. Even though the ICT industry started growing in India since the 1970s, its profit-potential came into limelight only in the late 1980s, when India gradually began to open up its economy. Out of the 30 sample entrepreneurs, only one had established an organization in the ICT sector prior to 1985. Most of the entrepreneurs had started their business after 1990, particularly between 1995 and 2005. Table 3.6 also shows that a majority of the sample entrepreneurs started their business when they were between 25 and 30 years of age. Our observation regarding age of founder(s) during start-up stage of their company also found resonance in the way in which today's large ICT companies of India got started. For example when HCL was started Shiv Nadar, the principal founder of the company, was 30 years old. Other founders were also in the same age group (Rediff, 2007).

Table 3.6

Age Distribution

Present Age (In Years)	*Age while Initiating Business (In Years)*				*Total*
	20–24	*25–35*	*36–45*	*46–50*	
20–30	Nil	1	Nil	Nil	1
31–40	3	8	Nil	Nil	11
41–50	Nil	6	5	1	12
51–60	Nil	3	2	Nil	5
61–70	Nil	Nil	1	Nil	1
Total	3	18	8	1	30

Out of the 30 sample entrepreneurs, 27 were married, two were unmarried and one was a widower. Even though family responsibilities quite often constrained individuals from taking risky decisions, at least 11 entrepreneurs[4] started their business career after their marriage. Table 3.6 clearly indicated that an individual's ability and/or interest in taking risk of starting a business initiative went down with age. Only one entrepreneur started a business initiative after crossing 46 years of age. Similarly, the number of people who started their business very early in life was also less: only three entrepreneurs started their business when they were between 20 and 24 years of age. This probably had to do with the level of maturity and experience that came with age after 25 years.

Motivation to Become an Entrepreneur

For individuals who were from traditional business communities, becoming an entrepreneur was considered as a normal route in professional life. However, those who were not from business families needed to take a conscious decision to become entrepreneurs. Often, becoming an entrepreneur involved heavy financial loss, at least in the initial stage. This was because, the money that an individual was capable of earning as salary in an established business was often much more than the revenue that a new business could generate. Therefore, in starting-up a business, often entrepreneurs were motivated more by non-monetary factors than by monetary factors, at least during the initial stage. The same was applicable for individuals from business families, who started a new business on their own, away from their family business. For N.R. Narayan Murthy it was the desire to develop good quality software in India (Murthy, n.d.). For Pradeep Kar of Microland it was the desire to be independent and thereby release his creative potential. However, earning possibilities was also one of the motivating factors for him (Kar, 2010). Subroto Bagchi of Mindtree, on the other hand, was motivated to create a business enterprise that is value-based, socially sensitive, and would make an upfront commitment to societies in which it works (Bagchi, n.d.). The interviews with the sample entrepreneurs revealed diverse motivating factors responsible for the emergence of entrepreneurship. They included the desire to be different, tenacity for freedom, excitement of being part of a high-technology-based industry, prospects of high returns, identification of specific business opportunity, and scarcity of suitable jobs as a result of global ICT slowdown. There was some similarity between the findings of the current research and that of Roberts (1991) in the USA. Roberts found that most technical entrepreneurs in the USA were fulfilling a long felt ambition of starting their own business in order to become independent, become their own boss, and search for new and bolder challenge.

Hindustan Computers Limited (HCL) was created because the founders, despite being paid well at Delhi Cotton Mills were unhappy with what they were doing at the Calculator Division of the Company and wanted to do more (Rediff, 2007).

Coming from a family where everyone excepting him was a doctor, Rajat Apte, founder of Magnatech Inc. wanted to be different. This dream he pursued by becoming an engineer, and not a doctor, and later by leaving a 'well-cushioned' job and becoming an entrepreneur. Coming from a middle-class family, where nobody prior to his generation ever became a graduate, it was interest in doing something different that also motivated Arjun Desai, founder of Win Infotech Ltd. and Kunal Raman, founder of Sharp Technologies Pvt. Ltd. to become entrepreneurs. However, for Kunal Raman, rational choice played an important role in identifying the field to venture into. He along with his brother chose to enter software industry because it required little investment when compared to other industries. Same was the reason that Jayant Srinivas, founder of Ahead Technologies Pvt. Ltd. had in entering high-technology industry as entrepreneur. However, what helped Kunal Raman and his brother in choosing the software industry was that the technical training that they had was suitable for doing business in industry. They, therefore, decided to jump into this industry even without identifying a business opportunity. Unlike Kunal Raman and his brother, Akhtar Hussain, founder of Communication Networks decided to become an entrepreneur only when he succeeded in identifying a business opportunity. Ability to identify a business opportunity was one motivating factor for Anil Despande, founder of Tech Writers Inc. and K. Padmakumar, founder of Frontech Ltd. as well.

Coming from lower-middle-class family, for S. Sivakumar, founder of Datainformatics Pvt. Ltd. the motivation to become entrepreneur emerged out of the desire to be someone big. Prospects of earning high revenue was the prime motivating factor for Akhtar Hussain, founder of Communication Networks, Raj Modi, founder of Softech, and Raj Software and Communications, Ullas Gowda, founder of Knowledge Solutions Pvt. Ltd., James John, founder of Spaceage.com, and Alok Dutta, founder of Silicon Networks Pvt. Ltd. For Raj Modi, founder of Softech and Raj Software and Communications, Jayant Srinivas, founder of Ahead Technologies Pvt. Ltd., and Vinay Reddy, founder of Software Consultants Pvt. Ltd., the motivation to join ICT industry also came from the thrill of being part of a new technology-based industry. For Vinay Reddy, this thrill developed out of his exposure as a part of his job to the potential that technology had in facilitating business operation.

For Anil Despande, founder of Tech Writers Inc., Ullas Gowda, founder of Knowledge Solutions Pvt. Ltd., Pankaj Sen, founder of Advanced Software Systems Pvt. Ltd., Vishnu Krishnaswamy, founder of Techvision, Chandan Sivaram, founder of Soft Solutions Pvt. Ltd., Kunal Raman, founder of Sharp Technologies Pvt. Ltd., and Sudha Sharma, founder of Design Lab, one important source of motivation to become entrepreneurs was fascination for independence. In the words of Kunal Raman, founder of Sharp

Technologies Pvt. Ltd., 'temperamentally I don't fit into any organized set-up or I don't like to follow rules laid down by other people. So I would like to be on my own. So that's the urge'. This was the kind of response that came from Anil Despande, founder of Tech Writers Inc. as well.

O.P. Nayar, founder of Accent Tech Solutions, Dinesh Marwari, founder of Ryze Softech Pvt. Ltd., Kirti Harlalka, founder of Knowhow, and Rupa Datta, founder of Infonet Pvt. Ltd. became entrepreneurs with the intention of doing something big. However, it was the expansion of job market in recent times that created an environment where entrepreneurs could take the risk of leaving their jobs in order to pursue their big dreams. This was because even if an entrepreneur was unsuccessful in business he/she could always go back to employment as plenty of jobs were available in the market. Such an understanding, developed while interacting with entrepreneurs like James John, founder of Spaceage.com and Jayant Srinivas, founder of Ahead Technologies Pvt. Ltd. However, experience of Gautam Apte, founder of Innovative Web Solutions Pvt. Ltd., gave rise to a completely different picture. It was the scarcity of suitable jobs in the ICT industry during 2001 due to global economic slowdown which motivated him to do something on his own. However, he could do it only because he had developed and maintained necessary professional contacts while working in the USA as an employee.

Gender and Entrepreneurship

In Israel, median successful high-technology entrepreneurs were male (Malach-Pines, Dvir and Sadeh, 2004). Considering the lack of visibility of women entrepreneurs in almost all industry segments in India, particularly in high-technology sectors like ICT (observed in course of this study), it could be presumed that the Indian statistics would be no different from that of Israel if relevant quantitative data was collected. This implied that gender played an important role in determining the possibility of an individual to become an entrepreneur. Entrepreneurship was oriented towards creating independence, which could be unacceptable in a patriarchal society like India, where women were concerned. This could be one explanation for near absence of women entrepreneurs.

We interacted with three women entrepreneurs for the purpose of this research. One interesting similarity among them was that all came from families that were involved in business.

Even though we met two of these entrepreneurs in Mumbai and one in Chennai, it was found that all were brought up in Mumbai. Two of these entrepreneurs hailed from Punjabi family. Out of these three entrepreneurs two were married and one was unmarried. Here also it was observed that in-laws of both the married entrepreneurs were involved in business. All these indicated that having a business background in family possibly created a somewhat conducive environment for the development of woman entrepreneurship. However, only one of these entrepreneurs received support from her family members from the beginning; the other two faced opposition from their family members initially. One of the married entrepreneurs had a child. She ran her business from home. The two married women entered business early on in their life, at the age of 27 years. Whereas, the third entrepreneur got into business at the age of 46 years, after a long career as a professional. Even though the number of women entrepreneurs was too less to identify a widespread pattern, influence of gender on an individual's experience in entrepreneurship was clearly visible.

It was found that, when it came to business activities, married women entrepreneurs laid more emphasis on their relationship with family members in comparison to their male counterparts or the unmarried woman entrepreneur. For example, Rupa Datta, founder of Infonet Pvt. Ltd. said, 'My husband had been my biggest backing. He has been supporting and (acting as a) sounding board and putting me into place .... I have a very supportive family. So that obviously helps'. Similar statements were rare to come from male entrepreneurs. Although few male entrepreneurs like Mangalam Srinivas, founder of Global Technologies Pvt. Ltd. emphasized the importance of family support, it was more important for them in entering business. While Pankaj Sen, founder of Advanced Software Systems Pvt. Ltd., Chandan Sivaram, founder of Soft Solutions Pvt. Ltd., and S. Ram of Integrated Software Solutions mentioned the supportive role played by their wives, unlike married women entrepreneurs, family support was not so important for male entrepreneurs in running business on a day-to-day basis. This was true also in case of N.R. Narayana Murthy of Indian ICT major Infosys (Murthy, n.d.). Interestingly, while founding Infosys the founders (all male) had taken a decision that their wives would not be part of this venture. Following Narayana Murthy other founders took this informal decision so as to ensure the balance between home and office given the extensive engagement that an enterprise demanded at its initial stage from the founding team (Iype, n.d.).

One more reason for which family support was essential for married women was that families had a lot of expectations from women at home, particularly if they were married. Therefore, without agreement from family to share responsibilities, it was difficult for a woman to function as an entrepreneur. For example, Rupa Datta, founder of Infonet Pvt. Ltd. said,

> Support from my family has been good ... (Getting support from) my parents was very easy, obviously, because it was their daughter (who was) trying it. My in-laws have also been very supportive ... . I don't have to worry about the house ... . I don't (bear) many family obligations ... . And people have accepted it, you know. So very honestly put I am supposed to be a woman who is very concentrated at work ... they have, I guess, accepted that. So acceptance from them has come very easily.

Being married and having a child to look after, Kirti Harlalka wanted to work from home. That was how she got the idea of founding Knowhow, a freelancer-driven organization, as opposed to taking up a job, which would have required her to travel. Interestingly, she felt that gender worked in her favour in business. She said,

> In fact one of my biggest enablers is the fact that I am not a man! ... because if I were a man I ... (had to bear) the responsibility of running a household. So my husband being the earning member, I don't have to worry about earning the bread. So that is a big pressure off my head. Whatever pressure is there to earn is self-created. So in that sense it is nice.

Entrepreneurs in the ICT industry formed a diverse group in terms of the various criteria mentioned above. It was observed that background influenced performance of an entrepreneur in business. However, this was not to say that the ICT entrepreneurs needed to come from a specific kind of background. For example, although an entrepreneur's family background in business often helped her/him by making various necessary resources available, most of the entrepreneurs sampled for this study did not have any family background in business. This indicated that, in order to explain the variation that existed in the business performance of entrepreneurs, there was a need for reflecting both on entrepreneurs' background and on the nature of the enterprise founded by them.

Notes

1. For detailed profiles of entrepreneurs and enterprises founded by them, see Appendix.
2. The number before decimal implies year and the number after decimal implies month. For example, 2.1 would mean two years and one month.
3. Following the rules of Registrar of Companies, Government of India closing down of non-operational companies was extremely difficult, if not impossible. Therefore, companies continued to exist on Government record, even though they were not operational.
4. Data on this is not available for all entrepreneurs.

References

Bagchi, S. (n.d.). Making of the Mindtree. *IDG Ventures India*. <http://www.idgvcindia.com/html/Mindtree%20Article.pdf.> Retrieved 21 June 2014.

College of Business, San José State University. (n.d.). Dell supply chain. *College of Business, San José State University*. <http://www.cob.sjsu.edu/reade_c/187.Chap016.ppt#398,10,Dell's%20Suppl y%20Chain.> Retrieved 14 January 2009.

Dicken, P. (2000). A new geo-economy. In D. Held and A. McGrew (eds), *The global transformations reader: An introduction to the globalization debate*. Cambridge: Polity Press, 251–258.

Iype, G. (n.d.). The amazing Infosys story: How Infosys was born. *Citehr*. <http://www.citehr.com/118434-amazing-infosys-story-how-infosys-born.html.> Retrieved 21 June 2014.

Kar, P. (6 October 2010). Leveraging Technology. *Entrepreneur*. <http://entrepreneurindia.in/people/coverstory/leverag-ng-technology/4954/.> Retrieved 22 June 2014.

Kar, P. (n.d.). Reinventing Microland. *Leadership Insights, Colorshots*. <http://leadershipinsights.colorshots.co/reinvent-ng-microland-pradeep-kar/.> Retrieved 21 June 2014.

Malach-Pines, A., Dvir, D. and Sadeh, A. (2004). The making of Israeli high-technology entrepreneurs: An exploratory study. *The Journal of Entrepreneurship*, 13(1), 29–52.

Marico Innovation Foundation. (n.d.). Wipro global command centre. *Marico Innovation Foundation*. <http://www.maricoinnovation foundation.org/awards/pdfs/winners_wiprogcc .pdf.> Retrieved 16 January 2009.

Murthy, S. (n.d.). Story of Infosys. *Voofin.* <http://voofin.tripod.com/infosys.htm.> Retrieved 22 June 2014.

Parthasarathy, B. (2004). India's Silicon Valley or Silicon Valley's India? Socially embedding the computer software industry in Bangalore. *International Journal of Urban and Regional Research*, 28(3), 664–685.

Rediff. (9 June 2007). The amazing story of the birth of HCL. *Rediff.* <http://www.rediff.com/money/2007/jun/09bspec1.htm.> retrieved 22 June 2014.

Roberts, E.B. (1991). *Entrepreneurs in high technology: Lessons from MIT and beyond.* Oxford: Oxford University Press, 47–49.

Wipro. (n.d.). Wipro global command centre. *Wipro.* <http://wipro.com/webpages/itservices/infrastrucmgmt/gcc.htm.> Retrieved 16 January 2009.

4

Customers, Business Development, and Social Capital

Development of business involves a wide variety of activities including identification of business opportunity, exploration of prospective customers, getting customers, retention of existing customers and managing crisis. These functionalities demand engagement with a range of economic actors with special attention towards the customers. Embedded relationships and networks of various types play an important role in influencing an entrepreneur's ability to develop the necessary relationships. Considering the resource value of relationships it appears that embeddedness and networks may be considered as platforms for development of social capital in this context. However, business development also concerns spheres where interpersonal relationships play little or no role. Therefore, it would be important to understand their significance in order to secure a comprehensive understanding of the process of business development. To facilitate this process of understanding I would utilize knowledge gained from different small and medium entrepreneurs with whom I had extensive conversation.

Identification of Business Opportunity

Success of any initiative depends on the strength of the guiding idea. One important component of that idea revolves around identification of a right opportunity to take initiative. This is particularly relevant in profit-oriented enterprises, where it is also referred as 'market opportunity' (Soh, 2003; Ramachandran and Ray, 2006). Many entrepreneurs consider identification of a business opportunity as the most significant challenge in business. Mangalam Srinivas, founder of Global Technologies Pvt. Ltd., a software product company, mentioned that the most important challenge in his business was to create a product roadmap keeping the market dynamics in mind. K. Padmakumar, founder of Frontech Ltd., also took a similar position when he said that the trajectory of business development in his company was decided by changes that took place in the business environment and pattern of customer expectation. The issue that remains critical here is the way in which an entrepreneur develops an understanding about the market. Interaction with different entrepreneurs indicated that their educational and/or professional background and their interpersonal relationship with professional colleagues, friends, and family members played a critical role here. However, interpersonal relationship with family members was useful in business primarily for entrepreneurs with business family background.

Educational Qualification and Professional Background

Educational background of an entrepreneur often played an important role in identifying business opportunity in a technology-based industry like ICT. Entrepreneurs like Rajat Apte, founder of Magnatech Inc., Anil Despande, founder of Tech Writers Inc., and Pankaj Sen, founder of Advanced Software Systems Pvt. Ltd. felt that choosing to enter this industry was a natural progression from their educational background in engineering and work experience in the same field. However, it is important to understand that while technical knowledge is significant for an individual to function successfully as an entrepreneur in the ICT industry, not every individual acquired such knowledge through education. This was true for entrepreneurs who did not have any educational qualification related to ICT, for example, Ajay Aggarwal, founder of Netware Pvt. Ltd., Raj Modi, founder of Softech and Raj Software and Communications, Hitesh Patel, founder of Knowledge Software Pvt. Ltd., and Naresh Ponnaiah, founder of Sunshine Technologies Ltd. Each of them, interestingly, had an educational background in the discipline of Commerce. Educational qualification did not play any significant role for them in identification of business opportunity. Furthermore, it was also pointed out that at times, suitable educational qualification could become a dark resource obstructing an entrepreneur's ability to identify the best business opportunity. Speaking about himself S. Sivakumar, founder of Datainformatics Pvt. Ltd., said,

> ... thinking that one is an engineer is a liability ... (Being an engineer) I was always more interested in doing something technical, and was not at all interested in trading ... (while) I knew that only trading was going to give big money .... (However) I didn't have that attitude, because I was always thinking that I am an engineer and I can do much more than trading.

Professional background of an entrepreneur could also play an important role in identifying appropriate business opportunity. Subroto Bagchi, one of the key founders of well-known ICT services company Mindtree Consulting, wrote that it was an opportunity to work on a strategic study of the future of Indian software industry as an employee of Lucent Technologies in Bangalore that made him understand the scope of software services in the 21st century. It is this understanding that later motivated him to think of starting Mindtree (Bagchi, n.d.). Arjun Desai, founder of Win Infotech Ltd., got his idea of starting a business venture in the area of ICT training while being on his last job as a part of which he was responsible for setting up franchisees of an ICT training institution all over South India. Arjun Desai's business idea evolved from his perception of opportunity in doing what his then employer was doing. In contrast, Akhtar Hussain got the idea of founding his company, Communication Networks, by perceiving what his then employer was not being able to do. To put it in his own words,

> I was working with an ICT company in the Customer Support segment .... (I found that companies) were mostly into selling computers .... They were not able to deliver ... quality service, specially to the ... small and medium enterprises. They were concentrating largely on the big corporates .... So I found ... there was a segment of customers who were ready to give ICT services contract even to new entrepreneurs.

Naresh Ponnaiah, founder of Sunshine Technologies Ltd., felt that even though there are exceptions, it is quite common for first generation entrepreneurs to develop an enterprise in an area where entrepreneurs have professional experience.

Naresh Ponnaiah's statement appeared largely valid, as out of the entrepreneurs who did not highlight their professional background while talking about the process of identification of business opportunity we found people who discussed about the significance of their family background in business. This included Ajay Aggarwal, founder of Netware Pvt. Ltd., Amit Sharma, founder of Sindh Infotech Pvt. Ltd., and Hitesh Patel, founder of Knowledge Software Pvt. Ltd. Even though for these entrepreneurs family played some role in identifying business opportunity in ICT industry, it is not that their family had a business background in the same industry. Prior to starting their business venture these entrepreneurs had never worked in ICT industry. This was not true, however, for all entrepreneurs who had a business family background. Raj Modi, founder of Softech and Raj Software and Communications, Dinesh Marwari, founder of Ryze Softech Pvt. Ltd., and Kirti Harlalka, founder of Knowhow, who came from business families, had worked as employees in their relevant industry segments. They utilized knowledge they developed as a part of their professional career in conceptualizing their business idea. On the other hand, there was Jayant Srinivas, founder of Ahead Technologies Pvt. Ltd., who was neither from a business family, nor had any work experience in ICT industry to fall upon in conceptualizing his business idea. He began his professional career with a business venture which he was running when I interacted with him. Experiences of the entrepreneurs mentioned above represent the widespread diversity that exists in the impact of educational and professional background on identification of business opportunity.

Rational Choice

While entrepreneur's background was found important in exploring market opportunities, economic action, particularly business decisions were, to a large extent, outcome of conscious rational calculations. This included rationally choosing the industry segments to venture into by comparing the various options. Entrepreneurs had diverse justification for choosing an industry. Amit Sharma, founder of Sindh Infotech Pvt. Ltd., decided to enter ICT industry as he felt that it was an industry of the future; it was clean, appeared interesting, had growth potential, and had lower government interference. In order to adopt a rational decision an entrepreneur collected necessary information through different avenues like attending industry symposium (as done by Amit Sharma, founder of Sindh Infotech), studying market trend reports (as done by Ullas Gowda, founder of Knowledge Solutions Pvt. Ltd.), observing current market trends in the USA and Europe (crucial markets for ICT industry) to understand the future business possibility in India (as done by Pankaj Sen, founder of Advanced Software Systems Pvt. Ltd.), or making a comparative analysis of growth of different industry segments during periods of economic recession (as done by Kunal Raman, founder of Sharp Technologies Pvt. Ltd.). However, identification of business opportunity was not a one-time process which ended once a business opportunity was identified at the beginning. Instead, it was found to be a continuous process of business activity. Therefore, it involved considerable research in market trends on a regular basis.

Ability to make rational choice depended on availability of diverse information needed for making a precise cost-benefit analysis. However, such information was hardly available about new business areas where most of the opportunity existed. Therefore, 'hunch' often played an important role in business decision-making. However, usually entrepreneurs validated their hunch by collecting as much information as possible. Ajay Aggarwal, founder of Netware Pvt. Ltd. could get the confidence to go ahead with his hunch about the existence of a business opportunity in web designing because he had the moral support of his father who was a businessman and he could also consult his uncle who was a professional in the ICT industry in the USA. It appeared that hunch could play a more important role among entrepreneurs who were willing to diversify their already existing businesses. First-timers often depended more on rational calculation in order to avoid the risk of incurring loss. Even then hunch could become important in specific cases. Rational choice was important for every entrepreneur. But, the extent to which an entrepreneur could become rational depended on the situational limitations of entrepreneurs. For example, an individual could initiate a business venture in an industry segment only if he/she had developed some understanding about that segment. In the same way, availability of necessary finance could determine the level of rationality that an entrepreneur could reach in identifying a business opportunity. Therefore, the rational choice that an entrepreneur succeeded in adopting in business varied.

Serendipity

Rational choice had its importance for any business. However, often it was serendipity that played significant role in business decision-making process. In case of ICT industry, identification of client industry played an important role in locating business opportunities. Quite often identification of client industry happened by chance. This was clear from the experience of Amit Sharma, founder of Sinch Infotech Pvt. Ltd. He identified a particular area of business and thought of specializing in it only when he got a chance to serve a client from that specific industry segment. Rajat Apte, founder of Magnatech Inc. and Arjun Desai, founder of Win Infotech Ltd. also had similar experiences whereby the business opportunity that they identified evolved out of their engagement with and understanding of the business area of their initial clients. However, these engagements did not evolve out of any conscious decision taken by the entrepreneurs. Back then, being new in business, they had to accept any client who was ready to offer them some work. Given such role played by serendipity entrepreneurs like Kunal Raman, founder of Sharp Technologies Pvt. Ltd., felt that chance was much more important for business than anything else including advance business planning. Kunal Raman also emphasized the need for practical considerations like entrepreneur's resource capacity while identifying a business opportunity.

Interestingly, Dinesh Marwari, founder of Ryze Softech Pvt. Ltd., was candid enough to make it clear that, even though business decisions were often taken by chance, it was important to project them as an outcome of careful consideration. Regarding the process through which Ryze Softech Pvt. Ltd. chose telecommunication as an industry to focus on, he said,

> See most companies will actually say that it was a well defined strategy and things like that. So if I am giving a press interview that's what I will say. But I can guarantee you that every company at least while starting out will define their strategies based on opportunities that come to them .... We were going after any client that we could get. It just so happened that many of our clients were in the communication space. So by default, you build expertise and build referenceability in that industry ... now if ... I have got ten clients in this industry and I have got one client in the banking industry, if I am talking to a new customer in the banking industry, its much more difficult for me to convince him to work with me

> than if I am getting a new customer in telecom industry, where I can tell him, listen I have ten other customers – this is what I have done ... and he has ten people to talk to if he wants to validate what we have done in the past. So its ... much more easier for us to get a customer in this space and it gives us a good focus and a good platform to talk to a customer. So that's how everybody builds their vertical focus area. That's how we have done it.

Such a position, in a way, questions the rationale for formulating a business plan to start a venture. In this connection, Rupa Datta, founder of Infonet Pvt. Ltd., said that when it came to implementation, her business model changed drastically from what she had written in the business plan that she had prepared and submitted to her investors. Looked at in this way, a business plan could be perceived as a process document rather than a finished product which is ready for implementation. The business plan document could be viewed as a tool through which business ideas evolve over time. However, one must also understand that serendipity was found to be crucial for ICT industry as it is largely a service-based industry in India. Without denying the significance of serendipity it may be said that the findings could have been different if the study was concentrated only on software product companies.

Professional Relationships

Developing and maintaining professional relationships was found to be tremendously important for any business. Such relationships could include people with whom an entrepreneur had worked in the past as co-worker during her/his career as employee in different organizations. It could also comprise of people who were not co-workers of entrepreneur, but whom the entrepreneur came across through her/his employment career, for example, independent professionals or people working as employee in other organizations with whom entrepreneur's then employing organization had some form of association. In addition, people known to the entrepreneur through various professional associations and meet-ups, where the entrepreneur participated could also be considered here. Professional relationships could also include people whom an entrepreneur came across through her/his own business, for example, customers, financiers, employees, etc. To a large extent, social capital required for business developed out of such professional relationships.

Importance of forming and maintaining relationship for developing business was emphasized by different entrepreneurs. Gautam Apte, founder of Innovative Web Solutions Pvt. Ltd. felt that for doing business it was essential to 'have contacts' and to 'keep in touch' with those contacts. Experience of Rajat Apte, founder of Magnatech Inc. was that informal discussion with existing customers could generate business ideas for future. However, it did not mean that discussion with professional colleagues always helped in developing a business idea. If a business idea was unconventional in nature, it was not easy for everyone to assess its worth. This was the experience of Anil Despande, founder of Tech Writers Inc. His company offered a service in the field of technical writing. Even today, the field of technical writing is not well-established as business. People are not sure whether a business can depend solely on technical writing service. The situation was even worse when Anil Despande started his business in this field. Being a new unconventional field, his then colleagues hardly had any idea about it. Social capital emerging out of professional relationships had the potential to become important for all entrepreneurs. However, entrepreneurs from business families, whose family members were strongly involved in their business, (for example, Ajay Aggarwal, founder of Netware Pvt. Ltd., Amit Sharma, founder of Sindh Infotech Pvt. Ltd., Hitesh Patel, founder of Knowledge Software Pvt. Ltd., and Dinesh Marwari, founder of Ryze Softech Pvt. Ltd.) were relatively less vocal about its importance.

Personal Relationships

Just like professional relationships, personal relationships also played an important role in developing business. Personal relationships included kindred connected directly or indirectly to the entrepreneurs either through blood or through marriage. It also entailed friends of an entrepreneur as well as that of her/his family member(s). Such personal relationships often led to formation of social capital for business. Considering utility of social capital in development of business, all entrepreneurs attempted to build them. This research work began with the presumption that ICT being a new industry no entrepreneur would have a family-based social capital in the same industry. This would have meant that every entrepreneur would have to develop necessary social capital with her/his own efforts. However, it came out that coming from business family background had its own advantage in terms of social capital development, irrespective of the industry the family members of the entrepreneur were involved in. This could happen in multiple ways. Even if an entrepreneur had family members who were involved in an industry different from the one in which the entrepreneur wanted to venture into, those family members could still be resourceful for the entrepreneur if they had connection with people from industry and/or professions relevant for entrepreneur as friends and/or professional colleagues. It was not necessary for such family members to be entrepreneurs. Even as a senior salaried professional, an individual could possess insider information about an industry.

As mentioned earlier, Ajay Aggarwal, an entrepreneur with a business family background, decided to found Netware Pvt. Ltd. based on such insider information received from his uncle who was a senior ICT consultant in the USA. However, to become social capital for business, family connection could be relevant even if it was in an industry different from the one in which the entrepreneur wanted to venture in. Family connection in other industries, particularly industry of prospective clients, could also turn out to be useful. This was quite clear from the experiences of Raj Modi, founder of Softech and Raj Software and Communications, who began his business with development of an accounting software. He mentioned that while pursuing this business opportunity he collected insider information from a friend of his father who was a Chartered Accountant. Such information was useful in order to understand the possible market value of this product by addressing questions like was there any requirement for such a product, would people buy it, what would be the price that people would be willing to pay for, etc. For social capital to emerge out of family relationships it was not always necessary to network with people who are well aware about the industry in which the entrepreneur wants to venture in. Social capital could also entail resources evolving out of entrepreneur's relationship with family members who have no connection whatsoever with the industry in which an entrepreneur wants to venture into. Entrepreneurs could identify a business opportunity just on the basis of their familiarity with the everyday activities of their family members. For example, Hitesh Patel, founder of Knowledge Software Pvt. Ltd., got the idea of developing a database software, a user-driven personal encyclopaedia, seeing the problem that his wife used to face on a regular basis in preserving and retrieving pieces of information that she would collect over time in order to conduct quiz competitions. However, he thought of converting the basic software that he had developed for his wife into a more sophisticated marketable product only when quiz contests gained popularity in the country through introduction of relevant popular shows on television. Hitesh Patel's experience showed how everyday life problems could give rise to business ideas. Initial ideas behind the various knowledge management software which he offered could be traced in the observations that he made in his personal life earlier on.

It was observed that entrepreneurs having a family background in business were more vocal about the resource potential of their personal relationships. This included entrepreneurs like Ajay Aggarwal, founder of Netware Pvt. Ltd., Raj Modi, founder of Softech and Raj Software and Communications, Amit Sharma, founder of Sindh Infotech Pvt. Ltd., Hitesh Patel, founder of Knowledge Software Pvt. Ltd., and Dinesh Marwari, founder of Ryze Softech Pvt. Ltd. However, not all entrepreneurs whose family members were involved in business emphasized the importance of their personal relationships. This included entrepreneurs like Pankaj Sen, founder of Advanced Software Systems Pvt. Ltd., Gautam Apte, founder of Innovative Web Solutions Pvt. Ltd., Naresh Ponnaiah, founder of Sunshine Technologies Ltd., and Kirti Harlalka, founder of Knowhow. That these entrepreneurs did not emphasize the relationship with their family members, even though the latter were involved in business, could probably be explained by the hiatus between the nature of business of these entrepreneurs and that of their family members. These entrepreneurs felt that as a result of this divide, their family members hardly understood the business they were involved in.

Educational and professional background was found to be playing an important role in the identification of business opportunity. At the same time, relationships developed and maintained as a part of one's profession or family also played an important role for many entrepreneurs in locating business ideas. In this context, outcome of such relationships could be considered as social capital. Often identification of business ideas were cumulative effect of multiple factors mentioned above. Discovery of business opportunity was frequently highlighted as an achievement of the entrepreneur reached through rational calculation. Even though the importance of rational choice could not be ignored, serendipity was found to be emerging as an important factor in the whole process. However, what was interesting was that entrepreneurs were unsure about publicly accepting this significance.

Locating Prospective Customers: Marketing Strategies

Often, if not always, a business opportunity is defined by notional presence of customers. Therefore, thought of starting a business venture and identification of prospective customers are often simultaneous processes. However, it was observed that depending on the nature of business initiative, the processes through which enterprises attempted to identify prospective customers varied considerably. However, broadly it was possible to locate certain considerations that entrepreneurs kept in mind in this process. Going by the experience of studied entrepreneurs a typical customer usually had considerable dilemma in depending on new companies or new products, due to lack of familiarity with their performance. However, as entrepreneur, one needed to find a way of convincing people and get new customers. For quite a few entrepreneurs in a technology-based industry like ICT identifying prospective customers was quite a challenge. The challenge was often more for people who entered this industry because they identified a technology solution, for example, entrepreneurs like Vinay Reddy, founder of Software Consultants Pvt. Ltd. and Naresh Ponnaiah, founder of Sunshine Technologies Ltd. Having to spend considerable amount of time and energy on technology such technopreneurs often had little time left to develop an understanding of the market, the ways of approaching it, procedure of persevering with a client, and closing a deal. The problem was more because at the seed stage they did not have the necessary resources to recruit people who could look after marketing.

Reference-based Marketing: Potential for Social Capital

References of various types played an important role in the marketing of products and services. Reference was the process through which an entrepreneur used another person, who was familiar with the entrepreneur and/or her/his business offering, as referee. Role of referee was tremendously valuable in developing confidence in the mind of people who were unfamiliar with the entrepreneur and/or her/his business offering. Quite often a referee could be a person who had once been a customer of the entrepreneur. Broadly, it was possible to identify two types of references. In the first type of reference, which was more prevalent, an entrepreneur mentioned about her/his association with the referee to a prospective customer in order to develop confidence in her/his mind. The referee could be personally known to these prospective customers. However, it was not necessarily so. In a second type of reference, which any entrepreneur valued much more than the first type, people familiar with the entrepreneur and/or her/his business offering could suggest other people known to them to avail the product or service offered by the entrepreneur.

Entrepreneurs applied different strategies to establish reliability. For example, during the early days of internet in India Ajay Aggarwal, founder of Netware Pvt. Ltd., a company offering web designing services, decided to design websites for various industry associations, like Builder's Associations of India and All India Rubber Industries Association at a concessional rate in order to build references. The idea was that, once he had established a relationship with these associations, it would be easier to convince association members to hire him for doing their own web-designing work. This strategy helped Ajay Aggarwal in developing reputation about his work among prospective customers who never knew him personally. Here reputation was developed by using relationship-based social capital that existed between associations and their members. In case of nascent entrepreneurs, who were in the process of developing reputation in the market, social network could play an important role in identifying people whom entrepreneurs would like to approach for work. In such case, relationship could be used as a tool for earning the confidence of the customers.

Naveen Jayakumar, founder of Datamagic Pvt. Ltd., plunged into entrepreneurship and then started looking for business opportunity. He got his initial leads in business through social network of his founding partners. Kunal Raman, founder of Sharp Technologies Pvt. Ltd., recollected similar memories about his brother who was the founder of the first business venture with which he was associated. His brother used his relationship with friends, ex-colleagues, and acquaintances to meet senior managers at various companies in Bangalore to get initial projects so as to bootstrap the company. According to S. Ram, founder of Integrated Software Solutions, as an organization scaled up, the role that was played by personal social networks of entrepreneurs went down consistently. He felt that with time institutional effort like development of good websites and maturity in the formal marketing process should get priority. However, this did not mean that social network became unimportant. Development of network was a continuous process and it was non-negotiable. However, social capital emerging out of such network could have its own limitations. For example, while Alok Dutta, founder of Silicon Networks Pvt. Ltd., could use his Indian nationality to get business from companies in the USA by going through its employees belonging to Indian diaspora. However, he felt, 'the pressure of satisfying that kind of a customer is more than satisfying a totally unknown customer .... (When you are serving an unknown person) there is no emotional attachment. It's a job; you don't do well they let you go, you do well they come back to you .... Over here, the emotional aspects come in. And the pressure on you is more to do it ... because that employee's position is at stake'.

Reputation and Trust

In case of established businesses reputation is important for various aspects of business including the process of attracting customers. Reputation in the context of brand here depends primarily on the ability of a company to build a public image about the high quality of the company and/or its business offering. Customers' reliance on an established brand, however, does not depend on their familiarity with the functionaries of the organization that is offering a brand. Neither is it essential for a customer to use a brand in order to rely on it.

Engagement with emerging businesses/companies that were yet to establish themselves as brands brought out that till the time a company and/or its business offering became a brand, reputation could develop in two different ways. First, customers could begin to rely on the business offerings of a company either because they had availed it and were satisfied with it, or because their close acquaintances had similar opinion about it. Second, customers could also begin to depend on a company because they were familiar with the ability and/or the qualification of the functionaries of the company, particularly its founder. The second factor often became more important when a customer was dealing with a new organization whose business offering was yet to attain a reputation in the market.

Reputation was closely related with trust, which in this context primarily referred to reliance.

To put it in the word of Vishnu Krishnaswamy, founder of Techvision, 'nobody gets fired (from their company) for choosing IBM (as vendor)'. This was because IBM, as a company was a brand and, therefore, carried certain inherent reputation. Whereas, depending on a new company always involved some risk for the customers, as the credibility of the company was yet to be established in market. Rajat Apte, founder of Magnatech Inc., said that initial customers were generally individuals or companies who were willing to take the risk. Therefore, in the initial stage, it was necessary to know who the risk-takers were in the target industry. It was not necessary for such risk-takers to be organizations. They could be individuals in various organizations. According to Rajat Apte, in a technology product industry, one characteristic of these early users of new technology was that, even though they were not completely satisfied with what they were getting, they were confident that they could work with the manufacturers of that technology to take the product to the next level to make it useful for them.

While it was true that the initial customers took risk by depending on a new organization, customers often found a way of mitigating such risk with the help of familiarity with the entrepreneur as a person and/or her/his ability. This was clear from the experience of Gautam Apte, founder of Innovative Web Solutions Pvt. Ltd. One of Gautam Apte's initial customers, who knew his ability personally, decided to trust the reliability of Innovative Web Solutions Pvt. Ltd. because Gautam Apte was the person behind it. However, in the absence of initial customer's familiarity with the entrepreneur's ability, an entrepreneur (for example, Pankaj Sen, founder of Advanced Software Systems Pvt. Ltd.) could use her/his educational qualification, skill-set, and/or work experience in a reputed organization, to build her/his reputation in the mind of the customer. Of course it also came out from Pankaj Sen that such objective indicators of capability were not always sufficient to impress a customer. At times, it was also necessary to demonstrate capability by performing some work free of cost. Many of the initial customers of Pankaj Sen were companies for which he had provided some complimentary service at the beginning. This emphasis on ability in development of trust was comparable with the nature of social capital existing among Silicon Valley entrepreneurs (see Cohen and Fields, 1999).

'Cold-Call': Marketing without Reference

'Cold-calling' was a term used by entrepreneurs across cities to imply marketing initiatives where reference played no role. Such initiatives could either involve calling up prospective customers over the phone or visiting their offices. Depending on the nature of business 'cold-call' could play a significant role in business. For example, even though Ajay Aggarwal, founder of Netware Pvt. Ltd., decided to use his relationship with industry associations to enhance his reputation among their members he often had no reference to fall upon to reach these associations. Instead, he had to depend upon 'cold-calling'. Entrepreneurs often used a combination of reference-based calling as well as 'cold-calling' for identifying prospective customers. This was confirmed by Raj Modi, founder of Softech and Raj Software and Communications. When interviewed he was marketing a software targeted towards the stock-broking industry. For marketing this product, he contacted 'known' as well as 'unknown' stock-brokers. The word 'known' did not necessarily imply sharing any close relationship. It could just mean knowing someone by face. Anil Despande, founder of Tech Writers Inc., said he used 'cold-calling' to a large extent during the initial period. Whenever he visited the office of one company at an industrial estate he always carried some extra brochures about his organization. He would always try to walk into offices of companies in the same industrial estate and attempt to talk to person(s) concerned. Sometimes business did develop out of such visits. However, Raj Modi mentioned that 'cold-calling' did not work as a marketing strategy in all industries. In stock-broking industry it worked, because, according to him, it was an industry that was organized around formal institutions. But in diamond industry, for example, which was the target industry for his previous software product, 'cold-call' did not work, because diamond industry was entirely based on informal relationships. In diamond industry all business transactions were dependent on references. Even in industry segments where 'cold-calling' worked, a large part of such initiatives could result in rejection. Only sometimes business would develop out of it.

In organized industries it was relatively easy to identify who would become prospective customers. Vishnu Krishnaswamy, founder of Techvision, identified his prospective customers from multiple sources like top 200 companies listed by *Data Quest* (a premiere news magazine about the ICT industry), membership list of Software Technology Parks of India (STPI), and companies listed in different online and offline ICT directories. Anil Despande, founder of Tech Writers Inc., had learnt the process of identifying prospective customers through his previous work experience as a marketing professional for a software product. Being in the profession of technical writing he extensively went through product catalogues, business catalogues, yellow pages, and trade magazines in order to identify organizations that could require his service to prepare documentation for their product. However, among all companies which could require his service he chose to focus on electronic product manufacturers considering his related educational background. These experiences and strategies indicated that entrepreneurs continuously attempted to adopt an eclectic approach towards marketing by mixing strategies involving trust and 'cold-call'.

Mass Marketing and Serendipity

In addition to 'cold-call' and 'reference', prospective customers could be identified through mass marketing as well. Mass marketing implied marketing strategies using various mass media. Mass marketing became essential when entrepreneurs were not sure who could become their customers and, therefore, could not use 'cold-call' or reference in order to market their business offerings. Such a challenge was generally faced by entrepreneurs who were attempting to market some new technology. Naresh Ponnaiah, founder of Sunshine Technologies Ltd., said about his product that it was disruptive in nature: when the product was launched there was no established market for it; instead, market had to be created by disrupting the existing nature of technology. Traditional marketing strategy through mass media would include advertising in television, newspaper, or radio. However, it was not feasible for many small- and medium-sized companies lacking necessary financial support to go for such models of mass marketing. Therefore, new entrepreneurs identified various alternative strategies of mass marketing.

Hitesh Patel, founder of Knowledge Software Pvt. Ltd. had little idea as to who could be the prospective customers for his software products. Therefore, he tried to face this challenge by displaying the product at trade shows. However, simultaneously, he also interacted with software distributors as well as PC makers as prospective customers for his product. While he adopted mass marketing as a strategy, he also looked forward to create satisfied customers to use them for reference-based marketing. According to him, the marketing challenge was more in software product industry than in software service industry. In service industry the entrepreneur could find out from the customer what he/she required. However, in the absence of a ready-made customer in product business, the entrepreneur could only use her/his intuition to guess the needs of prospective customers. The situation was even more complicated in case of the non-conventional software which Hitesh Patel had built for maintaining a personal collection of jokes, quiz questions, etc. This was because in comparison to formally defined areas like accounting and statistics there were hardly any standard rules defining user behaviour in non-conventional spaces.

In India, since the end of 1990s and particularly since year 2000 internet emerged as an important medium of mass marketing. This promoted entrepreneurs like Kunal Raman, founder of Sharp Technologies Pvt. Ltd., to use internet as a cost effective means of communication. His idea was to make the product available on the internet for download so that people can try it out. While such a strategy was useful for smaller products it didn't work for elaborate products that required installation by the company that developed the product. Besides, given the degree of anonymity that was built into internet, as a technology, it was difficult for a company, which permitted the users to purchase and download a software online, to understand who was using their product and what were they using it for. In order to understand that entrepreneurs often created discussion forums. Once entrepreneurs had some understanding of the users and the utility it was possible for them to focus the attention of marketing there and even use word of mouth reference. It also facilitated the next level of development of this product. In addition to internet, Kunal Raman also had to adopt other affordable strategies of mass marketing like writing to editors of industry magazines about his software and going to trade shows to display his product. Depending on the nature of business offering traditional method of poster/banner-based mass marketing could also turn out to be useful. Arjun Desai of Win Infotech Ltd. began his career as an entrepreneur by opening a computer training centre. Having a local focus they began publicity through posters. At times, entrepreneurs identified new spaces for their business just by chance while interacting with a prospective client. That's how Anil Despande, founder of Tech Writers Inc. got into preparing help text for software industry even though at the outset his focus was on electronics product industry.

In identifying prospective customers, the role of serendipity was more important when entrepreneurs lacked clear vision of who their prospective customers were. Entrepreneurs in software product industry could lack clear vision about prospective customers when they developed an innovative product for which market was still unknown or less known. They could also face a similar situation if they started looking for business opportunity after plunging into entrepreneurship. In such cases, entrepreneurs could be more concerned about getting work than about the nature of work that they could get. When the nature of work took a backseat, entrepreneurs did not remain so focused in deciding whom they would approach for work. However, at times, like in case of Naveen Jayakumar, founder of Datamagic Pvt. Ltd., stable products developed out of certain commissioned work that the company had done just by chance for a customer. Kunal Raman, founder of Sharp Technologies Pvt. Ltd., also experienced the importance of serendipity in a significant way when he started marketing his data storage software product through internet. He said that while conceiving the product he never had those users in mind who were using his product more when I interviewed him. Prospective customers could be identified in multiple ways; using social capital was one among them. Other than social capital, one could use 'cold-call' or various strategies of mass marketing as alternatives. With reference to mass marketing, serendipity played an important role. However, serendipity was found to be important even in case of 'cold-call'. While looking for prospective customers, entrepreneurs simultaneously utilized multiple techniques. Out of different approaches which one would be successful in bringing customers was again, to some extent, a matter of chance.

Getting Initial Customers

Entrepreneurs simultaneously deployed various strategies for marketing their products and/or services. Even then, getting initial customers was a particularly difficult task as customers always had hesitation in dealing with entrepreneurs whose reputation in the market was not established. This was especially so when an entrepreneur was offering a new type of product/service. In many instances it was found that relationship played a particularly important role in getting the first customer. Interestingly, initial customers also came from 'cold-calling', where the nascent entrepreneur was able to convince an otherwise completely unknown person to become a customer.

Reference Led Social Capital

Entrepreneurs having family background in business often used some form of reference in getting their initial customers. Such references came through personal and/or professional relationships. Ajay Aggarwal, founder of Netware Pvt. Ltd., who was from a business family, said that his first customer was through a business contact of a friend with whom he had a relationship at stock market. Friendship was also important for Amit Sharma, founder of Sindh Infotech Pvt. Ltd. and Raj Modi, founder of Softech, and Raj Software and Communications. Raj Modi's first customer was his cousin's friend. However, it was not that for getting customers through reference an entrepreneur had to depend only on her/his acquaintances. Contacts established by employees could also be useful in identifying initial customers. This was true for Amit Sharma, founder of Sindh Infotech Pvt. Ltd. as managers in client organizations were known to managers of Sindh Infotech. An interview of Dinesh Marwari of Ryze Softech Pvt. Ltd. brought out how family-based social capital facilitated the process of getting customers. Mr Marwari was from a family which had more than one hundred years of experience in founding and running large-scale businesses in different industries. He could, therefore, fall upon his family while starting the business. He candidly admitted,

> (While starting business, I was a person) with (just) three-and-a-half years experience. May be a bright young chap, but the only reason someone would have given me business was because they trusted me, my capabilities, and not because of my experience or credibility, which I didn't have. So even till date most of large clients are relationships of mine that have been leveraged. You have to do a lot of networking, you have to do a lot of getting to know the right people and then sort of getting introduced into the right areas.

However, the importance of reference in identifying the initial customers was also visible for entrepreneurs who did not have a family background in business. For example, O.P. Nayar, founder of Accent Tech Solutions said that a new company could attempt to enter an already established market by offering lower price. However, that alone was not sufficient. Product/service had to be reliable. But, before delivery it was difficult to establish confidence in the mind of a customer about the dependability of a business offering. That's where reference became helpful. For this purpose many first generation entrepreneurs tried to utilize relationships developed by them in the course of their professional career, if that was relevant. This was also true for Indian software major Infosys. However, as one of the key founders of the company N.R. Narayana Murthy put it, this relationship could be capitalized only with competencies, commitments, and value systems of the company (BBC, 2011).

This was also true for entrepreneurs having family business background whose family members hardly participated in their business, for example, Gautam Apte, founder of Innovative Web Solutions Pvt. Ltd., and Kirti Harlalka, founder of Knowhow. Often decision to become an entrepreneur was facilitated by existence of a reference-based client. For example, Akhtar Hussain, founder of Communication Networks was familiar with his first client, who was a customer of the last company in which he was working. He knew that his employer organization was not able to cater to the requirement of this person. O.P. Nayar also utilized the relationships that he developed as a part of his professional career in order to find initial customers for his company Accent Tech Solutions. Even an entrepreneur's ex-employer could become one of the initial clients. This was the experience of S. Ram, founder of Integrated Software Solutions. Of people with whom I got an opportunity to interact Jayant Srinivas, founder of Ahead Technologies Pvt. Ltd., was the only entrepreneur who primarily worked with various government departments for their e-governance projects. In the initial phase, he got introduced to government organizations as customers through the founding partner of his company. The founding partner developed this association while he was doing his project work as a part of engineering degree at a government research organization. For Anil Despande, founder of Tech Writers Inc., the first customer was his friend. Entrepreneurs like Naveen Jayakumar, founder of

Datamagic Pvt. Ltd., felt that even though 'gut feeling' was required to start a business, without social network no business could be developed in the initial stage. His first business contract came from a friend, earlier his senior at an organization, who had started a business with some friend's connection in the USA.

ICT was one industry which succeeded in bringing down the importance of geographical distance to a large extent, primarily as a result of intensive use of new communication technology. Given this nature of ICT industry, networks did not remain restricted within the boundaries of nation state. Transnational networks, particularly with people/organizations located in the USA or Europe, did emerge as extremely important for developing business, even in getting initial customers. This was quite important with reference to ICT industry, as a large number of companies in India targeted overseas companies as customers. Gautam Apte, founder of Innovative Web Solutions Pvt. Ltd., as well as James John, founder of Spaceage.com testified this. They got their first customers through such transnational networks. Although initial customers often came through friendship relationships, such customers also needed to be convinced about what they were going to pay for. This was quite clear from the experience of Vinay Reddy, founder of Software Consultants Pvt. Ltd. He was into software product. About his first business transaction (which was with his friend) he said, 'if I could not have shown (the) product he would not have bought it, even if he was my friend'. First customer was important not only to initiate the revenue flow, but also to get subsequent customers. People and firm were understandably hesitant to be the first customers. Entrepreneurs therefore, often used their social capital to get their first customer. Once there was one customer, it was easier to convince others to become customers for the same product/service as they had the advantage of getting the feedback.

All types of social capital that were discussed so far were developed through social networks which were based on familiarity existing between two or more persons through either professional or personal life. However, embedded social capital could develop without existing familiarity as well: two completely unknown people could develop a close relationship on the spot after realizing that they shared special sentiment for or had trust in some third party. The experience of S. Sivakumar, founder of Datainformatics Pvt. Ltd., was illustrative of this. He said that when he and his partners were running around looking for business, they visited an organization. While talking to the person concerned, who was completely unknown to them, it came out that all of them had studied from the same college. That person was really happy to know that some students from his own college were trying to do something on their own. Therefore, he felt that he should do something for them in order to encourage their initiative. The work was small, but it was a good encouragement for them. In this way alma mater could facilitate formation of social capital. Another form of reference was visible in the case of Kirti Harlalka, founder of Knowhow. In her case, this reference led her to start her business. She said,

> Actually he (the first client) came through a reference. I had gone somewhere for a (job) interview after I had quit my last job. The interviewer happened to know me. He was actually my neighbour …. And after getting selected I realized that the job required travelling and I didn't want to travel. So I said that, you know, I would prefer to be a freelancer than take up a job which requires travelling. So he … told me about a person (who later became my first client).

Cold-Call

Initial customers for many businesses, particularly for entrepreneurs with a family background in business came from social networks. However, it was not necessarily so. Rajat Apte, founder of Magnatech Inc., lacked any family background in business. When he entered software service business he had to develop everything on his own. However, according to him, 'if you come across as genuine and good intentioned, people will tell you information that you are looking for'. In that context serendipity played an important role in his journey as an entrepreneur. When it came to making 'cold-call', an entrepreneur usually sought to identify customers in organizations whose nature of operation made them depend on services/products offered by the entrepreneur. Hitesh Patel, founder of Knowledge Software Pvt. Ltd., developed a knowledge management software which could be used for building an individual's word power. His first customer for this software product was a magazine, which had a section on building word power.

James John, founder of Spaceage.com, adopted a strategy which he jokingly called 'cold-walk' instead of 'cold-call'. He decided to look for prospective customer company's nameplate when he walked on the road. If he saw the nameplate of a company which could become his prospective customer he walked into their office. However, he admitted that not all companies permitted that. He got his first customer through one such 'cold-walk'. Another way of getting initial customers without reference was by applying in response to an advertisement about a contract. It is never the case that an entrepreneur could depend completely on reference at the cost of 'cold-call' or vice versa. Entrepreneurs kept attempting to get customers through different avenues. However, different kinds of relationships brought customers in diverse context. Sometimes, it was difficult to distinguish between 'cold-call'-based and reference-based business relationship. For example, when I asked Ajay Aggarwal, founder of Netware Pvt. Ltd., how he got his first customer, he said, 'it was ... marketing call directly and then what helped a little bit was I knew the ... son of the owner of that organization .... So ... (we) had made a presentation .... And then having known each other helped convert that'.

Mass Marketing: Importance of Serendipity

It has already been mentioned that mass media was important in getting customers when an entrepreneur was trying to launch a business offering which was new in the market. Given the financial constraints that start-up companies faced, internet-based advertising or maintaining a company website on the internet emerged as a viable option. Often initial customers came through internet. Vishnu Krishnaswamy, founder of Techvision, got his first customer who contacted him by perusing the information provided on his company website. However, entrepreneurs had to bank upon a combination of multiple channels. While Mangalam Srinivas, founder of Global Technologies Pvt. Ltd. used his old contacts, he depended on the marketing channels which he had set up. This included setting up offices in the USA and UK, which his company identified as potential markets. At the same time, his company also appointed associates in the Asian region, who would function as marketing channels. Exhibitions quite often functioned as channel for establishing acquaintances that led to business development. This was the experience of K. Padmakumar, founder of Frontech Ltd. His company developed a database application during the late 1980s. However, he hardly could find any customer for that application in India. Then he went to the USA, stayed there for four months, and searched for customers there. During his stay, he attended a technology launch programme by IBM in Chicago. It is in that exhibition that he met a person who later purchased all rights for his product.

Although for conceptual purpose the channels for accessing customers have been categorized into reference, 'cold-call' and mass marketing, in reality these boundaries often get blurred. While entrepreneurs utilized different means for getting initial customers, social capital in the form of references often turned out to be indispensable. The way in which entrepreneurs utilized social networks to secure their initial customers depended completely on the social network-based resources accessible to them. Availability of such resources depended on social as well as professional background of the entrepreneurs and their network partners. However, in terms of strategies adopted by entrepreneurs in securing initial customers, no difference was visible among entrepreneurs in terms of their backgrounds.

Retention of Customers

Strategies that entrepreneurs adopted for getting customers were quite different from the strategies that they adopted for retaining them. Getting customers had a lot to do with the ability of the entrepreneurs and/or their representatives to convince people to become customers, whereas, customer retention depended largely on the capability of the entrepreneurs and/or their organizations to satisfy the customers. Customer retention was extremely important for maintaining the revenue flow of the enterprise. Besides, it had a close bearing on the ability of the organization to build reputation in the market and thereby attract more people to become customers. Rupa Datta, founder of Infonet Pvt. Ltd., said that her existing customers even helped her in finding a financial investor. Retention took different meanings in different organizations. For a large number of organizations, retention implied that customers continue to regularly pay for using the product or the service which they offer. It could also mean that a customer got back to the company with a new requirement. For a small number of organizations (primarily organizations that sold products requiring little or no support from the producer) retention implied that the customers continued to use the product after purchasing it. In the latter case, customers paid a one-time fee in the beginning and no fee thereafter, but could continue to use if for life.

Reputation and Retention

The ability of an entrepreneur to retain a customer depended to a large extent on the level of satisfaction of the customer, which was contingent on the quality of the business offering. The reputation of an entrepreneur was largely dependent on the level of this satisfaction. There were many techniques that entrepreneurs used in understanding how satisfied a customer was. For example, Raj Modi, founder of Softech and Raj Software and Communications, said,

> See first of all if I get my cheque for AMC (Annual Maintenance Contract) that means my service is okay. And if I am able to sell two more products through that client that means my product is okay .... One is to satisfy someone and another is he is so satisfied that he will recommend it some others.

Customer's ability to trust the quality of business offering was extremely important in formation of reputation. In case of a service-driven company this, to a large extent, depended upon the quality of human resource who worked for a client. Considering the high level of attrition that characterized the ICT and ITES industry, maintaining the quality of human resource was quite a challenge for the entrepreneur. At the same time, this was a problem for the client as well. If the employees in service provider's organization kept changing, the clients could never be sure of quality. It was the entrepreneur's responsibility to certify that the delegated employee was capable of fulfilling the client's requirement. Making a valid judgement there was vital for the entrepreneur. This was because if the customers found those employees to be useful, they trusted the entrepreneur's judgement and remained with the entrepreneur as client.

Anil Despande, founder of Tech Writers Inc., sent technical writers to work onsite at his client's office. He experienced that trust on the company and/or its founder resulted in trust on the employees. Punctuality, which was important for all industries, had a special significance in ICT industries. For most of the clients, ICT was an infrastructure that they required for building their business. Therefore, growth of the client's business depended on completion and operation of the ICT project on time. The ability to complete the project punctually helped in building the reputation of a company. Anil Despande felt that the ability of his company to deliver projects on time made it easier for him to secure references from his clients. Customer retention took a different character when it came to software product companies. Amit Sharma, founder of Sindh Infotech Pvt. Ltd., offered an ERP (Enterprise Resource Planning) software product for the export industry. He said, that unlike software services, where the entrepreneurs hoped for the customer to come back to them, in the case of software product the company walked out of the client's office after installing the software. The only form of contact that sometimes remained with the customers in case of some software product companies was the annual maintenance contract or some support contract. However, it was important that the customer should continue to use that product satisfactorily. That helped in building and maintaining the company's reputation.

Software products developed by Techvision, founded by Vishnu Krishnaswamy, required regular support. Here, the reputation of the organization, which was needed for retaining the customers, also depended upon the quality of the support. Vishnu Krishnaswamy said, 'We always go the extra mile to make sure our products are up and running all the time. We are talking to our customers periodically'. Even if there was no need for support, maintaining relationship with customers was found to be important for a software product company in case the company produced multiple products. According to Vinay Reddy, founder of Software Consultants Pvt. Ltd., customer could require some other software product in future. Kunal Raman, founder of Sharp Technologies Pvt. Ltd., said that, this was valid for any kind of product company, not necessarily software. Customers considered continuing their relationship with a company whose one product they have found trustworthy. This opinion was also endorsed by Mangalam Srinivas, founder of Global Technologies Pvt. Ltd., a software product company. He said, '... many a time the technology that you are developing undergoes phases of upgrade. You might introduce a technology for three/four years. Then it could change. And if your customers are confident of your roadmap they are going to stay with you for their next product also'.

Knowledge Software Pvt. Ltd. produced various knowledge management software for end users. Though this company broadly came under business-to-customer (B2C) category, it had little contact with the end users. Instead, it tried to reach the end users through various other organizations which had their own channels of mass marketing. For example, a computer-selling company purchased many licenses of one of their software products for providing it to their customers as a part of bundled software. Similarly, a popular magazine also purchased many licenses of one of their software products in order to add value of their magazine for their customers. For Hitesh Patel, founder of Knowledge Software Pvt. Ltd., retention of customers meant whether those organizations like the computer-selling company or the magazine came back to his company for buying more licenses or not. He mentioned that the computer-selling company did come back to them for buying more licenses.

Relationships and Trust

At the end of the day, the possibility of retaining a customer was decided by the organization's ability to cater to customer's requirement. But relationships played an important role in the background. It was in this context that trust was vital in customer retention. Trust took different forms in different contexts. For example, Rajat Apte, founder of Magnatech Inc. visualized trust as an outcome of honesty. He acknowledged, 'Trust is a very important thing in the industry. If people can trust you, if people can like you, they will do business with you ... . (A match between) what you say and then what you deliver is very important. If you are not able to deliver, its important that you pick up the phone ... and tell people .... That's trust! .... People respect that .... So that's what helps you sustain'.

Similar observation was also made by Vinay Reddy, founder of Software Consultants Pvt. Ltd. In the initial phase, till a company became a brand, the name of the company was not sufficient to attract customers. In this context, personal relationships played an important role in getting customers. However, such relationships were not always developed by the entrepreneur. At times, it was developed by employees. Permitting the employees to grow relationships was necessary for expanding the company, as otherwise the company became entirely dependent on the entrepreneur. However, in the case of employee-developed customer relationships, if the relationship with the individual employee became more important than the relationship with the employer enterprise there was a chance of losing the customer if that particular employee left the enterprise. Ajay Aggarwal, founder of Netware Pvt. Ltd., faced this crisis in the initial phase. One of his employees, while leaving, took away two of his customers. Thereafter, he decided to meet each of the customers personally. While the phenomenon of employees taking customers away happens at companies of all scale it naturally affects the small enterprises more given the low volume of their business. Faced with such a situation what Ajay Aggarwal did ensured the continued existence of his enterprise. However, the trade off here was that possibly it was the same strategy that stunted the growth of the company by making it entrepreneur-dependent. Therefore the dilemma that entrepreneurs in small enterprises had in deciding freedom of the employees could be considered as a strange vicious cycle which restricted their growth while protecting their existence. It would be worthwhile to explore how entrepreneurs who have taken their company from start-up to growth stage have succeeded in breaking away from this cycle. Trust may be a critical framework from which this phenomenon may be looked at.

Flexibility in approach played an important role in retaining a customer, particularly in the case of service-based companies. It helped in building goodwill. 'Personal touch', as mentioned by entrepreneurs was important even in formal business transactions. Flexibility took different meanings in different contexts. According to Ajay Aggarwal, founder of Netware Pvt. Ltd., in any service driven company flexibility often took the shape of complimentary extension of credit limit or service to the customer beyond the decided period. Sometimes such a culture of extension of complimentary privileges helped the entrepreneur in retaining customers in times of crisis. Being customer-centric is an important requirement for retaining customers. Rajat Apte, founder of Magnatech Inc., a well-established middle-size company, said that even he spent fifty per cent of his time with the customers. Being customer-centric was often understood as sharing customer's problem as one's own and, therefore, 'going out of the way' to take care of that problem. It was emphasized that as a strategy 'going out of the way' helped in building goodwill with the customer. Such goodwill often helped in retaining the customers even when for a temporary period an entrepreneur was unable to meet the requirement of the customers. Chandan Sivaram, founder of Soft Solutions Pvt. Ltd. also believed in similar kind of customer-centric strategies. According to him, if an entrepreneur adopted such strategy, customers could show patience when the entrepreneur was going through troubles like employee attrition. Ranjan Raghavan, founder of Bangalore Technologies, also agreed with this. But he said, 'if you build a reputation ... I think that would earn the goodwill ... in cases where ... you had some setbacks and stuff like that I think the good past will certainly give you a little bit of latitude. But I think you will run out of that eventually, unless you buckle up in and then get back on track'. This was also supported by Naresh Ponnaiah, founder of Sunshine Technologies Ltd. when he said,

> ... when projects go into trouble your final (strategy) is to invoke the relationship. I think that's more like a reserve. You shouldn't be using (it) all the time. It's a very precious thing and you need to use it absolutely only when it is needed. And because its the most expensive option, once you have used it you do not have anything else to fall back on. That's your last resort. So I think we tend not to use it most of the time and we tend to be more of the opinion that we will accept our mistakes rather than use the relationship or something like it and cover it up.

K. Padmakumar, founder of Frontech Ltd., however, disagreed with the possibility of benefiting through existing relationships during the bad phases of business: 'When you are falling nobody is there to help you. So the customer is not going to show you mercy at all because he is paying money'. The experience of Dinesh Marwari, founder of Ryze Softech Pvt. Ltd. supports this argument:

> ... (With) the first client we had we completely messed up. It was our fault. It was not at all the client's fault. I mean, he was supporting us in whatever way he could. You know, you may get introduced through the chairman of the company and you can get the client, but, at the end of the day, you have to also prove your worth. So in a few cases we were not able to prove our worth and we got chucked out.

Being in the same field (ICT infrastructure management), the experiences of Akhtar Hussain, founder of Communication Networks, and Arjun Desai, founder of Win Infotech Ltd., were more or less the same, though they were located in two different cities: the former in Mumbai and the latter in Bangalore. Both of them emphasized the importance of maintaining relationship with customers in developing goodwill. For developing goodwill, often the entrepreneur was required to go out of the way to take care of the requirements of the customers. This, in the case of Arjun Desai, could mean solving the problems of client's home computer systems, though that was not part of the formal contract. This could also mean serving the client late in the evening or even at midnight in case of emergency. All this, in the words of Arjun Desai, was 'relationship management'. According to Arjun Desai, various out of the way services which he offered for his clients helped in building a relationship of trust which, in turn, helped him in retaining the customers. His account of the old business relationships that his company Win Infotech Ltd. had was a testimony to the importance of goodwill and trust in retaining customers: 'mainly relationship go bad if trust goes out of control ... it has not come so often but whenever it has come at all levels we have gone and we have personally seen that those issues are resolved and we apologized. We have shown a lot of care'. As mentioned earlier, Ahead Technologies Pvt. Ltd., founded by Jayant Srinivas, took up projects on e-governance from various governmental agencies. Jayant Srinivas also experienced the importance of long-term relations in building trust and, thereby, in retaining customers. According to him, many of the governmental functionaries he dealt with were averse to risk and, therefore, preferred to utilize the services of people about whose ability they were familiar through past association.

Being customer-centric did not only mean offering out of the way service. It also meant responding to customers call for support. Business relationships, just like personal relationships, depended on the people who were involved in the relationship. It took time to build a relationship. Therefore, if people involved in a relationship kept changing because of the high level of attrition in an organization, the relationship did not get the opportunity to get strong. Therefore, keeping the level of attrition low helped in strengthening a relationship and could ensure customer retention. The impact of low level of employee attrition in an organization on its ability to retain customers was pointed out by different entrepreneurs including Gautam Apte, founder of Innovative Web Solutions Pvt. Ltd. and Arjun Desai, founder of Win Infotech Ltd. Kirti Harlalka founder of Knowhow also came up with a related thought. Talking about the advantage of being small, she said,

> ... one decisive factor is that since we are a very small organization I am the person who approaches the organization, introduces it, gets the business, executes it, gives the updates – so I am the one point contact for everything. I think that is the very big factor as to why they like to deal with us.

However, such factors became functional in retaining customers only when the quality of business offering was dependable. Gautam Apte said, 'we gave our customers the importance they needed .... Because we realized if we are not spending on sales-marketing our customer is our brand ambassador. So lets execute well, lets keep the customer happy, lets retain the customer and this customer will give us more customers'.

Customer retention implied that the same organization remained as a customer. However, many a time relationship developed not between organizations but between individuals in organizations. Therefore, even if individuals moved into other organizations the relationship could continue and that would also be considered as customer retention from the point of view of the entrepreneurs. This came out clearly from the experience of Alok Dutta, founder of Silicon Networks Pvt. Ltd. Despite all effort, customers could still leave an entrepreneur due to other reasons. Naveen Jayakumar, founder of Datamagic Pvt. Ltd., said that, in a fast changing industry like ICT, technological changes could make an entrepreneur's reputation or relationship redundant. If entrepreneurs were not upgrading in terms of technology, many clients could outgrow them. In that case, even though personal relationships continued to exist they would not be useful in any way for business. Whereas, social capital in the form of relationships was the foundation for an entrepreneur's ability to secure initial customers, it was just a facilitator when it came to retaining those customers. With reference to customer retention, reputation emerging out of the quality of an entrepreneur's business offerings played the most important role. However, what came out was that quality was not all about quality of work. It was also about quality of relationship.

Getting Subsequent Customers

During the inception of a business initiative, entrepreneurs used their educational qualification, work experience, and their acquaintances to build confidence in the mind of initial prospective customers. However, once they got a few customers, the situation changed. Besides the existing channels of sourcing customers, one new channel developed, namely getting customers through existing satisfied customers. On the one hand, satisfaction of customers increased the reputation of the entrepreneur's business offering and this increased entrepreneur's referenceability. No doubt the quality of business offering played a more important role in building reputation, but the importance of relationships could not be ignored. When asked about the importance of relationships at a later stage in business, S. Ram, founder of Integrated Software Solutions, said,

> Definitely as you grow, to scale you will need a whole lot of organizational processes and structures and so on. But still the personal comfort level cannot be substituted with anything else. (At the same time) your personal relationships will have some limitation. Of course you have to expand that personal network. You have to (see that) they still play a part. But that is backed by a strong institutional effort actually. So you must have good websites and so on.

O.P. Nayar, founder of Accent Tech Solutions, also emphasized the limitation of relationships in business in the long run. He said, 'Relationship will work for few customers. But beyond that it is all about what you know. It is not about who you know .... So then relation will not take you to build a big business'. Even Kirti Harlalka, founder of Knowhow, who was in the initial stage of her business, said that in order to get more business she registered her curriculum vitae in various relevant websites. However, it should not be construed from such arguments that relationships did not play any role in getting customers at the later stage. Instead, the nature of relationship required for business developed out of business reputation rather than personal relationships. This was also the experience of Sudha Sharma, founder of Design Lab.

Although serendipity played an important role in the initial stages of business in making inroads into a particular industry, an entrepreneur's sustenance in that industry depended upon her/his ability to perform in that industry. It is in this context, that an entrepreneur's performance with initial customers became important. This was clear from the experience of Akhtar Hussain, founder of Communication Networks, who was into ICT hardware infrastructure management. He felt that he could get many customers in the stock broking industry because by serving his first customer, who was also in the same industry, he learnt to understand and speak the language of that industry. Diversification was a common strategy for expansion of business activities. Diversification could imply entering a new target industry or developing business in a new geographical region. In the initial stages of diversification the challenges that entrepreneurs went through were similar to those which they had to face during the inception of business. Therefore, relationships could play an important role in initiating business diversification as well. This was clear from the experience of Ajay Aggarwal, founder of Netware Pvt. Ltd., when he started his business in the USA. He felt that he could not have developed his business in the USA if his uncle, a senior ICT consultant, was not located there to vouch for the company during its initial stage. The later customers, however, largely came through his initial customers who have been proactive in promoting the company within their own circles. However he also said, 'if your service quality is not up to the mark you are not going to be able to retain that customer'. Ability of a company to satisfy its existing customers and thereby retain them increased its referenceability and chance of getting more customers in future. Whereas, inability to satisfy customers created a bad reputation and an entrepreneur had to live with it. As Rajat Apte of Magnatech Inc. mentioned, 'once you are out in the market for better or for worse you have a reputation'.

In order to get a customer it was important to prove one as reliable. For many small companies word of mouth reference remained important even for subsequent customers. At the initial stage, and definitely at later stages, prospective customers were more interested in finding out whether anyone known to them had utilized this product/service and what was her/his response. Prospective customers tried to find this out by asking 'Do we have any relationship?'. This meant, 'Have you worked for our organization earlier?'. Different entrepreneurs addressed this question differently. For this purpose Anil Despande of Tech Writers Inc. started a three-day training course on technical writing. Many people from reputed companies pursued that course. When he approached these companies for getting any business, he used the names of those employees, whom he had trained, to prove that he already had a relationship with that company. The company then would check up his trustworthiness with those employees. According to Anil Despande, such reference worked because insider reference was given more importance. In addition to offering a training course on technical writing, Anil Despande also took other initiatives which incidentally helped him in developing confidence in the mind of his later customers. He was the owner of a mailing list in his field for a long time. Association with a wide variety of people through this mailing list helped him in building a sense of reliance in the mind of people who were familiar with the mailing list, though many had never met him personally.

However, Alok Dutta, founder of Silicon Networks Pvt. Ltd., mentioned some of his experience which contradicted the importance given by different entrepreneurs to reference in getting the later customers. When interviewed he said that in 17 years of his business career he had hardly got customers who came through reference of previous customers. Arjun Desai, founder of Win Infotech Ltd., on the other hand, felt that for his company word of mouth reference had played an important role in getting later customers within India. However, it did not play any role when it came to getting international customers. K. Padmakumar, founder of Frontech Ltd., said that it was important to build relationships. However, he felt that such relationships were necessary more for finding out organizations where there was a demand for services being offered by him or the right persons in those organizations. However, it was not necessary that persons giving such information would have any social relationship in that organization which would be important enough to get an order from that organization. It appeared that importance given to relationship in getting subsequent customers varied depending on different criteria like nature of business offering, the location of market, and nature of target customers.

Crisis Management

Crisis, particularly those emerging from transformation in business environment, is an integral part of business activities. Therefore, each business has a history of dealing with crisis. In a fast changing industry like ICT diversification is often used as a strategy for dealing with crisis. Discussing about egurucool, an established e-learning company that got acquired later on by National Institute of Information Technology, founder Vivek Agarwal mentioned that the Company constantly responded to the dynamics of the market and changed its business model several times to adapt to the changes (Behl, 2004). I found similar currents in my own research as well. For example, for an entrepreneur with whom I interacted, Amit Sharma, founder of Sindh Infotech Pvt. Ltd., entry into ICT sector itself was a response to the crisis faced by his family business. Each business went through phases of stability and crisis. Stability was easy to conceptualize, but crisis could be multi-dimensional. While crises like an organization's inability to secure sufficient number of customers could be unique to an individual organization, sometimes these kinds of crises could be the outcome of broader phenomena like global economic slowdown, crash of ICT industry, etc. In that case, the paucity of customers would not be faced by a single organization. Instead, it would be faced by a large number of organizations in the same industry. Depending on the nature of crisis and that of the organization which was facing it, the way in which the situation was tackled or managed differed considerably. It was important to understand the various factors which influenced the way in which a crisis was managed. It was interesting to observe how entrepreneurs utilized social capital developed by them through various interpersonal relationships in order to bail their organizations out of situations of crises. However, leaving aside social capital, there were other factors which influenced entrepreneur's ability to manage crisis.

Often business ran into a crisis as a result of large-scale factors completely external to business. Iraq War in 1990 played such a role for Alok Dutta, founder of Silicon Networks Pvt. Ltd. As a result of this development few companies in the USA with whom he was having business conversation decided to put a hold on to it. Then as a strategy he started identifying companies in India using his business contact. Besides, through Indians working in the USA he also tried to identify the companies in the USA that were likely to outsource. Like Gulf War, another widespread phenomenon which affected a large number of organizations in ICT industry, if not all of them, was the rise and fall of 'dotcom' companies (popularly referred to as 'bubble boom' and 'bubble burst'). The term 'dotcom' was a general expression to imply the various internet-based businesses that developed during the second half of 1990s, which often had names ending with '.com'. This wave of global development of dotcom companies came down sharply during 2001. While this phenomenon of 'bubble burst' directly affected the dotcom companies, many other companies, which were in some or other way associated with the dotcom companies, got affected by it. After the crash of software industry in 2001, Alok Dutta, founder of Silicon Networks Pvt. Ltd., had fallen back on his social network to get some work from the research wing of a large company. No entrepreneur utilized only one procedure for searching customers. Specifically, during situations of crisis, an entrepreneur attempted to go all out and try to get clients through multiple channels. Experience of Gautam Apte, founder of Innovative Web Solutions Pvt. Ltd., was similar. In the initial period, his company was completely dependent on one US company for getting business.

That company was the only customer that they had. During the dotcom burst that US company found it difficult to sell its products. So, eventually, they decided to close down. At that point of time, Gautam Apte's company was already formed and they had a couple of employees on their payroll. He had no intention of closing down the company's operations and, therefore, he had to become active in getting new customers. He started looking for new customers through the transnational networks that he had developed as a part of his professional career in the USA.

However, such predicaments faced by entrepreneurs were not always an outcome of large-scale economic crises. When Amit Sharma founded Sindh Infotech Pvt. Ltd., his plan was to visit the USA in order to get initial customers. However, at the same time, he had discussions with some managers of a large Indian software company who showed strong interest in offloading some part of their work to Sindh Infotech. The work being substantial Amit Sharma gave up his plan of going to the USA in order to get initial customers. The managers of that company asked Amit Sharma to get a team of freshers who would be trained by them to perform their job. However, the situation became critical in the last moment when as a result of a leadership change the client company decided to back out. Amit Sharma had to then go all out to find substitute customers. And in doing so he did a lot of 'cold-calling' in India and abroad. They then managed to get their first customer through one such 'cold-call'. Diversification of business activities was one of the strategies that were adopted by the entrepreneurs to reduce business crises. When ICT industry went down Akhtar Hussain, founder of Communication Networks, attempted to diversify out of his business in the hardware PC market. He did that by identifying business opportunities in newer fields like data recovery and networking where entry barriers existed in terms of technical know-how. By lowering competition he could increase revenue in this way.

Crisis was also the motivation for Pradeep Kar, founder of well-known Indian ICT company Microland, to start new business. Initially in India Microland started as an authorized implementation agent for multinational companies that were into manufacturing computer networks equipments. This business was facilitated by substantial reduction in import duties as a result of implementation of New Economic Policy in India in 1991. However, in 1996, as internet economy got more consumerized Pradeep Kar sensed that the need for an intermediary, what Microland was back then, would go down. Therefore, in 1998 Microland decided to move into the business of internet economy offering different services including website development (at Planetasia) or content development for youth (at Indiya.com) or software development for networking and communications equipment providers (at Net Brahma). However, in 2001 when the internet economy crashed Microland had to reinvent itself again. And this time the idea was to leverage export business by exploiting the cost advantage of India. That's how Microland decided to get into remote management of IT operations in 2002 (Kar, n.d.).

Besides diversification, another way of facing sudden financial crisis was to restructure thrust areas of a business. Alok Dutta, founder of Silicon Networks Pvt. Ltd., started his career as an entrepreneur in the semiconductor industry. Later on, he diversified into the software industry. After the burst of dotcom bubble he decided to migrate back to semiconductor. The experience was similar for Arjun Desai, founder of Win Infotech Ltd. post World Trade Centre crash. His company was then involved in business process outsourcing (BPO), software development, and ICT infrastructure management. Faced with crisis emerging out of closure of some of his main clients in the US his company decided to close down the software and educational services division and instead focused only on BPO and ICT infrastructure management division. He said, 'That really helped. We had so many customers in the ICT infrastructure management. That was the bread and butter. That took care of the survival of the company'. Same was true for Dinesh Marwari, founder of Ryze Softech Pvt. Ltd. He began his career as an entrepreneur in business consulting space. However, after failing to serve the first client, he realized that he did not have the appropriate capability and infrastructure for offering service in business consulting. In that situation of crisis he moved to software consulting instead.

In a fast changing high technology-based industry like ICT, entrepreneurs needed to continuously update not only their knowledge, but also their business offerings. This was clear while talking to Akhtar Hussain, founder of Communication Networks. To a large extent, the success of an entrepreneur in retaining customers depended upon the quality of product and/or service offered by her/him. Poor quality of business offering often led to customer attrition, giving rise to business crisis. This was the experience of Ullas Gowda, founder of Knowledge Solutions Pvt. Ltd., who offered service in e-learning segment. When Ullas Gowda understood that the quality that they were offering was poor he needed to act urgently in order to resolve such a crisis. For this purpose, he had to develop expertise in core areas of his business that was production about which he hardly knew anything earlier. He was only looking into business development. Although entrepreneurs continued to do business, they were not successful in all situations to wrest themselves out of crisis. For example, Raj Modi, founder of Softech and Raj Software and Communications, has almost given up one part of his business which involved selling an accounting software produced by him. This happened in the face of the competition he had faced from a similar product produced by another company which became a big brand. Another reason for his business crisis was the widespread software piracy. Controlling piracy was beyond his capability.

Experience of the entrepreneurs brought out that social capital played an important role in each aspect of business development. In the context of entrepreneurship in ICT industry social capital primarily implied the resources emerging out of interpersonal relationships that entrepreneurs had with their social network partners as well as various relationships in which they were embedded. However, in comparison to interpersonal networks we could find much less presence of embedded networks in this industry. Although social capital played an important role in all aspects of business development, the level of importance varied across activities. It was observed that getting initial customers was one activity where social capital played the most important role. When it came to other aspects of business, for example, developing business idea, identifying prospective customers, retaining customers, getting later customers, and managing crisis social capital was more of a lubricant (similar to Anderson and Jack, 2002). That meant social capital, by itself, was often not sufficient to get the work done. However, presence of social capital was found to be necessary for handling situations where other components like worth of business offering played a more important role. Social capital was not only functional within the enterprise; its utility was also visible in the environment in which the enterprise functioned. Therefore, it would be important to reflect on different aspects of business environment with a specific emphasis on locating the role of social capital in them.

References

Anderson, A.R. and Jack, S.L. (2002). The articulation of social capital in entrepreneurial networks: A glue or a lubricant. *Entrepreneurship and Regional Development*, 14(3), 193–210.

BBC. (4 April 2011). Start-up stories: NR Narayana Murthy, Infosys. *BBC.* <http://www.bbc.com/news/business–12957104.> retrieved 22 June 2014.

Bagchi, S. (n.d.). Making of the Mind Tree. *IDG Ventures India.* <http://www.idgvcindia.com/html/Mindtree%20Article.pdf.> retrieved 21 June 2014.

Behl, R. (2004). Making of egurucool. com. *Global Business Review*, 5(2), 277–289.

Cohen, S.S. and Fields, G. (1999). Social capital and capital gains in Silicon Valley. *California Management Review*, 41(2), 108–130.

Kar, P. (n.d.). Reinventing Microland. *Leadership Insights, Colorshots.* <http: //leadershipinsights.colorshots.co/reinvent-ng-microland-pradeep-kar/.> retrieved 21 June 2014.

Ramachandran, K. and Ray, S. (2006). Networking and new venture resource strategies: A study of information technology start-ups. *The Journal of Entrepreneurship*, 15(2), 145–168.

Soh, P.H. (2003). The Role of networking alliances in information acquisition and its implications for new product performance. *Journal of Business Venturing*, 18(6), 727–744.

5

'Business Ecosystem' and Social Capital

Success of an entrepreneur in executing a business idea depended on the environment within which the business operated. The importance of wider environment was discussed to some extent in the previous chapter under crisis management. Business crises, largely an outcome of failure of expectations, were often unavoidable as business depended on multiple relationships of interdependence. Entrepreneurs often used an umbrella term 'business ecosystem' to refer to these forms of interdependence in business. 'Business ecosystem' included various aspects like availability of financial investments, need for physical infrastructure, nature of human resource, development of collaboration, and relationship with state. While the overall context of business was common for all enterprises there was scope for individual enterprises to manipulate that environment with the help of unique resources accessible to them. Social capital could be one such resource. However, the nature of relationship that could become important for formation of social capital varied contextually.

Financial Investments[1]

Execution of any business idea depended to a large extent on the availability of necessary financial resources. Traditionally, the founder of a business venture was responsible for arranging the necessary financial capital by investing her/his personal resources or resources borrowed from other individuals or financial institutions. That was how the word capitalist came to be used as synonymous to founder of an organization oriented towards making profit. Later, with the development of capitalism, particularly with the creation of joint stock companies, various alternative models of financial investment evolved, where people other than the founder started investing financial resources in an organization. The traditional way of securing external finance through loan required the founder to submit some property as collateral to the creditor in order to negate the risk of loss for the creditor. That continues even today (for example, Amit Sharma founded Sindh Infotech Pvt. Ltd. with a bank loan received against collateral). However, the limitation of this model was that only those people, who possessed sufficient property to submit as collateral could secure loan for giving shape to their business idea. Whereas, the alternative models of finance, which became popular only recently, did not have any such requirement. This naturally increased the scope for investment.

Given that these alternative models did not require collateral, they naturally carried considerable risk for the financier. An investor was ready to bear high risk only when there was a potential for high return. Popularity of these models of financing started increasing as the opportunity for securing high return began to gain momentum. Emerging wave of high-technology-based business initiatives was one of the major developments to create this momentum in the recent decades. Two models of financing start-up companies gained popularity: venture capital and angel investment. Venture capital was the money that was provided by professionals who invested alongside management in young, rapidly growing companies that had the potential to develop into significant economic contributors. Professionally managed venture capital firms generally were private partnerships or closely held corporations funded by private and public pension funds, endowment funds, foundations, corporations, wealthy individuals, foreign investors, and the venture capitalists themselves (India Infoline, n.d. a).

Business angels, on the other hand, were important links in the entire process of venture capital funding. This was because they supported a fledgling enterprise at a very early stage – sometimes even before commercialization of the product or service offering. Typically, an angel was an experienced industry-bred individual with high net worth. Angels provided funding by 'first round' financing for risky investments – risky because they were in young/start-up companies or because financial track record of those companies was unstable. Angel financing was typically used to prepare a company for 'second round' financing in the form of an initial public offering (IPO). Angels were people with less money orientation, who played an active role in making an early-stage company work. They were people with enough hands-on experience and were experts in their fields. They understood the field from an operational perspective. An entrepreneur needed this kind of expertise. He also needed money to make things happen. Angels brought both to the table of an entrepreneur (India Infoline, n.d. b).

Leaving aside the financial support that investors brought along, presence of a well-established individual/firm as financier also helped the entrepreneurs in convincing people to become customers for their business offering by bringing greater visibility and reputation. In recent years a large number of venture capital firms and angel investors entered the financial market. While that surely helped the emerging high technology enterprises having potential for high return, raising finance was still not an easy job. Convincing individuals/firms to part with their money was always a challenging task. Rejection rate was very high: only about 10 in 100 got beyond pre-evaluation stage, and only 1 in 100 got funded (India Infoline, n.d. c). Therefore, it required substantial strategizing on behalf of the entrepreneurs desirous of raising finance. A large number of entrepreneurs found no other option but to build up their ventures with their own finance, either coming through bootstrapping or from family. Such challenges made dynamics of financial investment an important component of business ecosystem. For analytical convenience, we categorize financing into five apparently watertight compartments here, namely, bootstrapping, family funding, angel investment, venture capital investment, and bank loan. To be sure, empirically, these categories were not completely watertight. Significance of social capital could be explored in the structure and functioning of each financing model.

Bootstrapping

In the absence of availability of financial support from family or investors, many first-generation entrepreneurs found bootstrapping to be the only viable option for financing their business venture. However, given that bootstrapping was time consuming, it was workable when the entrepreneur had time to wait for the finance to be generated. This model was applicable more in software service than in software product industry, as product required quicker and larger one-time investment. Raj Modi, founder of Softech and Raj Software and Communications, however, bootstrapped to generate fund for executing his first business idea, that is, development of an accounting software. He supported his software development work by taking up certain data entry job. Kunal Raman, founder of Sharp Technologies Pvt. Ltd., also bootstrapped to develop a software product. He bootstrapped the money for developing this software product from the software services business of which he was a part previously.

Family Funding: Reliance on Strong Ties

Family funding was accessible mostly to entrepreneurs who were from business families, which had resources to invest. One more criteria for family funding was that family members needed to be ready to bear certain risk by investing their family resources in business being initiated by their family members. It was primarily because of the second reason that many well-to-do families lacking business background were often not interested in investing such resources in business. One more constraint for families (including business families) to invest was non-comprehension of revenue models of new business areas. For business families, investment was primarily governed by reliance on strong ties (Granovetter, 1973). Ajay Aggarwal, founder of Netware Pvt. Ltd., and Dinesh Marwari, founder of Ryze Softech Pvt. Ltd., who came from business families, started their organization with family funding. On the contrary, despite having a family business background Naresh Ponnaiah, founder of Sunshine Technologies Ltd. (developing a software product), and Kirti Harlalka, founder of Knowhow (offering business research services) did not begin their businesses with family funding. Their family members, who were primarily involved in traditional businesses like trading or building construction, had little or no idea about the area of their business operation. However, father of Ajay Aggarwal, founder of Netware Pvt. Ltd., who was an entrepreneur in import-export trading, was strongly involved with Ajay Aggarwal's entry into ICT industry, a sector completely different from his own. Initially, his father was not familiar with ICT industry, but he used his own contacts to find out opportunities in this area. Therefore, while starting Netware Pvt. Ltd., the entire funding came from the family.

While family funding was received mostly by entrepreneurs from business families, it was not necessarily so. To begin with, it is now part of the industry legend that iconic Indian ICT entrepreneur N.R. Narayana Murthy began Infosys by borrowing $250 from his wife Sudha Murthy (Iype, n.d.). Among the entrepreneurs whom we interviewed Arjun Desai also accepted funds from his wife's family while founding his first company Win Infotech Ltd. Likewise, Anil Despande while founding Tech Writers Inc. also received some token funding from his family members, his in-laws. By the time I interviewed him some of his friends had started showing interest in investing in his organization.

Angel Investment: Role of Relationships

Considering the difficulty of securing venture finance, impossibility of family funding and time consuming nature of bootstrapping, angel investment often emerged as a practical option for many individuals who decide to become entrepreneurs after a career as a professional. While talking about the difficulty of securing venture capital funding K. Padmakumar, founder of Frontech Ltd., said,

> If your demands are higher ... then people are willing to go through the scientific process and do everything, analysis and business projection and all that. But when you are looking at one million, two million nobody is interested in giving. Because they don't see one million going into hundred million. The growth of that is not very attractive. So when you want a not too high figure you only have to connect through networks and friends like that.

Angels, as it has already been mentioned, are individuals who are experienced professionals in the industry of an entrepreneur's interest. Their interest in funding a business venture primarily develops out of their understanding of the potential of a business idea by virtue of their experience in that field, and their familiarity with the potential of the entrepreneur executing that business idea. Both these aspects were visible from recollection of Rajat Apte, founder of Magnatech Inc.,

> I had little bit of track record in the market, having started my consulting business and having delivered good results through

> consulting contracts in this space. When I wanted to raise money ... I said to myself the best people to raise the money from are the people who understand your business. Its hard enough to ask somebody to part with their money. Its even harder if you also have to explain to somebody what your business is. So my earliest investors were a couple of individuals from (my target) industry, (that is) the pharmaceutical and life science industry. In fact they were couple of ... (senior employees of well-established companies from this industry) who, on an individual capacity, looked at the concept I had put together and said this makes tremendous sense and agreed to invest some personal money and come in as angel investors .... These people were my customers ... I had developed (a personal relationship with them).

Personal relationship also helped Raj Modi, founder of Softech and Raj Software and Communications, to secure financial support for developing his business idea. In the initial phase he had bootstrapped to generate resources for developing his accounting software, but later on he managed to secure some angel financing. It came from the company for which he was working previously. His ex-employer had requirement for an accounting software; he had asked Raj Modi to develop it. For developing that software, there was need for substantial finance. Raj Modi's ex-employer proposed to invest in his company in the form of shareholding. According to Raj Modi, this happened mainly because his ex-employer was familiar with him.

Like Rajat Apte, founder of Magnatech Inc., Arjun Desai, founder of Win Infotech Ltd., and Ranjan Raghavan, founder of Bangalore Technologies, also got angel investment from their customers. Arjun Desai said,

> (Among the funders) there are two different organizations ... (We) by chance bumped into them and one of them was our customer actually. At that point of time, in 1999–2000 everyone wanted to get into the IT industry ... . So there were many manufacturing organizations who were our customers who showed interest in, wanting to invest on us, because we were performing consistently to get a lot of credibility. At that point of time we must have been a seventeen-years-old organization. We were always there with them. So they made some investments .... (What impressed them) was delivery capability. They knew we could deliver. Next thing is, of course, good relationships.

Relationship with clients also turned out to be useful for Vishnu Krishnaswamy, founder of Techvision. He got an angel investor who was referred by one of his Indian clients in the USA. Financial investment was just one of the reasons why Vishnu Krishnaswamy valued his association with this angel. What, according to him, was more important was the extensive experience that the angel had in successfully running relevant business in the USA. His involvement with Techvision in an advisory capacity helped the founder in expanding the diversity in the managerial team which till then consisted of just the founder and his wife.

Like customers and their references, ex-superiors at previous workplaces could also become an angel investor for an entrepreneur. This was the experience of Naresh Ponnaiah, founder of Sunshine Technologies Ltd. He said,

> ... We needed somebody to put some money into (our company). So I went back to my ex-boss ... I (had) some relationship with him ... (I also) went back to another (ex-boss of mine) who was in the US. So using them as angel investors ... we started the company .... (Investing is) ultimately a matter of trust .... When people decide to give you control they expect two things. One is ... they need to believe that you have the capability to do it. The second thing is they really (need to) trust you as an individual (so that) they (can) give you control.

Whereas, the relationships that previously mentioned entrepreneurs utilized for getting their angel investors was built up as a part of their professional/entrepreneurial career, an entrepreneur could use their family relationships as well for this purpose. Such was the case for Alok Dutta, founder of Silicon Networks Pvt. Ltd. He used his father's relationship for getting an angel investor. He said,

> ... my Dad was able to introduce me to another gentleman of his generation .... So both of them didn't understand semiconductor business or even software probably. So they just looked at it as something called IT. The other gentleman had a group ... that could invest fund. They asked me how much I would need and so that's how we started ... I would say it was a very low level of seed investment.

While looking for more angel investors, Rajat Apte, founder of Magnatech Inc., utilized his association with The Indus Entrepreneurs (TiE).[2] Association with TiE helped him in developing reputation. It also gave him access to people, approaching whom otherwise would have been difficult. He said,

> How I approached additional investors is actually quite interesting. Two things I will mention, approach and solution. One was TiE. TiE was being found right around that time. That was in (19)95–96. There was only one chapter (of TiE) at that point. It was the TiE Silicon Valley. I made a presentation (of my business plan) at the TiE Silicon Valley chapter ... to a gathering of about 150 people .... After the presentation ... two or three individuals stepped up, came and said, we want to talk to you. I was quite thrilled. They said, 'we are from (your target) industry, we are part of TiE and (your business idea) makes a lot of sense'. So I followed up with them. They eventually became investors and that's the way I started making a network of angel investors over next three to four months period. Then they completed the initial round of financing.

The second component which helped Rajat Apte in developing a reputation was his aptitude in playing a musical instrument, namely, Tabla. As he played Tabla in the USA and India with many well-known Indian artists it helped him in developing an informal relationship with many people, particularly those from Indian diaspora. Many such people willingly vouched for him as they knew him as a person. He said,

> Even some of the TiE members knew me first as a good Tabla player, as a musician, and then knew me as a businessperson. And I leveraged that as much as I could .... They were comfortable enough to say yes I will help you, I will vouch for you.

Venture Capital: Reference as Lubricant

Decision to approach a venture capitalist (VC) and decision of a venture capitalist to support an enterprise was governed by diverse factors. There were multiple concerns on both the sides. Writing about the experience of Mindtree, Subroto Bagchi mentioned that in choosing a venture fund they assessed the value that the partner brought other than cash. He felt that in international business in ICT industry the credential of the funder often influenced the credibility of a new enterprise (Bagchi, n.d.). On the other hand, as it has already been mentioned, venture capitalists were extremely fastidious in making a decision to fund a business venture. They give considerable value to references from their trusted sources about an entrepreneur. It would not be possible for entrepreneurs to secure such references unless the referees are intimately familiar with them professionally and personally. However, at times, intimate relationship with VC also created hesitation in the mind of entrepreneurs. For example, writing about the initial days of conceiving Mindtree, Subroto Bagchi wrote, 'As our business plan progressed, I felt awkward to speak to either Som (Das) or Sudhir (Sethi) (both from Walden International, a California-based reputed venture fund) as it might look like I am taking advantage of a lifetime of relationship' (Bagchi, n.d.: 15). However, finally Subroto Bagchi had to overcome this hesitation in order to get ahead with the company as past relationship worked as an incentive.

Subroto Bagchi could begin with a relationship thanks to his long and illustrious professional career. For many entrepreneurs who did not have that advantage at the beginning had to depend considerably on references. Rajat Apte, founder of Magnatech Inc., said,

> ... once you get going, once you have some customers, so on and so forth then approaching the venture (capitalist) community becomes a bit easier ... you can talk to them. Even then when I got my initial sort of venture meetings they were always through somebody. I chose not to go to a single VC directly. Either I approached them because somebody had given me a reference. I said so and so person that they knew recommended that I talk to you because he felt that you would be interested in looking at my business. Or had the same people who were my well-wishers talk to the VC and tell them have you looked at this company? You should look at this company because they are doing something pretty nice. So you get call from them saying, hey we want to talk to you.

Rupa Datta, founder of Infonet Pvt. Ltd., also had similar experience while getting connected to a venture capitalist. When asked how she got in touch with the venture capitalist firm, she said,

> There's somebody, a family friend, who recommended. We just had gone to this person, a friend's father, to ask for advice, and he said, I have somebody who might be interested in your project. So why don't you put a project plan together .... I was told to go and approach Aavishkaar ... luckily for me, my idea, or what I said, hit home with Aavishkaar on my first meeting.

So far, we have discussed the role that relationship plays for an entrepreneur in building the initial connection with VCs. But relationship continues to play an important role in securing finance from VCs even after the initial introduction is over. Rajat Apte, founder of Magnatech Inc., said,

> ... to raise money is to build competition among investors. Investment is a herd mentality. Its either feast or family. Meaning either everybody wants to invest in you or nobody wants to invest in you .... If you can't get somebody to invest in you or interested in investing in you, nobody is interested in investing in you .... So you have to create a feast scenario. But there's only so much you can create. The fundamentals of business need to be attractive enough for it to look like a feast to people. If the business in itself looks like a family you can not create feast. But you still have to employ a strategy to make it look as much a feast as you can so that you can attract lot of investors. That's how you create competition .... That's the way you create the sense of confidence ... . To bring the confidence you need to also have enough investors in the pipeline ... . Investors don't want to be the first one (to invest) .... So in fact you have to sort of herd them in along the same time and in a matter of few days. So that's the strategy .... (The prospective investors) talk to each other before they invest, and also after they invest. The investment community is very close-knit. So you have to be consistent in your message .... It should be a true picture, but the true picture has to be managed in a strategic way to maximize the closure of the deal.

Relationship, thus, needs to be built up not only between the entrepreneur and the VC, but also among different VCs who are considering investment in the same organization. A VC's decision to invest is based on her/his assessment of the worth of the business idea, and it is supported by her/his familiarity about the personality and aptitude of the entrepreneur, knowledge about which essentially comes through relationships.

Experience of Mangalam Srinivas, founder of Global Technologies Pvt. Ltd., showed that the basis of a VC's decision to invest varied depending on the maturity of an organization seeking investment. Whereas, during the initial phase of development of a company, investors are interested in knowing about the earlier professional performance of the founder, in the later phase of a company, investors are interested in knowing about the performance of that company. Interestingly, relationship played an important role in identifying a prospective investor at any stage of business. While narrating his experience, Mangalam Srinivas said that the three/four people whom he had contacted for raising the first round of finance were known to him. Those people also knew other members in the management team of the company. This familiarity helped in building confidence between the two sides. In comparison to the first round, the second round of financing was based more on data related to number of products that were created, number of patents that were filed, number of customers, revenue and its projection, the quality of the people in the team, etc. However, even here Mangalam Srinivas and his team members decided to approach only those investors with whom they had the most comfortable relationships.

With larger number of entrepreneurs approaching VCs, these days professionals or organizations have emerged which specialize in connecting the entrepreneurs with suitable VCs. Such mediations in some way institutionalize the information network. Jayant Srinivas, founder of Ahead Technologies Pvt. Ltd., found his investor through one such professional. Ullas Gowda, founder of Knowledge Solutions Pvt. Ltd., also approached such a professional. However, unlike Jayant Srinivas, he was not successful in finding a financier through such mediation. When asked about the role played by relationship in such mediation Jayant Srinivas said, '(These organizations) have relationship with the venture capital firms. Because, they would have got other deals to them ... that relationship is transformed into our paying this guy to do the job ...'.

While attempting to secure funding from external sources start-up companies often receive offers for buy out. However, not everyone is ready to sell their company. In this context Anil Despande, founder of Tech Writers Inc., said,

> There were three attempts to buy my company. I did not agree to any one of them. At that point of time I did not see a point in giving away that company to somebody who has no understanding of this business, who looks at it as an investment more than a passion, who has no emotional attachments and who might actually sell it away to somebody else if he gets a better price within six months. Then what happens to me, my people, the team that I have developed as on. I always believe that one can have money. But to have a team is very difficult. And if you have the right kind of team money will follow.

Loan

The way in which organizations/individuals think about generating finance for their business ventures has changed considerably in the recent years with the hype over stock investments by angel investors and venture capitalists. However, loans from banks or other traditional financial institutions still remain an important source of finance for entrepreneurs. Business loan situation has now become relatively more favourable for the debtor, with banks considering the possibility of offering loan with less or no collateral. With banks willing to take risk, the dependence on social capital in the form of assessing trustworthiness and creditworthiness of an organization or an individual entrepreneur is increasing as a way of reducing risk. This was clear from the experience of Ullas Gowda, founder of Knowledge Solutions Pvt. Ltd. He said that in a bank even if branch manager changes there are other staffs in the bank to introduce an entrepreneur to the manager and to vouch for them based on past records of banking. According to Ullas Gowda these insider references play a crucial role in financial transaction at bank.

Trustworthiness remained an important requirement in dealing with bank or for that matter, any financial institution. Ullas Gowda felt that reputation also helped (for example, by way of getting overdraft facility) in bad times. However, at the same time, he said, 'If you keep taking this kind of benefit everyday (the bank manager won't give it)'. Despite transformation in orthodox banking policies entrepreneurs including Pankaj Sen, founder of Advanced Software Systems Pvt. Ltd., Vishnu Krishnaswamy, founder of Techvision, and Chandan Sivaram, founder of Soft Solutions Pvt. Ltd. were critical of banks as well as governmental financial institutions for being averse to giving loans without security. Chandan Sivaram felt that banks were also biased against small enterprises and primarily preferred to lend money to corporates.

Another way of raising finance, which became particularly popular among a large number of companies in the ICT industry, specifically prior to 'dotcom burst', was launching the Initial Public Offering (IPO) in the share market. Of all the entrepreneurs whom I interviewed K. Padmakumar, founder of Frontech Ltd., was the only one who raised finance through this channel. This channel of raising finance was possible only after a company had performed for some time in the market. For all other channels of accessing financial resources, social network or interpersonal relationship of various forms often played a significant role. However, depending upon the type of financier, the role played by relationship varied considerably. Whereas, family funding was relationship intensive, in others, relationship primarily played the role of facilitation. Relationships functioned as social capital for securing finance. The basis of such relationships could vary considerably: they could develop out of an entrepreneur's family, career as a professional, career as an entrepreneur, participation in business associations, and participation in activities outside her/his profession.

Various resources that were embedded in these relationships included financial resource itself as well as reference to connect to financiers. An individual's willingness to provide finance to an entrepreneur or to refer her/him to someone else depended on the trustworthiness of the entrepreneur assessed through relationship. In that way, trust played an important role in getting finance. Trust could be understood in two ways: trust on capability of an individual, and that on the person. Trust, as it was observed, developed out of certain current/past interpersonal relationships shared by individual actors, for example, superior-subordinate in an organization, supplier-customer, family member, friend/friends family members, etc. Once developed, trust played an important role in strengthening the relationship and thereby in facilitating the access to various resources including finance.

Physical Infrastructure

It is well known that virtual space plays a significant role for many organizations in ICT industry. This, however, did not reduce the importance of geographical place and physical infrastructure for them. Office location and allied set-up were important for the establishment and growth of a large number of organizations in the ICT industry. Quality of such infrastructure not only ensured the worth of the business offering, but also helped attract and retain customers and appropriate human resource by creating confidence in their mind. In addition to location of office, infrastructure could also include office interiors, stationery, and technology. Quality of such infrastructure depended upon the financial strength of an organization, which was contingent on the scale of operation of an organization. However, given the fact that ICT is an industry based on technology it was not possible for any organization to compromise much on technology. As a result, when it came to developing cost-effectiveness, quality of other infrastructural components often got compromised to some extent. Leaving aside the organizations, which from the initial phase itself received strong financial support, most of the organizations, at least in the initial phase, needed to compromise on the quality of other infrastructure in order to remain cost-effective. At this stage, often entrepreneurs depended upon resources emerging out of strong ties.

Most of the entrepreneurs started their business around the year 2000. At that time, the cost for buying a computer and/or renting an internet connection was much higher. For the entrepreneurs who started in the 1990s or even earlier the cost was quite prohibitive. However, entrepreneurs had no other option but to spend that money, as their business depended on that. Besides, back in those days provision of computers with internet connection, personal email ids was also a way of attracting prospective employees. While the general trend was to spend heavily on acquiring technology Ullas Gowda, while founding Knowledge Solutions Pvt. Ltd., attempted to reduce his expenditure on technology in a different way. He said, 'we didn't start the business with buying all the computers or buying all the furniture. Everything was rented'.

One component where many entrepreneurs attempted to reduce their cost, at least till the time their business grew, was quality and size of their office accommodation. In the absence of sufficient resources, entrepreneurs often utilized space available through their family relations. Ajay Aggarwal, founder of Netware Pvt. Ltd., said that he began his business from the garage at his residence. Starting business from home was apparently quite common among entrepreneurs in ICT industry because of the concern with cost effectiveness. Today's icon in Indian ICT industry Infosys also began its operation from the residence of its key founder N.R. Narayana Murthy (Murthy, n.d.). Other entrepreneurs who started their business operation from home included Anil Despande, founder of Tech Writers Inc., Naveen Jayakumar, founder of Datamagic Pvt. Ltd., Ranjan Raghavan, founder of Bangalore Technologies, Sudha Sharma, founder of Design Lab, and Jayant Srinivas, founder of Ahead Technologies Pvt. Ltd. When the flow of resources increased, Anil Despande decided to shift his office out of home considering the practical limitations of functioning out of home. K. Padmakumar, founder of Frontech Ltd., on the other hand, was against mixing office and home from the beginning.

Entrepreneurs who had a business background before starting their company in the ICT industry often utilized their existing resources from other business to set up their ICT business. This included Amit Sharma, founder of Sindh Infotech Pvt. Ltd. and Hitesh Patel, founder of Knowledge Software Pvt. Ltd. Both of them were from business families. This worked out for S. Sivakumar, founder of Datainformatics Pvt. Ltd., as well, though he was not from a business family. However, one of the co-founders of his first company was from a business family. That co-founder's father wanted to encourage his son and his friends in business and, therefore, supported them by providing some facilities. Rupa Datta, founder of Infonet Pvt. Ltd., also received strong infrastructural support from her father, who was a Chartered Accountant. She said,

> I started at the back of my dad's office on a single table. I was lucky that initially only he gave me some space, space being the main thing that you need in Bombay (she was located in Bombay). Then I was lucky that we had an office which was lying around, which was not really being used and I could pay rent and I could start. So I have been lucky ... that I had family-owned properties that I could move in. And then I was even further luckier; when I decided to move to a bigger place my dad said I will buy the property, you give me rent.

Some of the other entrepreneurs like Vinay Reddy, founder of Software Consultants Pvt. Ltd., and Gautam Apte, founder of Innovative Web Solutions Pvt. Ltd., started their business operation with minimal office set-up. Gautam Apte said that because he started the company with very basic set-up it was difficult for him at that stage to convince people to join the company as employees.

Seed investors for start-up companies often helped the entrepreneurs with an office space. Ex-employer of Raj Modi made a seed investment when Raj Modi founded Softech. In addition to finance, this investment also included arranging an office space for the company. The investor had an extra office, which he made available for Raj Modi. Same was true for Alok Dutta while founding Silicon Networks Pvt. Ltd. The investment came through a person whom Alok Dutta had met through his father. Other than office space, the investment also took care of initial advertisement, initial hardware that Silicon Networks purchased and few months of payroll. For Akhtar Hussain, founder of Communication Networks, it was one of his customers who helped him in getting an office space as they were symbiotically related. Akhtar Hussain said,

> ... we had to be (located) close to the customer. That was our core criteria ... so that we could reach the customer very fast ... most of our customers are in this South Bombay locality. So our office had to be in South Bombay. But offices in South Bombay are very costly. That's a problem. Again the customer helped us. I realized its always a two-way relationship. The customer also benefits when you are very close to him. So they help you in locating, in finding out an office or probably (by renting out an extra office that they have at a) lesser rent. So they don't mind leasing out to you at a lesser rent.

Entrepreneurs, in order to begin their business operations, needed to develop some physical infrastructure from the start-up stage itself. However, the challenge for the new entrepreneurs was to find a way to balance that requirement with the limited availability of financial resources. Whereas, in order to find such balance some entrepreneurs tried to bring down their cost of infrastructures like office accommodation; while others, who had a choice, tried to use interpersonal relationships to compensate for their scarcity of resources. Thus, access to physical infrastructure was another resource that was embedded in interpersonal relationships. In this way also interpersonal relationships functioned as social capital. However, it was not necessary for entrepreneurs to come from business family to have access to such social capital. Often entrepreneurs without business family background started their business operation from their residence. It came out from the discussion that entrepreneurs utilized various kinds of relationships for arranging their office accommodation. Such relationships included those existing between family members, employer-employee and supplier-customer. Here relationships were used to access infrastructure directly rather than being used as reference.

Human Resources

An entrepreneur's ability to execute a business idea satisfactorily depended, to a large extent, on the quality of the human resource available to her/him. Here the concern was not only about an entrepreneur's ability to attract appropriate kind of human resource, but also her/his ability to retain them. In fact, in the recent years, with the growth of the ICT industry, attracting and retaining human resource became a challenging issue for all entrepreneurs, big and small. However, smaller players were usually at the receiving end of an unequal competition when it came to salary structure. As a result, many start-up companies were compelled to hire freshers only. This came out from discussions with James John, founder of Spaceage.com, Raj Modi, founder of Softech and Raj Software and Communications, Akhtar Hussain, founder of Communication Networks, Naveen Jayakumar, founder of Datamagic Pvt. Ltd., and Chandan Sivaram, founder of Soft Solutions Pvt. Ltd. However, salary, to be sure, was not the sole determinant of an individual's choice of employer; nature of work as well as work atmosphere played an important role in this decision-making process. In the absence of access to huge financial resources start-up companies often attempted to attract and retain employees with the help of various non-monetary rewards of joining the company. Non-monetary rewards were also components by which larger companies attempted to motivate their employees. For example, reputed ICT company Mindtree spent significant resources during its initial phase to design 'thematic' office spaces and build a brand in order to attract talent. In addition, the company also put considerable emphasis on developing a common value system, an atmosphere of openness where employees were encouraged to speak up openly, and a culture of innovation. However, they also supplemented these non-monetary components with financial incentives like employee stock option from day one (Kumar, 2010).

Attracting Human Resources

Attracting an individual to become an employee was relatively easier in a new ICT service company in comparison to a new ICT product company, as product development involved certain amount of risk in terms of longevity till a customer base developed. While talking about his software consulting firm, Rajat Apte, founder of Magnatech Inc., said,

> It was a lot more straightforward (in comparison to software product business). You take a project and then hire either people as your employees or you bring in consultants ... if you are able to build a project pipeline then you hire employees. If you don't have a project pipeline then you hire consultants.

Initial recruits for Rajat Apte's software product company were handpicked. This was similar to word of mouth technique which he had applied while recruiting initial employees for his software consulting company. However, the relationship that existed between Rajat Apte and his product company employees was different from that of his consulting company. Not only that Rajat Apte picked up those individuals because he trusted their ability, those individuals also joined Rajat Apte's company because they trusted his vision. Rajat Apte's recollection is a clear testimony to it,

> With (my software product company) we had a good idea. So I could sell the vision to any prospective employee that I was talking to. What I didn't have is a whole lot of money. I raised a little bit of money from investors which could last us, you know, for six to twelve months. And then we all knew we had to raise more money in a next round of financing to get us to the next milestone. But my challenge was I needed to fill some key hires for us to get to the next level. So here I had little bit of money where I could hire these people, but didn't have enough to guarantee them any security. Yet I needed them to get to the next level. So how do you get around this problem? ... I was very open and transparent to the prospective employees .... It was that faith I would say, it was that vision, that openness that helped me attract these people. Even with that it wasn't easy. Generally I had to meet their families because it was a big decision for some of these guys to leave a position where they are paid (well). Besides our target industry (that is pharmaceutical and biotechnology) is a very stable industry. People don't change those many jobs .... All of my initial hires were people I knew through my consulting business; they were customers of mine ....

Given the fact that Rajat Apte's company was developing during the time when 'dotcom' wave was rising, it was always a challenge for him to get the right kind of talent, as a large number of individuals were interested in working for dotcom companies. At the same time, valuation of 'dotcom' companies by investors was much higher. However, as Rajat Apte puts it, 'fortunately for us there were still enough people around who were saying, I don't want to touch that "dotcom" thing'. In the recent years, attracting experienced people to join smaller companies has become a serious challenge for entrepreneurs. Raj Modi, founder of Softech and Raj Software and Communications, who during the interview was developing a software product for the capital market said, 'People who will be my clients ... know their industry. A person who has a background of capital market only has to go and explain the software to them. To get those kind of guys in marketing is quite difficult'.

A large number of companies in the start-up stage used social network to find out prospective employees. Many of the initial employees of Raj Modi, founder of Softech and Raj Software and Communications and Kunal Raman, founder of Sharp Technologies Pvt. Ltd., were their ex-classmates who came through word of mouth reference. The same was true for Jayant Srinivas, founder of Ahead Technologies Pvt. Ltd., for the first four/five years. For Naveen Jayakumar, founder of Datamagic Pvt. Ltd., James John, founder of Spaceage.com, and Chandan Sivaram, founder of Soft Solutions Pvt. Ltd., social network was always the only mode of identifying prospective employees. Another channel that professionals who later became entrepreneurs adopted in the initial stage was to identify prospective employee from their social network of ex-colleagues. However, later on these entrepreneurs utilized other channels for recruitment as well. Gautam Apte, founder of Innovative Web Solutions Pvt. Ltd., Naresh Ponnaiah, founder of Sunshine Technologies Ltd., O.P. Nayar, founder of Accent Tech Solutions, and Ranjan Raghavan, founder of Bangalore Technologies belonged to this category. Individual social networks and social networks of initial recruits played an important role for these entrepreneurs during the initial period. As Gautam Apte said, during the early stage it was otherwise difficult for them to attract a completely unknown person to the company because of the unimpressive office infrastructure that they had. However, he said that over the years the company developed its recruitment team and employed people from the market by taking the service of different employment portals.

Mangalam Srinivas, while founding Global Technologies Pvt. Ltd., also identified the core team from his ex-colleagues who came from multiple disciplines and who shared the same passion to build a world-class product company. However, after forming the core team, when it came to recruiting engineers, Global Technologies Pvt. Ltd. depended on regular advertisement. Naresh Ponnaiah, founder of Sunshine Technologies Ltd., on the other hand, said that his organization continued using reference for recruitment beyond the initial period. He felt that it helped them in sharing a common understanding and passion about the company and about their work. Knowhow, founded by Kirti Harlalka, was dependent on freelancers. Kirti Harlalka used different techniques in identifying such freelancers. She said, 'Some of them were people we have worked with before, who have been our colleagues, colleague's friends and references'. However, Kirti Harlalka also supplemented that with CVs downloaded from internet.

However, the strategy of recruiting through use of social network did not work well for Akhtar Hussain, founder of Communication Networks. Therefore, initially as an option he tried recruiting from IT training companies. However, given that the response was not so satisfactory he moved into advertising vacancies. A few entrepreneurs, other than Akhtar Hussain, mentioned that advertisement in print media was one of the most useful ways of identifying prospective employees. Such entrepreneurs included Amit Sharma, founder of Sindh Infotech Pvt. Ltd., Alok Dutta, founder of Silicon Networks Pvt. Ltd., Mangalam Srinivas, founder of Global Technologies Pvt. Ltd., Gautam Apte, founder of Innovative Web Solutions Pvt. Ltd., and Hitesh Patel, founder of Knowledge Software Pvt. Ltd.

According to Dinesh Marwari, founder of Ryze Softech Pvt. Ltd. majority of the recruitments in his organization did not happen through word of mouth reference. He felt that social network could play an important role in recruitment when the pool of professionals from which possible recruits were to be identified was much smaller, so that people knew each other fairly well to refer. According to him, that was not the case in ICT industry. Besides, he felt that had his organization been involved in software products and not software services, reference could have played a more important role. He said,

> If I were a product company then the kind of guys I would attract is software researchers, architects – the guys that are called nerds, who want to build something new. In that kind of a company word of mouth would play a great role because ... they would tell their classmates that I have got this great job .... It's the kind of community that will want to attract more and more of this similar type of people, researchers, academic-oriented software engineers, and those types of things.

In addition to using reference of his existing employees, Amit Sharma, founder of Sindh Infotech Pvt. Ltd., and Pankaj Sen, founder of Advanced Software Systems Pvt. Ltd., utilized the service of prominent recruitment companies for identifying employees for his company. Alok Dutta, founder of Silicon Networks Pvt. Ltd. recruited freshers by going to campuses of academic institutions and also used job advertisement. However, he felt that over the years, with increase in opportunities, it has become more difficult to get employees with right kind of talent. This was also felt by Pankaj Sen, founder of Advanced Software Systems Pvt. Ltd. He and Arjun Desai, founder of Win Infotech Ltd., also recruited from campuses of engineering colleges and computer training institutes. In addition, Arjun Desai used recruitment portals and network of placement agencies. Pankaj Sen, founder of Advanced Software Systems Pvt. Ltd., Rupa Datta, founder of Infonet Pvt. Ltd., and Gautam Apte, founder of Innovative Web Solutions Pvt. Ltd., also used recruitment websites. Rupa Datta said, she also used mailing list, discussion boards, etc. to identify prospective employees.

Uniqueness of the business area often played an important role in attracting employees. Jayant Srinivas' Ahead Technologies Pvt. Ltd. functioned in developing e-governance assignments for government departments. He said, 'we find lot of people who are interested in this kind of work which primarily brings some social relevance to the work that they are doing. So that definitely attracts people'. Kunal Raman, founder of Sharp Technologies Pvt. Ltd., felt the same way. He said, given that he began his entrepreneurial journey with ideas of software products, it was easier for him to attract talents, as in India opportunities in software product companies were relatively less. However, at the same time, it was his relationship with his classmates that made them join his organization. He said,

> Finally it all boils down to whether ... they are comfortable with you or not ... I know some of these people for long ... finally it boils down to whether they believe in you ... most of my friends trust me for what I say ... I try to be open, straightforward and speak my mind. Some people like that quality. So that was one of the reasons my friends joined me, not because there is a big opportunity, but because they seem to like working with me.

Mangalam Srinivas' Global Technologies Pvt. Ltd. was a software product company which primarily worked on a technology that was not used by many companies in India. Association with that technology itself had a capacity to attract people to join the company. In the absence of the ability to provide a high salary, smaller companies had to identify non-monetary rewards according to their capacity that they could offer to the prospective employees. Vishnu Krishnaswamy, founder of Techvision, said,

> When we bring them (freshers) in, we say we offer you a lot of freedom, we have internet available 24/7. You have email

> available. We don't block email like large companies. So lot of freedom and you will learn, learn a lot .... And we treat them well, where they are not just bodies. There's quite a bit of personal rapport, if you can say that. I would call to check with them when somebody is sick ... ask them to go home and get rest. So people really like that personal rapport. When (you are in) large companies you are like one among ten thousand or twenty thousand. You are just a number there.

Retaining Human Resources

Considering the existence of large companies in ICT industry who offer high salary package, smaller companies with weaker financial strength often accept the fact that they need to be satisfied with freshers. This is because people with experience will get higher paying jobs in this industry. However, this implies that a large number of individuals who join a smaller company in order to gain experience move on to better paymasters as soon as they get some experience. According to Raj Modi, founder of Softech and Raj Software and Communications, this problem with retention in ICT industry began after 1998/99 with the boom in the dotcom business. High attrition rate among ICT industry employees for joining jobs with higher pay was a reason for considerable grievance for founders of many smaller companies.

Given the problem that organizations face in their ability to retain employees entrepreneurs adopt different strategies for retention. Vinay Reddy's organization, Software Consultants Pvt. Ltd., being a small firm, also faces the problem of retaining employees. Therefore, he has adopted a strategy of recruiting freshers and keeping them attracted to his organization by creating a learning atmosphere. According to Vinay Reddy, in a smaller organization, creation of such a learning atmosphere depends a lot on the level of knowledge of the entrepreneur. Ranjan Raghavan, founder of Bangalore Technologies, also supported this argument. While talking about what retains employees in his organization, he said, 'very strong senior management team who understands not only numbers, money, and business, but understands the work they are doing'. Akhtar Hussain, founder of Communication Networks, also agreed with it. He said,

> I tried to give them more value in terms of the technical knowledge which I had. For example, I had been working for

> many years in a IT company, where I had gained some amount of knowledge .... Usually, the new engineers do not have so much expertise or exposure. So you try to pass on your knowledge to them. They get certain value out of that .... You are mostly taking freshers to begin with. It is difficult to retain experienced people.

Chandan Sivaram, founder of Soft Solutions Pvt. Ltd., a relatively small company, also tried to create a learning atmosphere, which, according to him, was missing for the juniors in large organizations. He said that in larger companies junior employees often didn't understand the purpose of the work that they were made to do. He claimed that in contrast, almost everyone working at his organization understood the project on which they were working. Being a small organization they also got chance to directly interact with the customers and were respected for their work. With reference to employees Vivek Agarwal, founder of egurucool.com, a well-known elearning company that got acquired later on by National Institute of Information Technology, also mentioned the significance of learning environment in an organization. This, according to him, added to the future growth of the employees. He also mentioned some of the other areas of work culture on which emphasis was laid at egurucool.com. This included trust, openness, fairness, provision of equal opportunities to all, non-existence of autocratic and controlled regime, emphasis on work freedom and flexibility, promotion of 'open door' policy, and practice of constant communication (Behl, 2004).

Anil Despande's Tech Writers Inc. operated in technical writing space. Retention was a serious problem for him as well. He introduced the concept of training contract in order to counter that problem. He said,

> Unlike me other companies are incapable of giving good training to freshers .... So after I trained them these companies offered them salary which was three times the stipend that I provided to them as a trainee. I cannot retain them. And that continues to happen even now. One of the solutions that we have found is we take any person on a one year training contract. We tell them that ... we provide you training for one year. During this training you undergo classroom training, you undergo hands-on training. There is a series of assignments that we want you to do and so on. And then you work on the real job, live assignments, the real clients. And that gives you real good experience. And for that you pay us some seventy

> thousand rupees in advance. At any point of time you leave, you won't get that money. And if you don't leave, then I am paying you stipend, every month. So by the end of the year you would have got all your money back through your stipend, in fact more. But if you leave halfway, then at least my training cost has come out. But even after that people leave.

In a similar vein, Rupa Datta, founder of Infonet Pvt. Ltd., introduced a set of strategies for retaining the employees. She said that new junior recruits in her organization got opportunity to work with different projects, diverse technologies, and learn different styles of writing. This diversity excited them. Every junior recruit had a mentor in her organization. Earlier Rupa Datta used to be the mentor for all. As the organization scaled up, the responsibility of mentoring had to be devolved to other experienced employees. This mentoring was important in order to create a professional out of a college student. Rupa Datta said that in order to retain talents Infonet Pvt. Ltd. also created a policy of offering a financial incentive once in six months. And at the same time they also learnt to accept that even after adopting all possible measures some people will still leave.

According to Mangalam Srinivas, salary paid at Global Technologies Pvt. Ltd. was quite comparable with the industry. However, being a start-up company, the salary was not way over market so as to retain a lot of employees. What instead helped the company to retain the employees was the organizational culture of co-ownership that prevailed in the company. The concept of co-ownership was operationalized through different strategies. For example, same human resource policy applied to all employees starting from the engineers to the CEO. While patents were owned by the company, shares of the company were distributed among everyone in the company. Therefore, in effect, all employees had an ownership right over the intellectual property of the company. At the same time while patents were owned by the company they were granted in the name of particular engineers in the company. Similar argument was also articulated by Naresh Ponnaiah, founder of Sunshine Technologies Ltd.

Jayant Srinivas' Ahead Technologies Pvt. Ltd. worked with government departments to enable e-governance. For this, the organization developed set-ups in semi-urban areas in the state of Karnataka where they recruited local people, who were offered appropriate training. The retention rate among those people was considerably high given that in those semi-urban areas employment opportunity was not as high as in a metropolis like Bangalore. According to Dinesh Marwari, founder of Ryze Softech Pvt. Ltd., in order to remain with an organization, it was important for employees to share the vision of the organization. He said,

> I think the biggest thing in terms of retaining people is your ability to get them to believe that that they are part of something that is interesting, that is going to grow, and that will add value to their careers. As long as they feel that way, they will stay with you. If they feel that this is just another job and this is just another software services company, then it boils down to what is the project I am doing, what is the money that I am making and those are the bottom line. When you reach that point ... the relevance of the company disappears. I think that happens more with the junior developers, because they are not able to understand the vision. So its a continuous challenge to educate them about the vision of the company. Whereas its much easier for the management team to understand the vision.

The experience of Kirti Harlalka, founder of Knowhow, was quite unique, as her organization did not have any employee. Instead it had a team of around thirty-five freelancers. The issues with freelancers were quite different. She said,

> ... we can be excellent pay masters, but because we do not give continuous employment it may not work out as a good long term or a sole source of income as one would say ... the nature of the people we work with is transitory. They do not like to work with one organization. They do not like to do the same kind of work again and again. That is the reason that they are freelancers. Again they may not be available full time. So these things create obstructions, because the work is regular .... So matching the people to the business is difficult. It is difficult to find people who are willing to stay on even when there are lows in the business. Besides, it is difficult to get people who will maintain confidentiality with data .... Although we sign legal agreements with them, its really a matter of trust.

Arjun Desai, founder of Win Infotech Ltd. and Vinay Reddy, founder of Software Consultants Pvt. Ltd., felt that their organizations were successful in retaining at least most of the core team members, who were quite critical for the operation of their organization. Arjun Desai, like Vinay Reddy, felt that ability of his company to perform well was one reason for the employees to stay back. The other reasons included past career growth of these employees in the company and one on one relationship that top management had with the employees. Despite all these Win Infotech Ltd. did lose some employees due to different market dynamics and it even had to lay off some employees when the dotcom bubble bursted.

Whereas, a large number of entrepreneurs complained about high attrition rate in their organizations, entrepreneurs like Gautam Apte, founder of Innovative Web Solutions Pvt. Ltd., claimed that the retention rate for his employees was exceptionally high. Explaining his success in retention of employees he said, 'We are no longer a very small company. But still having one to one contact with our people helps. We paid them well, gave them challenging work, showed them opportunities for future, and made sure that they grow in the organization'. It appeared that when entrepreneurs talked about retention they mainly talked about retention of key employees, who were critical to the operation of their organizations. This came out from the discussion with S. Ram of Integrated Software Solutions as well. Attrition among rest of the employees, even if problematic, was considered normal.

A few entrepreneurs, including Arjun Desai, founder of Win Infotech Ltd., Gautam Apte, founder of Innovative Web Solutions Pvt. Ltd., Vishnu Krishnaswamy, founder of Techvision, and Vinay Reddy, founder of Software Consultants Pvt. Ltd., highlighted the role of maintaining a personal relationship between entrepreneur and employees in employee retention. Chandan Sivaram, founder of Soft Solutions Pvt. Ltd., on the other hand, said, 'Major efforts that we put in as an organization in retaining the employees include an attempt to give each and every boy an identity of his own'. When asked about what retains their employees, S. Ram of Integrated Software Solutions said, 'It's personal trust and care (emerging out of) relationship that we have with the people and transparency (that we practise) .... (We have) definitely given them a lot of leeway to operate. That's very important'. However, Vinay Reddy admitted that relationship alone was not sufficient for retaining an employee. Alok Dutta, founder of Silicon Networks Pvt. Ltd., felt that attempts to retain people were a losing proposition. He felt that it was better to prepare for a situation where attrition is normal. For example, he said that his company kept the customers informed that none of their core technologies rested on any one person. That unnecessarily increased the value of that person who, in any case, would leave the company some time in future. K. Padmakumar, founder of Frontech Ltd., also accepted that attrition was a regular process, particularly among the middle management. He said,

> ... it is futile to think we can build in idealistic values and keep them motivated ... . So the best way is to make the raw talent deliver what we want. There is enough raw talent in the country ... . Actually we welcome such things, because fundamentally for me managing youngsters is much easier than managing middle (management) people. And secondly, the energy level which they give is phenomenally high.

Attrition, as it came out, was a regular feature of ICT industry in general. Organizations attempted to retain their key employees, as performance of an organization was often dependent on them. Organizations adopted different strategies for retaining employees. Most of these strategies involved remuneration package, promotion policy, job profile, and organization culture. However, according to entrepreneurs, there were other non-material components of an employment which helped in attracting and retaining an employee in an organization. It was here that interpersonal relationships came to play an important role with reference to human resources. Relationship functioned as social capital in attracting human resource through word of mouth reference. It was observed that entrepreneur's interpersonal relationship with classmates and ex-colleagues was useful in identifying and attracting human resource. Interpersonal relationship facilitated formation of trust in the mind of an individual about another individual's ability and personality. However, as it appeared, interpersonal relationship was often more important in identifying prospective employees during the initial stage of the organization. In comparison, when it came to retention of employees, 'personal touch' was important in all stages. Entrepreneurs mentioned that maintaining a one-to-one relationship between entrepreneur and employees and treating the employees with trust and care helped an organization in retaining its employees. Interpersonal relationships functioned as social capital in this manner. However, it also came out that interpersonal relationship functioned more like a facilitator. It alone was not sufficient in retaining employees.

Collaboration

About a century ago, the French sociologist Emile Durkheim (1984), attempting to understand the basis of social solidarity and social transformation, associated the rise of modernity with the growth of industrial societies integrated by organic division of labour. Such 'organic solidarity', according to Durkheim, was an outcome of collaborative interdependence existing among individuals and/or collectivities who were unique in their own way. The importance of collaboration, which was always emphasized in every context, enhanced considerably in a globalized world. In the context of business, collaboration in the form of a symbiotic relationship among different economic functionaries became important in order to integrate business processes and thereby enhance effectiveness and efficiency. Primarily two different forms of collaboration were observed in ICT industry: first collaboration among founders for forming an organization, and second, collaboration for growing a business. Both these forms of collaboration were mostly among individual entrepreneurs. In comparison, visibility of collaboration among organizations was relatively less as most of the studied organizations were still centred around individual entrepreneurs. Collaboration, here, was often institutionalized in the form of a business contract. Even then, the strength of the collaboration often depended upon the nature of interpersonal relationship shared by the collaborators. Trust invariably played an important role in the formation and maintenance of such collaborations.

Collaboration for Founding an Organization

Some of the well-established companies in ICT industry were founded by teams of professionals (Neergaard, 2005). Companies like Infosys or Mindtree Consulting in India could be standing examples of such companies (Ramachandran and Ray, 2006). This is not to hypothesize that a company founded by a team of entrepreneurs would essentially perform better than a company founded by a single entrepreneur. To disprove such a hypothesis, one can easily point out a large number of well-established companies founded by single entrepreneurs. Nevertheless, there was no gainsaying that most entrepreneurs recognized the benefits of having a symbiotic team with members having expertise in diverse complementary areas. There was no essential need for such team members to be founders; they could be inducted later in the company as board members (shareholder or not) or even as employees. Having co-founders with similar mindset surely helped the entrepreneurs in facing the challenges from the initial stage of company operation. However, developing and maintaining such collaborative relationships required the entrepreneurs to share a relationship based on trust. The question remained how people built and strengthened such relationship (Forbes, et al., 2006).

Few entrepreneurs, who started their business without investment or other form of strong participation from family members were in a position to have 'outsiders' (individuals who were not family members) as co-founders. The reason for this could be traced to the difficulty of extending the circle of trust beyond the family, at least in the initial stage. Amit Sharma founded Sindh Infotech Pvt. Ltd. with partial financial support from his family of origin, whereas Anil Despande founded Tech Writers Inc. with partial financial support and considerable moral support from his in-laws. None of these entrepreneurs had any external member in their company board. Other entrepreneurs who started their business venture by receiving support of family members included Arjun Desai, founder of Win Infotech Ltd. (wife and brother-in-law as co-founders), Vinay Reddy, founder of Software Consultants Pvt. Ltd. (wife as co-founder), Vishnu Krishnaswamy, founder of Techvision (wife as co-founder) and, Rupa Datta, founder of Infonet Pvt. Ltd. (mother as co-founder). However, in case of Alok Dutta, founder of Silicon Networks Pvt. Ltd., it was a family member, his father, who helped him extend his boundary of trust by connecting him to his friend, who was a minority owner of a company and who later provided a seed fund for starting Silicon Networks Pvt. Ltd. In this context it would be worthwhile to note that when today's ICT giant Infosys was founded, all the seven founders (all male) had decided against involving their wives in running the Company (Iype, n.d.).

Relationship between ex-colleagues has often played a critical role in forming collaboration to start an enterprise. When Subroto Bagchi thought of getting into business (which later became Mindtree) the first person he interacted with was his ex-colleague at his previous workplace Wipro, Krishna Kumar. Explaining the reason for that Bagchi wrote,

> I was KK's internal customer (at Wipro) and we often worked issues together. There was a strong bond developing between the two of us, though we met socially only once in the ten years I spent in Wipro. Whenever I used to size up people, my highest rated person was typically one who would fill two conditions: someone I

> would love to work for and someone I would call first, if I ever got into my own business. KK met both criteria. (Bagchi, n.d.: 1)

Ex-colleagues were part of the founding team for Naveen Jayakumar, founder of Datamagic Pvt. Ltd., Dinesh Marwari, founder of Ryze Softech Pvt. Ltd., and Kirti Harlalka, founder of Knowhow. Raj Modi, while founding Softech also had one co-founder, whom he met as colleague at his last workplace. However, by the time Raj Modi founded his second company, Raj Software and Communications, this co-founder had left, as he had to look after his family business located elsewhere. A new person came in as co-founder. This person was introduced to Raj Modi by a Chartered Accountant friend of his father. Talking about the synergy that existed between him and his second co-founder, Raj Modi said,

> He was also developing some software ... . He is a science graduate .... He had may be five years more experience than me. He was basically a developer .... I am a marketing guy. If I am to write a code it will take time. For him it is much easy.

The second collaboration developed by Raj Modi for founding his second company was based on the symbiotic relationship that existed among the founders in terms of areas of expertise. The same was true for Naveen Jayakumar while founding Datamagic Pvt. Ltd., and for Vinay Reddy while founding his first company. For Vinay Reddy, it was a mix of relationship within and outside family. He said,

> ... there was a relative of mine who was already working in IT industry. So we went together, brought another local partner as a finance partner and started our first IT company in (19)86 ... the idea was to identify the three core areas for an IT company. That was technical, admin and finance. So ... he (that is his relative, who was already working in the IT industry) became the technical guy. I took over the admin. The third guy took over the finance functions.

Here he could extend the boundary of trust beyond family relations, as involvement of family members in his business was not that dense.

Friendship was a common basis for development of collaboration among individuals for the purpose of founding an enterprise. Before founding egurucool, an elearning company which was later acquired by computer training company NIIT (National Institute of Information Technology), founder Vivek Agarwal had collaborated with his friend Piyush Gupta, a Harvard Law School graduate, while starting Track India, a management consultancy organization, in 1997. Again, later on, when two of them thought of starting a new business they met Ashish Goyal, then an employee of Hughes Software Systems, through a common friend (Behl, 2004). In our study as well we found that Ullas Gowda teamed up with two other people, both his friends, while founding Knowledge Solutions Pvt. Ltd., primarily for the purpose of raising finance. He came to know them initially while working for one of his ex-employers. Both were his ex-employer's customers. Friends also formed the founding team for James John, founder of Spaceage.com and S. Sivakumar, founder of Datainformatics Pvt. Ltd. Team members of S. Ram at Integrated Software Solutions were his ex-classmates at Indian Institute of Science, Bangalore. Jayant Srinivas, on the other hand, while founding Ahead Technologies Pvt. Ltd., found a collaborator through his mentor. Ranjan Raghavan founded Bangalore Technologies with the financial support of a company for which he was doing technology consulting. However, other than this company his brother was also involved in founding the company. He said,

> I was consulting for a Swiss company. And we did a lot of work together and they were very happy with what I had done .... Then we became good friends .... Something had been running on my mind for several years, but I was not very serious about that .... The suggestion came from the customer and then we said sure why don't we do it? So that's how we started the business.

Kunal Raman, founder of Sharp Technologies Pvt. Ltd., said that earlier in his career as an entrepreneur he was part of the founding team of a company that his brother had founded. The formation of that company involved a symbiotic relationship between his brother and his brother's friend who was also a founder. He said,

> My brother's friends had ... just set up a company in the US .... It was a kind of one man show. He was trying to develop a product on his own. And back then ... we had a ten or fifteen people team. We were doing some consulting work .... So we all met and then we decided to work together ... my brother's friend's company and our company kind of merged and we created a new company.

Kirti Harlalka, founder of Knowhow, had similar experience:

> I think the most important factor (in formation of collaboration) was personal, as we say likeability or trust. Those are very

> subjective things. Second is a complimentary availability of skills. I didn't think I would be very good at business development. And she was very good at it because she had been a freelancer before and had sourced projects from other organizations. That was, I guess, the primary reason. Other factors were we had experience in a different kind of researches.

Collaboration for Business Growth

Collaboration was necessary not only for founding an organization, but also for that organization to attain maturity in terms of business growth. However, the nature of such collaboration differed from the one required for founding the business, particularly concerning the role of relationship. Trust played an important role in case of both types of collaboration, but it was often formalized in the latter. It was observed that, for founding a company, an entrepreneur often collaborated with individuals/organizations with whom he/she shared a strong tie, for example, family members, friends, ex-colleagues or ex-classmates or ex-customers who later became friends. Whereas, it was not necessarily so in case of developing collaborations for making the business grow. However, formal collaboration could develop with the intervention of an individual or organization with whom/which the entrepreneur shared a strong tie.

Development of business partnership was, at times, facilitated by the existing customers. This was the experience of S. Sivakumar, founder of Datainformatics Pvt. Ltd. S. Sivakumar was a reseller who dealt in Apple Computers and some software products. While explaining the way in which he had built such relationships, he said,

> Those days Apple Computers were sold by traders who did not have the technical background. Therefore, they could not technically support their customers ... . So one of the aggrieved customers brought a machine to us through some reference .... And we solved the problems .... That's when he felt that ... (he) should become our partner. So it started. Some of the users of these computers told us, why don't you sell Apple Computers? Because of, I would say, social pressures, customer encouragement, and motivation we took the dealership of this product and we could easily convince customers because ... we were genuine. Supporting these computers was more difficult than just selling. That really boosted our business.

The same was true when he became a sales agent in India for a German software products company. However, relationship was not essential for developing such business collaboration. About one of his business partners Hitesh Patel, founder of Knowledge Software Pvt. Ltd., said,

> ... they are an online software distributor. So we gave them the distribution rights for our software .... I didn't identify him. He identified us ... we were displaying the software at an exhibition in Germany. He walked into our booth. We had a small chat. He looked at it. He is a very experienced man in software business. He realized the importance of this is utility product.

Similar was the experience of Kunal Raman, founder of Sharp Technologies Pvt. Ltd., whose business collaborators contacted him by looking at his website.

Trust emerging out of strong ties shared by entrepreneurs or their acquaintances, played an important role in building collaborations. This was another reason for visualizing interpersonal relationships as social capital. Different forms of interpersonal relationships which were observed in this context included friendships and/or work relationships with family members, ex-colleagues, and customers and ex-customers. Often, such relationships were based on complimentary availability of skills among collaborators, thus giving rise to a symbiotic relationship. This was also the story of Indian ICT company Mindtree, which had an unusually large founding team of 10 members with each having complimentary skills (Kumar, 2010). In case of Mindtree what also facilitated collaboration among founders was the age gap that existed among them, thereby creating no crisis of leadership. Ashok Soota, the senior most both in age and experience was therefore the natural choice for the position of chairman of Mindtree (Kumar, 2010). It appeared that trust played a comparatively less important role in developing collaboration for business growth than in building collaboration for founding an organization. Sometimes, on the contrary, trust emerged out of collaboration for business growth. Collaboration for business growth could even develop among two individuals/organizations who shared no prior direct or indirect relationship. This was, however, never the case when it came to collaboration for foundation of an organization.

Relationship with Government

In India, as elsewhere, ICT industry has almost achieved an iconic status in the new economy. This is particularly true for many Asian countries which only recently have found an esteemed place on the economic map of the world. In India, ICT industry is often visualized as an offshoot of economic liberalization which began in the mid–1980s. The most significant landmark in this direction was the introduction of New Economic Policy in 1991. However, motivation to implement liberalization varied across the states of India. It has been hypothesized that such differential initiatives in states (as introduced by state as well as central governments) is largely responsible for varied development of ICT industry in India (see Heeks, 1996; Heitzman, 2004). On the other hand, orthodox state policies restricting operation of foreign companies like IBM in India favoured the initial development of personal computer companies like Hindustan Computers Limited (HCL). However, at a later stage the company benefited significantly when the central government in 1984 decided to open up the computer market and liberate import (Rediff, 2007). That particularly benefited the software companies like Infosys (BBC, 2011). Although arguments emphasizing governmental role in the development of ICT clusters in cities like Bangalore, Hyderabad, Pune, and New Delhi have been put across by academic analysts, entrepreneurs provided us with diverse impressions about the role of government in this industry.

Amit Sharma, founder of Sindh Infotech Pvt. Ltd., recognized the role played by the government in setting the foundation of ICT industry:

> In 1986 December the Department of Electronics held an annual symposium in New Delhi at Pragati Maidan. They held, a big seminar lasting two days in which particular focus was on computer software. And that came because Rajiv Gandhi in his first year did this fantastic job ... which people don't recognize. He laid the foundation for the IT industry.

Paradoxically, the same Amit Sharma, who appreciated the role of government in development of ICT industry later on mentioned that one of the reasons he decided to diversify into the ICT industry was that it had 'minimal government interference or even government awareness'. Dinesh Marwari, founder of Ryze Softech Pvt. Ltd. also had a similar negative impression about the government:

> In my personal opinion the farther the government stays from the industry the better it is. The government should and currently plays a role in policy setting ... I think, software industry is an

> example of an industry where the government was probably sleeping when it was created. So they did not have time to create frameworks and policies to regulate the industry. And that's the reason why we have been so successful. If you look at any other industry there's hundreds of regulations. And whenever we have regulations, its just another form of restriction and when there is restriction then you have to cross-hurdle, you have corruption. Software, as an industry, fortunately is an intangible industry in the sense that you are not showing something that you are producing. Its all on the computer. Its sent through the internet back to your clients. So there is nothing that you are showing. So its very difficult to get your hands around it. So in my opinion the government as a regulator need not do much in the software industry. They probably realized that now, that it's a great industry, its doing very well. If I do anything its probably going to mess with it rather than help it ... I think the software industry today has got a lot of potential. But I think the potential is being realized only by the top guys, the top companies in India. And there is a big challenge ... that a small company has to face to ... reach certain scale. So I think the government has to probably do something to help the Small and Medium Enterprises (SME) sector in some ways.

Like Dinesh Marwari, Kirti Harlalka, founder of Knowhow also argued in the same line. She felt that government does not have any way of facilitating the growth of educated women entrepreneurs like her who are functioning at a smaller scale in the service sector.

After 1987, the Department of Electronics (DOE) had developed the Software Technology Parks of India (STPI) scheme in order to attract offshore software production houses and 100 per cent export-oriented units by offering broadband communication networks, reliable infrastructure, tax reliefs, etc. (Heitzman, 2004). In the course of discussion, it came out that, for a large number of entrepreneurs, relationship with government meant relationship with STPI, as that was the only specialized governmental organization other than the Registrar of Companies and taxation departments that they had occasionally got in touch with. Vinay Reddy, founder of Software Consultants Pvt. Ltd., recognized the way in which he was benefited by his association with STPI in the past. He said,

> ... in those days to import a mainframe was a big task, so impossible. Foreign exchange wouldn't be released. Finally the Software Technology Park was set up where they imported one of the first

> machines to which even I had access. Otherwise everything was onsite ... till I would say (19)89/90 .... It was, otherwise, all restricted to a few large companies, who could import that kind of equipments with heavy investment and also provide guarantee that they will export as per government norms.

Similar observations were made by Ranjan Raghavan, founder of Bangalore Technologies. When asked about his association with government, he said,

> ... given that we are a STPI unit in a liberalized economy we have to comply with several statutory requirements and we also enjoy the benefits of customs duty waiver. So that helps .... We were definitely able to put together infrastructure at a price lower than we would have otherwise, if we had not been STPI unit. And then we keep getting ... leads and invitations from STPI for delegates that come to visit India from overseas. We haven't been able to turn that into an opportunity and business. But at least STPI tries on its part to help (with) friendly referrals and stuffs like that. So I think government has definitely played some part.

S. Ram of Integrated Software Solutions also highlighted the benefits of association with STPI:

> ... definitely some of the clearances are faster .... For example, here we have bonded warehouse. So ... to import certain items required for our work clearances are faster. Otherwise, you have to run to different government departments. STPI that way is a clean organization unlike many other government departments ....

He also mentioned how favourable taxation policy of the government has facilitated the growth of ICT industry in general even though he felt that it would be helpful if the taxation rules are made clearer.

Mangalam Srinivas, founder of Global Technologies Pvt. Ltd. also discussed his relationship with STPI. However, he did not mention about any specific way in which he was benefited by his association with STPI. He, on the other hand, elaborated on his relationship with the Registrar of Companies, which of course, any company needed to maintain. Naresh Ponnaiah, founder of Sunshine Technologies Ltd. also felt that relationship with government organizations was important:

> ... I would say that these government bodies are facilitating ... to make our life little easier .... For example, STPI helps us in getting

the network connectivity. And they are very lenient when it comes to payment. For example, we are a start-up company. If you are running through a private provider and if you don't pay your bills on time they will cut your connection. But because STPI is helping small companies to grow up they will tolerate us even if there is a little bit of delay in payment. Because they play that parenting ... incubating role and they are doing a fantastic job.

However, not each entrepreneur recognized any significant contribution of government in their business operation. Many organizations like Frontech Ltd. founded by K. Padmakumar had very little interface with government.

In each aspect of 'business ecosystem' discussed in this chapter interpersonal relationship functioned as social capital for entrepreneurs. Interpersonal relationship was valuable for entrepreneurs in getting direct or indirect access to various resources. With respect to indirect access, references often played an important role. The way in which relationship facilitated access to resources varied considerably depending on the nature of the resource the entrepreneur was seeking to access. For example, there was difference in the role of relationship in collaboration for founding an organization from collaboration for business growth. Role of relationship also varied depending on the maturity of a business. For example, relationship often played more significant role in identifying human resource in the start-up stage of business than during the growth stage. Role of trust was repeatedly mentioned by entrepreneurs in this context. Trust, as it appeared, developed out of interpersonal relationship. Once developed, trust played an important role in strengthening the relationship.

Notes

1. Content of this section was published earlier in Sengupta (2011).
2. For details about TiE see Chapter One.

References

Bagchi, S. (n.d.). Making of the Mind Tree. *IDG Ventures India*. <http://www.idgvcindia.com/html/Mindtree%20Article.pdf.> Retrieved 21 June 2014.

BBC. (4 April 2011). Start-up stories: NR Narayana Murthy, Infosys. *BBC.* <http://www.bbc.com/news/ business– 12957104.> Retrieved 22 June 2014.

Behl, R. (2004). Making of egurucool. com. *Global Business Review*, 5(2), 277–289.

Durkheim, E. (1984). *Division of Labour in Society*. New York: Free Press.

Forbes, D.P., Borchert, P.S., Zellmer-Bruhn, M.E. and Sapienza, H.J. (2006). Entrepreneurial team formation: An exploration of new member addition. *Entrepreneurship: Theory and Practice*, 30(2), 225–248.

Heeks, R. (1996). *India's software industry: State policy, liberalisation and industrial development.* New Delhi: Sage Publications.

Heitzman, J. (2004). *Network City: Planning the information society in Bangalore.* New Delhi: Oxford University Press.

India Infoline. (n.d. a). Venture Capital. *India Infoline.* <http://www.indiainfoline.com/bisc/veca/ch02.html.> Retrieved 12 May 2006.

India Infoline. (n.d. b). Venture Capital. *India Infoline.* <http://www.indiainfoline.com/bisc/veca/ch10.html.> Retrieved 12 May 2006.

India Infoline. (n.d. c). Venture Capital. *India Infoline.* <http://www.indiainfoline.com/bisc/veca/ch14.html.> Retrieved 12 May 2006.

Iype, G. (n.d.). The amazing Infosys story: How Infosys was born. <http://www.citehr.com/118434-amazing-infosys-story-how-infosys-born.html.> Retrieved 22 June 2014.

Kumar, S.P. (15 June 2010). The Mindtree way. *The Smart CEO.* <http://www.thesmartceo.in/magazine/cover-story/the-mindtree-way.html.> Retrieved 21 June 2014.

Murthy, S. (n.d.). Story of Infosys. *Voofin.* <http:// voofin.tripod.com/infosys.htm.> Retrieved 22 June 2014.

Neergaard, H. (2005). Networking activities in technology-based entrepreneurial teams. *International Small Business Journal*, 23(3), 257–276.

Ramachandran, K. and Ray, S. (2006). Networking and new venture resource strategies: A study of information technology start-ups. *The Journal of Entrepreneurship*, 15(2), 145–168.

Rediff. (9 June 2007). The amazing story of the birth of HCL. *Rediff.* <http://www.rediff.com/money/2007/ jun/ 09bspec1.htm.> Retrieved 22 June 2014.

Sengupta, A. (2011). Network strategy and access to business finance: Indian entrepreneurs in the Information and Communication Technology industry. *Journal of Entrepreneurship*, 20(1), 103–126.

6

Relationships as Resource

The book began with a broad question: *what is the background of the entrepreneurs who have managed to survive in the ICT industry,* and *what has helped only some entrepreneurs to survive in the ICT industry?* Having looked into the various dimensions of entrepreneurship in Indian ICT industry from the standpoint of entrepreneurs whom I interviewed and of those well-known entrepreneurs who have been interviewed time and again it appears important to go beyond the widely prevalent economic explanations of business experiences. A search for non-economic determinants leads us to look into two spaces, background of entrepreneurs and their relationships with significant others. The questions that are worth asking here are, is social capital the right framework for making sense of the resource value of these relationships and what is the appropriate way of operationalizing social capital in the context of business.

Entrepreneur's Background and their Business Experiences

For historic and ideological reasons business in the old economy developed, over the years, around specific religious/cultural communities and particular families. As a result, family and community background played an important role in understanding the development of entrepreneurship in India. While specific individuals did play important role in development of enterprises, their capacities as entrepreneurs were often understood in terms of their family/community background. However, the scenario changed with the development of high technology-based industries that did not have the legacy of being associated with particular families/communities. As a result, it became necessary to understand the individual entrepreneurs in terms of factors beyond their families and communities. With respect to entrepreneurship in ICT industry entrepreneur's background could be understood through demographic factors like age and gender. It could also be looked at through the educational qualification and work experience of the entrepreneurs, their family background in business, geographical location of business, and sources of motivation behind entrepreneurship.

The ICT industry, being based on advanced technology, emerged over the years, as a symbol of modernity for its proponents. It was probably this image that dissuaded entrepreneurs in this industry (whom I interviewed) from connecting their entrepreneurial journey with their socio-cultural heritage, particularly when that was understood in terms of their caste background. Given the context of ICT industry, it was politically correct to publicly distance oneself from caste backgrounds. Interestingly, entrepreneurs originating from traditional business families were not hesitant in discussing their community background. However, even this group of entrepreneurs also never mentioned about any community embedded business relationships that they enjoyed as entrepreneurs. Of course significance of family for development of business did get mentioned at times.

Studying the high-technology entrepreneurs in the USA E.B. Roberts (1991) found that two-thirds of the high-technology entrepreneurs in the USA had self-employed fathers. However, in India, the image that existed about the ICT industry was quite the opposite. It was portrayed as an industry that facilitated the development of first-generation entrepreneurs. Given the newness of the industry in India it was probably no surprise that no parents of interviewed entrepreneurs having business family background were involved in the same sector. As a result, none of these entrepreneurs had any advantage of learning about this business in their family. Nonetheless, entrepreneurs from business family had the advantage of learning general business acumen, if nothing else, from their families. Of course not every such entrepreneur was privileged in that sense. At times, there was insufficient support from family members due to their lack of awareness about the style of operation of the ICT business and its revenue model. This was particularly the case when family members were involved in traditional business activities like trading. Given the newness of this industry it was also not essential to have a business family background in order to become an entrepreneur in the ICT industry.

Researchers differed in their observations about the influence of gender on the style of business operation and/or ability to establish business and bring business growth (see Aldrich, Reese, and Dubini, 1989; Smeltzer and Fann, 1989; Cromie and Birley, 1992; Renzulli, Aldrich and Moody, 2000; Greve and Salaff, 2003). However, there was hardly any difference of opinion among them about the near absence of women entrepreneurs. Reasons for this virtual invisibility were quite understandable and could be traced to the obstacles created by patriarchal social structure. One ambition of entrepreneurship concerning women, which could be considered as particularly objectionable in a traditional society was independence. However, within this generic picture the scenario differed among industries. For example, while searching for women entrepreneurs in the ICT industry, I was often told that it would have been easier for me to find women entrepreneurs had I been interested in studying industries based on creative skills and not technology. Women entrepreneurs were particularly less in number in industries based on technology (which were traditionally classified as male domains); whereas, women entrepreneurs were more in industries based on creative skill (which was traditionally accepted as female domains).

It was interesting to find that indirectly (and also unintentionally!) patriarchal social structure could facilitate women entrepreneurship to some extent. In a patriarchal system earning of women was mostly considered as secondary income for family, whereas male member's earning was given primacy. As a result, family's concern about any loss experienced by a woman entrepreneur (in case, she was not the main earner) was much less when compared to the same experienced by the primary (mostly male) earner. This was because loss experienced by women entrepreneurs did not financially disrupt the family life. Such differential concern from family, at times, made it easier for women to leave a secure job and start a business venture which entailed risk. However, entry of a woman in entrepreneurship was strongly contingent upon family's concern about the possibility that entry into entrepreneurship would make a woman extremely busy and that would make it difficult for her to fulfil family responsibilities. Therefore, it was no surprise that both the married women entrepreneurs with whom I interacted felt that without the support of their family members they could have never become entrepreneurs. In some families, husband felt more comfortable in taking the risk of leaving a secure job and starting a business venture if his wife's earning was sufficient to financially support the family. On the other hand, some entrepreneurs felt that at a young age before marriage it was easier to take a risky decision like starting a business, as there were less of family responsibilities. One must note here that none of the entrepreneurs whose family members were into business and who participated actively in it considered business as a 'risky decision'.

The existence of a localized culture of innovation in the ICT industry in Silicon Valley, the USA is well-known (see Saxenian, 2000). This showed that, despite functioning within a standardized framework at a global level, there was a possibility for existence of unique localized business culture. However, the same was not true in India. To a large extent, local uniqueness was dependent on the growth of local business networks. Whereas, given the dependence of Indian ICT business on customers abroad, there was hardly any effort to develop strong local business connections. The dominating presence of transnational networks (Upadhya, 2004) was largely responsible for scarce existence of local uniqueness. Choosing to locate oneself in one of the many ICT hubs in India had more to do with the availability of necessary human resource there than with the local business culture.

Any industry depended on its own stock of knowledge. Being a high-technology industry, ICT demanded a high level of knowledge from the entrepreneurs as well as from the workforce. One channel through which people associated with this industry acquired necessary knowledge was formal education. This was visible from the pattern of educational qualifications of the entrepreneurs. Most of the entrepreneurs had some or other degree/diploma/certificate in the area of computer and allied fields. Till the time reputation of an enterprise developed, educational qualification of an entrepreneur as well as reputation of their *alma mater* was used as a credential in convincing a potential client. Educational credentials alone were not always sufficient to build reputation. It was also necessary to demonstrate skills, at times free of cost, to the prospective customers. According to many entrepreneurs here (quite similar to Cooper, 2002), work experience was more useful than formal education in order to learn such skills. This probably explained how despite being a technology-based industry ICT sectors had entrepreneurs from non-technical educational background. In Sweden as well, it was found that attending a course on business education and having previous experience of start-up as a team member was more useful in executing a business idea than having high formal education (Davidsson and Honig, 2003).

Other than forming reputation, relationships embedded in alma mater also facilitated the formation of social capital applicable for business. Having an educational degree from an institution/university located in the USA or some European country, where market for many Indian ICT companies was located, often helped an entrepreneur in building familiarity with markets abroad. Similar observations were made by other researchers (see Yoo, 2000; Schutjens and Stam, 2003; Upadhya, 2004; Upadhya and Vasavi, 2008). However, this did not imply that having an educational degree from overseas was essential for addressing foreign market. Many entrepreneurs interviewed for this research had degrees from state-level or, at the most, from national-level institutions in India. However, they were quite active in addressing markets abroad.

It was observed that entrepreneurship depended on the pattern of previous professional career that an individual entrepreneur had as an employee. Some of the entrepreneurs felt that having a professional career before becoming an entrepreneur was often useful in understanding the mindset of the employees, learning business acumen, and developing social capital in the form of membership in professional networks. However, having an employment with lucrative salary could also dissuade individuals from taking the risk of becoming an entrepreneur. While starting their business a large number of the studied entrepreneurs had work experience ranging between two and five years. This was quite different from the USA, where a typical technical entrepreneur had 13 years of work experience (see Roberts, 1991). Experience of having worked abroad as an employee of some large multinational company was quite useful in understanding the expectations of foreign clients. It was also advantageous in developing social capital in the form of membership in professional networks. For building such networks, many entrepreneurs found foreign exposure as an employee to be more useful than having the same as a student. However, entrepreneurs also received foreign exposure when they were sent abroad for short duration by their Indian employers or when they worked from India itself for foreign clients. This probably explained how many entrepreneurs were quite competent in developing and maintaining foreign business without having work experience abroad.

It was observed that entrepreneurs' background, specifically those emerging out of educational qualification and work experience, was often utilized for building business networks as well as reputation. One interesting connection between these apparently disconnected resources was that relationship often played an important role in their development. Therefore, there was a need to explore the possibility of bringing all these resources under one umbrella and investigate its importance for the ICT business establishment and growth.

Relationships, Trust and Business

Relationships were found to be useful in identification of business opportunities as many business ideas developed from discussions among people sharing different relationships. This supported the observations of previous researchers (see Lipparini and Sobrero, 1994; Soh, 2003; Julien, Andriambeloson and Ramangalahy, 2004; Arenius and Clercq, 2005; Eraydin and Armatli-Köroglu, 2005; Dyer and Hatch, 2006). People whom entrepreneurs found to be important for discussion included both family members and people outside the family. People outside the family included family friends, existing clients, colleagues at earlier workplace, as well as founding partners for their business ventures. Informal discussion with existing clients provided entrepreneur an opportunity to secure information about the business problems that were being faced by the clients. Listening to these problems helped some entrepreneurs in identifying business opportunities. Colleagues at workplace were found to be important discussion group members for some entrepreneurs in developing business ideas. However, in order to contribute towards identification of business opportunity it was necessary that the discussion partners understood the target business space. For some entrepreneurs, personal social relationships helped in identifying business opportunities by providing access to publicly unavailable information. Similar observations were also made by previous researches (see Burt, 2000; Tötterman and Sten, 2005). At times, entrepreneurs developed their business ideas while closely observing the challenges faced by their family members in their professional lives. Relationship with family members was also important in case an entrepreneur was dependent on family-based resources for executing her/his hunch about a business idea. Hunch was always based on some authentic information received from trustworthy sources. Knowledge about expertise of those sources was one mechanism through which trust developed. Interpersonal relationship was another channel for development of trust. Looked in this way it was difficult to identify spaces where relationships had no role to play.

Getting initial customers was the other challenge that the entrepreneurs had to deal with. Customers required rationale for trusting a new organization. Rarely were people interested in becoming the first customer. For example, in the service sector, an offer of lower price alone was not sufficient to convince customers to change from their existing vendors to new ones. The customers needed to be convinced about the quality of service. For that, word of mouth reference based on interpersonal trust was used as an important tool by many customers. Another resource on which any business depended was reputation. There were various ways of building reputation. Reference was one such way. It was also formed by building an association with individuals having high net worth in industry, for example, having a well-known experienced person as financier. Apart from any financial help, the investor also brought in other value like business advice, business contacts, and greater visibility. Other researchers (see Neergaard, 2005) also came up with similar observations. It was found that, after getting initial customers, reference from them was vital in getting the later customers. In facing business crisis emerging out of scarcity of customers, relationships with people outside the organization were found to be valuable. Partners of such relationships could be located abroad or could be located in geographical proximity. This observation contradicted the findings of some past researchers that entrepreneurs depended less on building external ties when they perceived uncertainty in the market (see Sawyerr, McGee and Peterson, 2003; Littunen, 2000).

Even though the use of social relationships facilitated business development in different ways, such benefits came with associated constraints. For example, securing an organization as customer through the use of reference from individuals who were employees there meant that the entrepreneur was obliged to take special care to satisfy the customer, as otherwise, it could affect the status of her/his referees in that organization. In comparison, business relationships developed through 'cold-call' were much easier to maintain.

While at the end of the day the possibility of retaining a customer was decided by an organization's ability to cater to customer's requirements, trust emerging out of relationships played an important role in the background. It came out from the discussion with entrepreneurs that people continued to do business only if they found each other trustworthy. Trust, for some entrepreneurs, emerged when one was able to deliver what he/she had promised. To remain trustworthy it was important to maintain transparency with customers, particularly in case things were going wrong. Business relationship, just like personal relationships, depended on the people who were involved in the relationship. It took time to build a relationship. Therefore, if people involved in a relationship kept changing, the relationship did not get the opportunity to become strong. And this could happen primarily when the level of attrition in an organization was high. Therefore, having low level of attrition helped in strengthening a relationship and this could ensure customer retention. Customer retention mostly implied an organization remaining as customer. However, many a times, customer relationships developed not with organizations but with individuals in organizations. Therefore, even when relevant individuals from client organization moved to another organization, the business relationship could continue if business developed with the new organization through the same individual. This was also considered as customer retention from the point of view of the entrepreneurs.

Social relationships played an important role for accessing financial resources. On the one hand, relationships with people who possessed financial resources gave access to financial resources. On the other hand, relationship was beneficial in getting references to access financiers. An investor's willingness to provide finance to an entrepreneur or to refer her/him to someone else depended on the trustworthiness of the entrepreneur which was often assessed through relationship. In that way, trust played an important role in getting finance. Trust was assessed in two ways, trust on capability of an individual and trust on the personality. Trust that was required for making an investment decision often developed out of interpersonal relationships among various kinds of actors, for example, colleagues in an organization, supplier-customer, family members, friend/friend's family members, etc. Similar observations were also made by other researches (see Cooper, 2002). Development of trust played an important role in increasing the strength of the relationship and thereby facilitating the access to various resources including finance.

For some entrepreneurs from business families having a close relationship with family members facilitated access to family's financial resources. Family relations were also found to be useful in getting in touch with angel investors as well as venture capitalists. However, having a good relationship with family was not sufficient to secure family's financial resources for investing in business. It was also necessary for family members to understand the nature of that business area. Often families involved in traditional businesses, particularly trading, found it difficult to understand the revenue models of ICT businesses. This was probably one reason for which the current research found some ICT entrepreneurs who were from business families, but whose business had developed without financial support from family. One more criterion for family funding was that family members needed to be ready to bear some risk by investing their family resources in business being initiated by their family members. It was primarily because of this reason that many well-to-do families lacking business background were not interested in investing family resources in business initiated by a family member. However, unlike some prior research (see Sanders and Nee, 1996; Smallbone, et al., 2003), having a business community background was not found to be important for accessing finance outside the family.

It was found that, while making an investment decision, angels gave considerable value to the ability of the entrepreneur. Angel investment decisions were also dependent on the ability of the angels to trust an entrepreneur as a person. Relationship was one way through which the angel investors secured such information. Often such relationships were developed by entrepreneurs during their professional career. Many entrepreneurs were familiar with their angel investors as colleagues, customers, employees of customer organizations, acquaintances of customers, ex-employers, and participants at business associations. Familiarity with angels as colleagues at previous workplace was also observed by Ramachandran and Ray (2006). For many entrepreneurs, the angel investors were their senior colleagues in organizations where they worked as employees. However, familiarity with entrepreneur's reputation was not sufficient to make an investment decision. It was also necessary for the angels to be familiar with the industry for which the entrepreneur was seeking investment.

Although a venture capitalist's final decision to invest was found to be based on an assessment of worth of the business idea, it was supported by knowledge about the personality and aptitude of the entrepreneur, which essentially emerged out of relationships. Primacy given by venture capitalists (VCs) to the worth of business ideas for making investment decisions was also found by Fiet (1995). Like elsewhere (see Jenssen and Koenig, 2002; Shane and Cable, 2002), in Indian ICT industry as well it was not necessary for the entrepreneurs to have personal relationships with VCs. Instead, it was quite useful to have relationship with influential people who could refer the entrepreneurs and/or their business ventures to the VCs. If more than one VC was investing in a venture, the relationship among them was also found to be important. However, it was not necessary for such relationship to be based on familiarity. It had more to do with an ability to cooperate.

While new models for financial investments developed with the rise of angel investors as well as VCs, a very large number of entrepreneurs depended on more traditional methods of raising finance, for example, bootstrapping and bank loan. In these methods of raising finance as well relationship played the role of facilitator. For example, while starting an ICT hardware supply business through bootstrapping, one of the studied entrepreneurs found it useful to have a close informal relationship with a client as that helped him in getting considerable monetary advance for delivering the required hardware. With banks agreeing to offer business loans against relatively less or no collateral, having relationship with bankers came to play an important role in getting bank loans. Here relationship was used in order to assess the trustworthiness and creditworthiness of the debtor. It was found that such relationship was also useful when entrepreneur was compelled to seek overdraft facility. However, frequent availing of such privileges reduced the utility of these relationships, as reputation of the entrepreneur went down. B. Uzzi (1999) also found relationship with bankers to be useful. Importance of social capital in the absence of physical assets to be offered as surety was also mentioned by Putnam (1994). However, unlike elsewhere (see Uzzi, 1999; Becker-Blease and Sohl, 2007) in Indian ICT industry gender did not seem to influence the access to finance.

Family relationships helped some ICT entrepreneurs in getting office accommodation. They began their initial business operations from home or garage at home or office space owned by family members. Those who began from home finally decided to move out when their workforce increased and when they generated sufficient resources for affording an external office space. However, not all entrepreneurs began their business at family owned spaces. At times, investment, particularly at seed stage, also came in the form of provision of an office space. This was one way in which relationship outside family turned out to be useful for entrepreneurs in getting office accommodation. For some entrepreneurs, such external relationships also developed through family members. It also developed during one's career as an entrepreneur. Some entrepreneurs even used office spaces which were rented out to them at a concessional rate by their family members or their clients.

Like elsewhere (see Neergaard, 2005), in Indian ICT industry relationship played an important role in getting human resource for a business venture, particularly during the initial stage of business. In the initial stage of an enterprise, recruiting by an employer and joining by prospective employees depended a lot on interpersonal trust and passion shared by the two sides. Initial key recruits were mostly handpicked on the basis of familiarity or on the basis of word of mouth reference by trusted informers. Handpicking was tremendously useful if one was looking for specific skill-sets. Such requirement was noteworthy in high growth oriented ICT product companies. These employees included individuals who were known to the entrepreneur as ex-colleagues, ex-colleague's friends and references, ex-classmates, and employees of her/his customers. They also included ex-colleagues of employees. Unlike in ICT product companies, initial recruitment in service-based companies took place once a work assignment arrived. Therefore, salary of the employees was assured. In a product company, continuation of employment was dependent on the successful execution of the product vision of the entrepreneur, which the prospective employee needed to trust. As a result, trust played more important role for an employee in joining a product company than in joining a service-based company. From entrepreneurs' side, it was necessary to keep future plans open and transparent in order to build trust.

Believing in the entrepreneurs vision was important for prospective employees in the initial stage of any business when the enterprise did not have impressive infrastructure or attractive salary packages to offer. However, this did not include enterprises which started with strong venture capital support. Of course, in such enterprises as well, relationship played an important role in identifying the key employees; for other positions recruitment often took place through advertisements. In such cases, besides salary and infrastructure, what attracted individuals to become employees were nature of technology, space and the worth of the business idea. The entrepreneur's efforts of showing 'personal touch' by establishing 'one-to-one contact' with employees was found to be useful to some extent in retaining employees by keeping them attracted to the workplace. However, 'personal touch' by itself was not sufficient to retain employees. It had to be supported by various other aspects like salary, scope for career growth, and job profile including nature of project and nature of technology.

Finally, relationship was found to be valuable for building collaborations to found companies and to develop businesses. Family members were the most common collaborators for founding a company, primarily because of the difficulty of extending the circle of trust beyond the family, at least in the initial stage. Similar observations were also made by Neergaard (2005). For many male entrepreneurs, such collaborators included their wives. Other family members who collaborated with the entrepreneurs for founding a company included brother, mother, in-laws, and brother-in-law. Collaborators other than family members included ex-classmates, ex-colleagues, own customers, customers of ex-employers, brother's friends, and individuals referred by family friends, family members, and mentors. It was found that whereas relationships based on blood and/or marriage facilitated trust formation with family members, friendship formed primarily through education and work mostly facilitated trust formation with collaborators outside the family. When it came to non-family collaborators for founding a business, entrepreneurs were also concerned about complimentarity of skills other than trust. This was an important consideration when mentors of entrepreneurs referred possible collaborator(s). Emphasis on complimentarity of skills was also observed by prior researchers (see Neergaard, 2005).

However, it should be noted that business did not depend just on relationship and trust. Other factors played crucial roles. For example identification of business opportunity also depended on human capital of the entrepreneur(s). Human capital was created by changes in persons that brought about skills and capabilities thereby enabling the individuals to act in new ways (Coleman, 1988). In Indian ICT industry an entrepreneur's human capital developed from their educational pursuit and particularly their work experience leading to growth of industry expertise of the entrepreneur. Human capital of this form played a significant role in the identification of business opportunity. Similar observations were also made by Cooper (2002). Utilization of knowledge emerging out of one's work experience was useful for many first generation entrepreneurs who did not have family background in business to bank upon. For entrepreneurs from business family background, such human capital was not essential for identification of business opportunity. It was, therefore, no surprise that all the entrepreneurs who did not mention about the indispensability of knowledge gained through education or work experience had some family background in business. Conversely, however, it was not possible to state that all entrepreneurs who had a family business background did not use their education and/or work experience for conceptualizing their business idea.

In a similar way, rational calculations and serendipity played an important role in the identification of business opportunity. Many entrepreneurs identified a business opportunity once they got to serve a customer in that segment just by chance. Rational calculation, on the other hand, was often based on industry reports, opinions of industry specialists, and observation and analysis of market trends. However, entrepreneurs' scope for application of rational calculation in choosing the right business opportunity mostly happened within the boundary set by domain knowledge of the entrepreneur and various other similar contingencies. These contingencies also played an important role in defining rationality. Rational decision-making was always subject to the availability of information with the decision-maker. Considering the fact that many a times such information about emerging business areas, where there was higher possibility for identification of business opportunity, was not available to the entrepreneur 'hunch' played a crucial role in business decision-making. However, it was possible to apply hunch extensively when the entrepreneur had sufficient financial resources to experiment with. Many a times, only entrepreneurs with family-business background or quite well-established entrepreneurs were at privilege with such supply of financial resources.

Relationship was also not the only way in which entrepreneurs got their initial customers. There were other alternatives as well. In fact, there were quite a few entrepreneurs who received their initial customers through 'cold-call', that is, marketing without any reference. Some entrepreneurs even attempted to find customers during a crisis situation by use of 'cold-call'. However, 'cold-call' did not work as a strategy in all industries. For example, in an organized industry like stock-broking, first of all, it was possible to identify prospective customers to call up by looking into business directories, yellow pages, and membership list of relevant associations, and secondly 'cold-call' was accepted there as a practice. However, 'cold-call' was not accepted in a traditional sector like diamond industry, which was entirely based on informal networks. There were also entrepreneurs who attempted to diversify their business in order to face business crisis. Entrepreneurs kept attempting to get customers through different avenues. They never depended completely on reference at the cost of 'cold-call' or vice versa. At times, it was difficult to distinguish between 'cold-call'-based and 'reference'-based marketing.

At the same time, there were business offerings for which even though a category of individuals were identified as prospective customers it was difficult to locate many such individual customers physically so that they could be contacted through 'cold-call' or reference. This was particularly true for business offerings for which per unit profit margin was low and, therefore, a business around it could be viable only if volume of sale was substantial. Most of the time, it was not possible for the entrepreneur to secure such a large number of customers through 'cold-call' or reference. In such cases, entrepreneurs needed to depend a lot on various strategies of mass marketing which included displaying a product at tradeshows, maintaining company website, and advertising on the internet and the print media. If the clientele was localized, poster- or banner-based marketing was also useful. Mass marketing also required an enterprise to set up offices in geographical locations of prospective market areas and build relationships with organizations that would function as marketing agency. One advantage of mass marketing was that, through this process entrepreneurs could even identify new categories of prospective customers.

Social relationship was often found to be more important for getting customers than for retaining customers. Ability of an entrepreneur to retain a customer depended to a large extent on the level of satisfaction of the customer, which was contingent on the quality of the business offering. Reputation about trustworthiness of an entrepreneur and/or her/his business offering was largely dependent on the level of this satisfaction. In case of a service-driven company, this, to a large extent, depended upon the quality of employees who worked for a client. For retaining a customer, it was extremely important to be customer-centric. Being customer-centric was often understood as sharing customer's problem as one's own and, therefore, going out of the way to take prompt care of that problem. Implemented appropriately, customer-centricity led to development of relationship which could facilitate customer retention.

While relationship played an important role in securing investors, alternative approaches did exist. There were organizations which specialized in finding investors for an enterprise. Such organizations, at the most, had professional relationships with different investors. Similarly, no clear importance of relationship was observed with reference to collecting financial resources through public offerings. On the other hand, while personal relationships often facilitated entrepreneur's access to infrastructure, it did happen without relationships also. Some entrepreneurs were against mixing home and office. At the same time, there were entrepreneurs whose entry into the ICT industry was driven by a need for diversifying from other businesses. Such entrepreneurs had the privilege of using their existing office accommodation itself for starting their ICT business.

It appeared that ability to use relationship for recruitment was also dependent on the strength of the network of entrepreneurs and their network partners. Besides, it was also contingent on the number of people to be recruited. If the number was high, depending only on references could prove to be time-consuming. In such situations, relationships had to be supported by other avenues like advertisements, campus recruitments, etc. Likewise, while relationships and trust were significant for developing collaboration to found a company, they were not important for forming collaboration that was needed for promoting business growth. It depended more on utility of association. For some smaller companies, formation of such collaboration was facilitated by people with whom both parties shared certain trusted relationship. In many cases such collaboration developed out of business calls, and trust developed after collaboration continued for some time.

Changes in Utilization of Relationship and Trust[1]

Forms of relationship and trust and their importance for business development were subject to constant modification. For example, it was found that as an organization scaled up, the role that was played by personal social networks of entrepreneurs went down consistently. Instead, importance of institutionalized networks, organization and processes increased. This did not mean that personal social networks of entrepreneurs became unimportant. Instead, the nature of relationship required for business developed out of business reputation rather than intimacy. There was no substitute for personal comfort level. The way in which a relational capital was utilized changed over time. For example, during the initial phase of business, it was often the reputation of the entrepreneur's ability that built trust in the mind of the prospective customers. With time, every growth-oriented company sought to reduce customer's reliance on this personalized reputation and instead built reputation of the organization and its business offerings. At the same time, business networks increased from networks established by entrepreneurs to networks established by organization, which included those formed by the employees as well as by the entrepreneur. This was because personal relationship had its limitation in expanding the business beyond one level. Though personal relationship continued to play an important role, there was need to back it up with institutional effort. This observation was similar to the findings of previous researchers (see BarNir and Smith, 2002; Shaw, 2006).

It was found that the basis of a venture capitalist's decision to invest varied depending on the maturity of an organization. Whereas during the initial phase of development of a company, investors were interested in knowing about the earlier professional performance of the founder, in the later phase of a company, they were interested in knowing about the performance of that company. Interestingly, relationship played an important role in identifying a prospective investor at any stage of business. In the early stage, investors also used relationships to assess the individual track record and trustworthiness of the entrepreneur. These relationships were often built up with entrepreneurs when they were working as employees. Investments at later stages were driven more by performance data. However, while approaching the investors, entrepreneurs were guided by their comfort level with the investors.

It was mentioned earlier that, during the initial stage of business, relationship played an important role in identifying human resource. In fact, for most enterprises each and every initial key appointment was relationship-driven. However, as business started growing, other channels began getting prominence. These channels included advertisements, recruitment portals, recruitment agencies, and campus placements at academic institutions. This did not mean that relationship became unimportant; it became one of the many channels. In slow growth businesses, however, relationship continued to remain the sole channel of recruitment. In moderate growth companies as well there was a possibility for dependence on relationships for recruitment. These relationships included relationships of employees in addition to relationships of entrepreneurs. Involvement of entrepreneurs in the recruitment process also changed with time. Whereas during the incubation period entrepreneurs were involved in all recruitments, as enterprise started growing entrepreneurs participated mostly in key recruitments; rest was looked after by the recruitment team of the enterprise. Over a period of time, network with founding partners transformed from social to business relationship. During the same time, network with customers and financiers changed from business to social relationship. Similar observations were also made by Schutjens and Stam (2003).

Relationship, Trust, and Entrepreneurial Social Capital[2]

While reviewing a wide variety of conceptualizations of social capital in Chapter One of this book it was observed that one commonality that cut across the diverse interpretations of the concept was everyone's concern about resource-potential of human relationships. An exploration of different resources required for the growth of entrepreneurship clarified that appropriate relationship could play an important role in supporting access to each of them. Therefore, in conceptualizing entrepreneurial social capital, it would be a futile effort to list down resources which could be accessed by use of relationships. Instead, it would be interesting to identify the resources which emerged primarily out of relationships.

It was found that reference was one resource which primarily emerged out of relationship. Reference indicated the process through which an individual, who was familiar with the entrepreneur and/or her/his business offering, acted as referee in the decision-making process of economic actors significant for an entrepreneur's business development, for example, a potential customer, a prospective financier, etc. The task of the referee was to vouch for the trustworthiness of the entrepreneur and/or her/his business offerings. Trust here involved reliability of entrepreneur as a person, worth of an organization, and effectiveness and efficiency of a business offering. Confidence to act as a referee developed primarily through relationships. This did not mean that such relationships were essentially based on personal intimacy. In fact, a large number of such relationships were purely formal business transactions. A referee could be a person who had once been a customer of the entrepreneur. Even though, having a business relationship helped an individual develop familiarity about a product/service, having a personal relationship was essential for knowing the entrepreneur.

Broadly, it was possible to identify two types of references. In the first type of reference, which was more prevalent, an entrepreneur could mention about her/his association with the referee to others in order to develop confidence in their mind. Those 'others' could, in turn, seek reference by getting in touch with the referee, even though they were not personally known to each other. In the second type of reference, which any entrepreneur valued much more than the first type, people familiar with the entrepreneur and/or her/his business offering vouched for them in their own circle. Reference became a resource in establishing reputation by acting as a bridge over a 'structural hole' between 'non-redundant contacts' (Burt, 1992).

In the Indian ICT industry, it was found, 'non-redundant contacts' of entrepreneurs included 'strong ties', relationships which need to be maintained by spending considerable time and which were characterized by high emotional intensity and reciprocity. This included relationships with family members and friends who provided an entrepreneur with the access to their own resources and external resources through valuable references. This finding questioned M. Granovetter's (1973) argument that 'strong ties' could only be a source of support and not external resources. At the same time, considering the intensity of relationships, it could be deduced from Granovetter (1973) that the level of trust would be higher in 'strong ties' as compared to 'weak ties'. I found that provision of access to resources in Indian ICT industry was strongly dependent on the level of trust among the partners. If so, it would be impractical to think that 'weak ties' would give access to valuable resources. However, it was observed that sharing of less important informational resources was feasible even among 'weak ties'. At the same time, the findings of current research endorsed the existing idea (see Granovetter, 1973) that 'strong ties' were sources of support. Observations in Indian ICT industry also supported arguments advocated by researchers about the importance of strong ties for business development (see Luo, 1997; Brüderl and Preisendörfer, 1998; Davidsson and Honig, 2003).

While relationship was one primary channel through which reputation developed, it was not the only channel. Reputation of a product/service also developed through the process of branding which was not contingent on relationship. Whatever way reputation developed, in order to refer, a referee needed to trust the referred, which meant, trust preceded reference. Again, reference in turn, created trust in the mind of others. Considering that reference was one form of social capital, in the sense that it was a resource which emerged from relationships, it could be concluded that the connection between trust and social capital was cyclical. Therefore, the debate about whether social capital preceded trust or trust preceded social capital (see Putnam, 1994; Fukuyama, 1996; Dasgupta, 2003) was pointless. It would be more appropriate to categorize the relationship between social capital and trust as supportive of each other.

Like reference, goodwill was another resource which emerged out of relationships. However, unlike reference, which could, at times, emerge even without relationships, goodwill could emerge only through relationships. Goodwill often developed through demonstration of what could be called 'favour'. However, it was observed that for many entrepreneurs, 'favour' was a politically incorrect word. Instead, some entrepreneurs preferred the term 'demonstration of flexibility'. Goodwill in the form of flexibility was found to be particularly useful in retaining a customer in a service-based company. If the entrepreneur showed flexibility he/she could expect flexibility in return from the customer, and the customer was also obligated to reciprocate. However, such a relationship developed only if norm of 'reciprocity' existed in the social structure. Considering the resource value of such reciprocity emerging out of 'convertability of capital' (Bourdieu, 1997), goodwill could be termed as social capital. This also supported findings of earlier researches (see Fukuyama, 1996, 2000; Lin, 2003; Frazier and Niehm, 2004; Anderson, Park and Jack, 2007).

Flexibility could take different meanings in different contexts. One strategy for such flexibility was termed as 'going out of the way'. This included helping a customer solve some problems even if the customer was not paying for it. Another related strategy was termed as 'showing personal touch'. This implied considering customer's problem as one's own. Entrepreneurs 'went out of the way' for 'showing personal touch'. If an entrepreneur adopted such strategies, there was a chance that customers would show patience when the entrepreneur was going through internal troubles like employee attrition. However, not all entrepreneurs agreed that relationship took care of all business problems. Goodwill, according to some entrepreneurs, had limited effect in the sense that it could take care of immediate disturbances. However, if one did not rectify the problem and did not get back on track, goodwill soon got exhausted. Relationship was a reserve which was to be considered as the last resort. It was tremendously precious, because once it was used to cover up some mistake, the entrepreneur was left with no protection.

Considering that social capital resources developed out of relationships, it was necessary to know what was the nature of such relationships. Considerable variation was observed in the nature of relationships maintained by entrepreneurs. A large number of these relationships emerged out of interpersonal familiarity. Commonly, these relationships were referred as social network. This included actors who are family members of entrepreneurs and actors outside entrepreneurs' family. Social network partners within entrepreneur's family included wife, husband, parents, siblings, cousins, uncle, and in-laws. Whereas social network partners outside family included customers, customers of earlier employers, previous employer, employees of customers, co-members of business associations, business acquaintances, well-wishers, individuals referred by trusted mediators, family friends, ex-colleagues, and ex-classmates. No relationship was observed between the type of social network and the resource potentiality of networks. However, it was observed that irrespective of their nature, social networks became resourceful only when certain intimacy developed in them.

It was not found necessary for the partners of social networks to have geographical proximity. However, it was observed that geographically distant network partners were usually in proximity at one point of time. That is when their relationship developed. For partners who had never been in proximity, the partnership was, at times, developed through a trusted mediator enjoying geographical proximity with one of the partners. In any case, distant partners needed periodic proximity. This observation suggested a middle path between researchers who endorsed the need for proximity in building entrepreneurial networks (see Keeble et al., 1998; Saxenian, 2000; Cooper, 2002; Neff, 2005; Tötterman and Sten, 2005; Bönte, 2008) and those who emphasized the need for global networks for promoting innovation (see Eraydin and Armatli-Köroglu, 2005; Lorentzen, 2008). It was found that for many entrepreneurs in this industry, networks were transnational in nature, with network partners located in the USA and in Europe, where there were large markets. Importance of mediators in formation of trusted relationship among distant partners was also highlighted by Hara and Kanai (1994). However, it was found that it was not sufficient to just build relationships. In order to gain out of it in terms of resources, one also needed to maintain them by 'keeping in touch'.

Another form of entrepreneurial relationship evolved from actors' embeddedness in various aspects of social structure (see Anderson and Jack, 2002). Unlike elsewhere (see Batjargal, 2003), in Indian ICT industry social embeddedness did not seem to reinforce social obligations and expectations that limited the freedom of economic agents to recognize and exploit new opportunities. Such embeddedness in Indian ICT industry developed from common diaspora (among people located abroad), family (particularly for business families), and alma mater. One component of social structure which was conspicuous by its absence from the list of criteria for embeddedness was community background of entrepreneurs. This was despite the fact that studied entrepreneurs included people from traditional business communities like Marwaris. In comparison, embeddedness in family was found to be of importance for all entrepreneurs, more for those from business families. Among immigrant ethnic entrepreneurs in the USA as well, it was found that for the purpose of developing business, family was more important than community (see Caulkins and Peters, 2002). When compared with traditional industries which had clear community characteristics, entrepreneurship in the ICT industry was not a community-based profession yet in India.

It was observed that social capital emerging out of social network was more prevalent in entrepreneurial relationships when compared with those emerging out of embeddedness. This questioned the perception of social capital as a collectivity-owned resource, as advocated by various researchers (see Bourdieu, 1997; Cooke and Wills, 1999). However, like elsewhere (see Coleman, 1988; Burt, 2000) we found that in Indian ICT industry as well social capital existed in the structure of relations among actors. At the same time, observations on ICT entrepreneurship in India also endorsed existing viewpoint that social capital was a by-product of other social activities (see Fukuyama, 2000; Anderson and Jack, 2002). However, writing on a different context we, naturally, differed from F. Fukuyama in terms of the nature of such social activities. Whereas, Fukuyama opined that such social activities included religion, tradition, and shared historical experience, none of these was important for us. Instead, social activities like work, education, family life, and expression of diasporic sentiments became crucial here.

One critical feature of social capital was its exclusivity. By its very nature, social capital was never available to everyone. The value of social capital primarily lied in its scarcity. It was this scarcity which facilitated social capital to become a tool for 'control' (Burt, 1992). Because of this scarcity value, entrepreneurs sought to keep the flow of social capital restricted. It was found that family-based social capital was primarily accessible to entrepreneurs who originated from business families. Coming from a business family was beneficial even if an entrepreneur had family members who were involved in an industry different from the one in which the entrepreneur had ventured into. Having family members lacking respective industry background could still be resourceful for the entrepreneur if the family members had connection with people from entrepreneur's target industry as friends and/or professional colleagues. It was not necessary for such family friends or colleagues of family members to be entrepreneurs. A salaried professional could also possess considerable insider information about an industry.

Usually, in case of an entrepreneur who was from a business family, if the business was strongly supported by her/his family, the number of important family-based networks in business was more. However, this did not include entrepreneurs whose families were involved in traditional businesses that did not understand new technology-based businesses and, therefore, did not participate in them even if their family members started one. In such cases, family-based networks were not important at all. Thus, it was not the family background of the entrepreneurs, but the participation of the family members in business that mattered. This was probably the same reasons why Dodd, Jack and Anderson (2002) found that having self-appointed parents did not have any effect on the size of entrepreneurial networks.

For understandable reasons, having social network with ex-classmates was useful mostly for entrepreneurs whose education was connected with their business pursuits. Similarly, having a social network with ex-colleagues was beneficial only if there was parity between entrepreneur's professional career and sphere of her/his business venture. Having a relevant professional career was found to be particularly useful for entrepreneurs lacking family business background. For the purpose of business, having a social network with clients and employees of clients was possible only for individuals who already had entrepreneurial experience. There was very little uniqueness in the social network structure of women entrepreneurs in ICT industry except that for the married women entrepreneurs the founding partners were women and with reference to business they gave a lot of importance to their relationship with family members when compared with male entrepreneurs, both married and unmarried. In comparison with the married women entrepreneurs, the lone unmarried women entrepreneur did not consider her relationship with family members to be that important for business. These observations (like that of Smeltzer and Fann, 1989; Cromie and Birley, 1992) differ from the arguments advocated by researchers (see Aldrich, Reese and Dubini, 1989; Renzulli, Aldrich and Moody, 2000; Greve and Salaff, 2003) who found gender bringing critical difference in the nature of social network of entrepreneurs. Many male entrepreneurs, on the other hand, had their wives as founding partners.

In the context of Indian ICT industry, entrepreneurial social capital could thus be conceptualized as resources emerging from entrepreneurs' social networks within and outside their family and from the embeddedness of entrepreneurs in various aspects of social structure like their diaspora, family, and alma mater. Relationships emerged out of trust and, at the same time, they generated trust. No resource flow took place among actors without the presence of trust in relationships. Having such trusted relationship directly with individuals who possessed resources that entrepreneurs required for developing business was useful as a source of support. However, relationship with others could also be useful for business if it gave rise to unique relationship-based resources like reference and goodwill, which were useful media for accessing resources from significant others. This implied that relationships by themselves were not social capital. They became social capital only when resources like support, reference, or goodwill emerged from them.

Researches utilized different indicators for measuring social capital. These included number of external relationships, frequency of contact, longevity of social network, reciprocity, goal sharing, level of intimacy, trust, commitment (Zhao and Aram, 1995; Frazier and Niehm, 2004; Tötterman and Sten, 2005; Rindova, Petkova and Kotha, 2007), ownership of business by family members, membership in business networks, experience as a member of a start-up team (Davidsson and Honig, 2003), frequency of church attendance, and marital status of the entrepreneur (Honig, 1998). Indicators for measuring social capital of immigrant ethnic entrepreneurs included retention of ethnic identity, residence patterns, frequency of social events, retention of native language, dependence on group assistance, self-sacrifice for group success, role differentiation based on sex, class hierarchies, conflict resolution mechanism, unequal inheritance distribution, and presence of endogamous marriage (Caulkins and Peters, 2002).

However, a careful observation indicated that in measuring entrepreneurial social capital what researchers actually measured was entrepreneur's access to relationships that could have resource potential. Considering that potential was often not realized, it was not appropriate to measure resource potential of a relationship for measuring social capital. Even if such measurements could have some reliability, their validity was questionable. The reason for attempting to measure entrepreneurial social capital in such an indirect way by measuring the nature of social relationships could be found in the difficulty of identifying indicators for measuring entrepreneurial social capital, given their fuzzy nature. From the observations on ICT industry in India I would like to propose a solution by advocating three forms of entrepreneurial social capital, namely, support, reference, and goodwill, whose measurement was practicable. Identification of these new forms would make it possible to assess entrepreneurial social capital by measuring the resource *outcome* of social relationships instead of computing resource *potential* of the same.

It was not possible to conclude that it was only because of social capital that performance of entrepreneurs differed in the ICT industry. Although social capital was necessary for an entrepreneur to survive in the ICT business, it was not sufficient as an instrument. It needed to be supported by various other factors which had little to do with relationships. At this juncture, the conclusion would be both partial and probable. All other essential components being present, without social capital, entrepreneurs could not survive in the ICT industry. Further exploration of certain related aspects which could help us develop a better understanding of this issue were inter-firm alliance and process of investment decision-making from the point of view of investors.

Notes

1. Content of this section was published earlier in Sengupta (2010).
2. Part of the content of this section was published earlier in Sengupta (2010).

References

Aldrich, H., Reese, P.R. and Dubini, P. (1989). Women on the verge of a breakthrough: Networking among entrepreneurs in the United States and Italy. *Entrepreneurship and Regional Development*, 1(4), 339–356.

Anderson, A., Park, J. and Jack, S. (2007). Entrepreneurial social capital: Conceptualizing social capital in new high-tech firms. *International Small Business Journal*, 25(3), 245–272.

Anderson, A.R. and Jack, S.L. (2002). The articulation of social capital in entrepreneurial networks: A glue or a lubricant. *Entrepreneurship and Regional Development*, 14(3), 193–210.

Arenius, P. and Clercq, D.D. (2005). A network-based approach on opportunity recognition. *Small Business Economics*, 24(3), 249–265.

BarNir, A. and Smith, K.A. (2002). Interfirm alliances in the small business: The role of social networks. *Journal of Small Business Management*, 40(3), 219–232.

Batjargal, B. (2003). Social capital and entrepreneurial performance in Russia: A longitudinal study. *Organization Studies*, 24 (4), 535–556.

Becker-Blease, J.R. and Sohl, J.E. (2007). Do women-owned businesses have equal access to angel capital? *Journal of Business Venturing*, 22(4), 503–521.

Bönte, W. (2008). Inter-firm trust in buyer-supplier relations: Are knowledge spillovers and geographical proximity relevant? *Journal of Economic Behavior and Organization*, 67(3–4), 855–870.

Bourdieu, P. (1997). The forms of capital. In A.H. Halsey, H. Lauder, P. Brown and A.S. Wells (eds), *Education: Culture, economy and society*. Oxford: Oxford University Press, 46–58.

Brüderl, J. and Preisendörfer, P. (1998). Network support and the success of newly founded businesses. *Small Business Economics*, 10(3), 213–225.

Burt, R.S. (1992). *Structural holes: The social structure of competition*. Cambridge, Mass. Harvard University Press.

Burt, R.S. (2000). The network entrepreneur. In R. Swedberg (ed.), *Entrepreneurship: The social science view*. New Delhi: Oxford University Press, 281–307.

Caulkins, D.D. and Peters, C. (2002). Grid-group analysis, social capital, and entrepreneurship among North American ethnic groups. *Cross-Cultural Research*, 36(1), 48–72.

Coleman, J.S. (1988). Social capital in the creation of human capital. *American Journal of Sociology*, 94 (Supplement), S95-S120.

Cooke, P. and Wills, D. (1999). Small firms, social capital and the enhancement of business performance through innovation programmes. *Small Business Economics*, 13(3), 219–234.

Cooper, A.C. (2002). Networks, alliances, and entrepreneurship. In A.M. Hitt, R.D. Ireland, S. M. Camp and D. Sexton (eds), *Strategic enterprise: Creating a new mindset*. UK: Blackwell Publishers, 203–222.

Cromie, S. and Birley, S. (1992). Networking by female business owners in Northern Ireland. *Journal of Business Venturing*, 7(3), 237–251.

Dasgupta, P. (2003). Social capital and economic performance: Analytics. In E. Ostrom, and T.K. Ahn (eds), *Foundations of social capital*. Cheltenham: Edward Elgar Publishing Limited/Inc., 309–339.

Davidsson, P. and Honig, B. (2003). The role of social and human capital among nascent entrepreneurs. *Journal of Business Venturing*, 18(3), 301–331.

Dodd, S.D., Jack, S. and Anderson, A.R. (2002). Scottish entrepreneurial networks in the international context. *International Small Business Journal*, 20(2), 213–219.

Dyer, J.H. and Hatch, N.W. (2006). Relation-specific capabilities and barriers to knowledge transfers: Creating advantage through network relationships. *Strategic Management Journal*, 27(8), 701–719.

Eraydin, A. and Armatli-Köroglu, B. (2005). Innovation, networking and the new industrial clusters: The characteristics of networks and local innovation capabilities in the Turkish industrial clusters. *Entrepreneurship and Regional Development*, 17(4), 237–266.

Fiet, J.O. (1995). Reliance upon informants in the venture capital industry. *Journal of Business Venturing*, 10(3), 195–223.

Frazier, B.J. and Niehm, L.S. (2004). Exploring business information networks of small retailers in rural communities. *Journal of Development Entrepreneurship*, 9(1), 23–42.

Fukuyama, F. (1996). *Trust: The social virtues and the creation of prosperity*. London: Penguin Books.

Fukuyama, F. (2000). *Social capital and civil society*. International Monetary Fund Working Paper, WP/00/74, 1–18.

Granovetter, M.S. (1973). The strength of weak ties. *American Journal of Sociology*, 78(6), 1360–1380.

Greve, A. and Salaff, J.W. (2003). Social networks and entrepreneurship. *Entrepreneurship: Theory and Practice*, 28(1), 1–22.

Hara, G. and Kanai, T. (1994). Entrepreneurial networks across oceans to promote international strategic alliances for small businesses. *Journal of Business Venturing*, 9(6), 489–507.

Jenssen, J.I. and Koenig, H.F. (2002). The effect of social networks on resource access and business start-ups. *European Planning Studies*, 10(8), 1039–1046.

Julien, P., Andriambeloson, E. and Ramangalahy, C. (2004). Networks, weak signals and technological innovations among SMEs in the land-based transportation equipment sector. *Entrepreneurship and Regional Development*, 16(4), 251–269.

Keeble, D., Lawson, C., Smith, H.L., Moore, B. and Wilkinson, F. (1998). Internationalization processes, networking and local embeddedness in technology-intensive small firms. *Small Business Economics*, 11(4), 327–342.

Lin, N. (2003). *Social capital: A theory of social structure and action*. Cambridge: University of Cambridge.

Lipparini, A. and Sobrero, M. (1994). The glue and the pieces: Entrepreneurship and innovation in small-firm networks. *Journal of Business Venturing*, 9(2), 125–140.

Littunen, H. (2000). Networks and local environmental characteristics in the survival of new firms. *Small Business Economics*, 15(1), 59–71.

Lorentzen, A. (2008). Knowledge networks in local and global space. *Entrepreneurship and Regional Development*, 20(6), 533–545.

Luo, J-D. (1997). The significance of networks in the initiation of small businesses in Taiwan. *Sociological Forum*, 12(2), 297–317.

Neergaard, H. (2005). Networking activities in technology-based entrepreneurial teams. *International Small Business Journal*, 23(3), 257–276.

Neff, G. (2005). The changing place of cultural production: The location of social networks in a digital media industry. *Annals of American Academy of Political and Social Science*, 597, 134–152.

Putnam, R. (1994). *Making democracy work: Civic traditions in modern Italy*. Princeton: Princeton University Press.

Ramachandran, K. and Ray, S. (2006). Networking and new venture resource strategies: A study of information technology start-ups. *The Journal of Entrepreneurship*, 15(2), 145–168.

Renzulli, L.A., Aldrich, H. and Moody, J. (2000). Family matters: Gender, network, and entrepreneurial outcomes. *Social Forces*, 79(2), 523–546.

Rindova, V.P., Petkova, A.P. and Kotha, S. (2007). Standing out: How new firms in emerging markets build reputation. *Strategic Organization*, 5(1), 31–70.

Roberts, E.B. (1991). *Entrepreneurs in high technology: Lessons from MIT and beyond*. Oxford: Oxford University Press.

Sanders, J.M. and Nee, V. (1996). Immigrant self-employment: The family as social capital and the value of human capital. *American Sociological Review*, 61(2), 231–249.

Sawyerr, O.O., McGee, J. and Peterson, M. (2003). Perceived uncertainty and firm performance in SMEs: The role of personal networking activities. *International Small Business Journal*, 21(3), 269–290.

Saxenian, A.L. (2000). The origins and dynamics of production networks in Silicon Valley. In R. Swedberg (ed.), *Entrepreneurship: The social science view*. New Delhi: Oxford University Press, 308–331.

Schutjens, V. and Stam, E. (2003). The evolution and nature of young firm networks: A longitudinal perspective. *Small Business Economics*, 21(2), 115–134.

Sengupta, A. (2010). Social capital and entrepreneurship: An analysis of methodological issues. *Sociological Bulletin*, 59(3), 323–344.

Shane, S. and Cable, D. (2002). Network ties, reputation, and the financing of new ventures. *Management Science*, 48(3), 364–381.

Shaw, E. (2006). Small firm networking: An insight into contents and motivating factors. *International Small Business Journal*, 24(1), 5–27.

Smallbone, D., Ram, M., Deakins, D. and Baldock, R. (2003). Access to finance by ethnic minority businesses in the UK. *International Small Business Journal*, 21(3), 291–312.

Smeltzer, L.R. and Fann, G.L. (1989). Gender differences in external networks of small business owner/managers. *Journal of Small Business Management*, 27(2), 25–32.

Soh, P.H. (2003). The Role of networking alliances in information acquisition and its implications for new product performance. *Journal of Business Venturing*, 18(6), 727–744.

Tötterman, H. and Sten, J. (2005). Start-ups: Business incubation and social capital. *International Small Business Journal*, 23(5), 487–511.

Upadhya, C. (2004). A new transnational capitalist class? Capital flows, business networks and entrepreneurs in the Indian software industry. *Economic and Political Weekly*, 39(48), 5141–5151.

Upadhya, C. and Vasavi, A.R. (2008). Outposts of the global information economy: Work and workers in India's outsourcing industry. In C. Upadhya, and A.R. Vasavi (eds), *In an outpost of the global economy: Work and workers in India's information technology industry*. New Delhi: Routledge, 9–49.

Uzzi, B. (1999). Embeddedness in the making of financial capital: How social relations and networks benefit firms seeking financing. *American Sociological Review*, 64(4), 481–505.

Yoo, J-K. (2000). Utilization of social networks for immigrant entrepreneurship: A case study of Korean immigrants in the Atlanta area. *International Review of Sociology—Revue Internationale de Sociologie*, 10(3), 347–363.

Zhao, L. and Aram, J.D. (1995). Networking and growth of young technology-intensive ventures in China. *Journal of Business Venturing*, 10(5), 349–370.

Appendix

The Entrepreneurs and their Enterprises: Case Profiles

Table 1

The Entrepreneurs: Demographic Profile and Educational Background

No.	Name of the Entre-preneur	Designation and Enterprise	Age of Entre-preneur at the Time of Data Collection (In years)	Gender	Education
1.	Ajay Aggarwal	MD, Netware Pvt. Ltd.	34	Male	He completed BCom in 1992 from Mumbai. Afterwards, he had joined a LLB programme at Government Law College, Mumbai, but left it midway.
2.	Akhtar Hussain	Proprietor, Communication Networks	36	Male	After SSC he completed a Diploma in Industrial Electronics in 1989 from Sabu Siddhi College in Byculla, Mumbai.
3.	Alok Dutta	MD/CEO, Silicon Networks Pvt. Ltd.	44	Male	He completed BE degree in Electronics and Communications in 1985 from Birla Institute of Technology, Mesra. Later on, in 1987, he completed M.S. in Computer Engineering (with specialization in Micro Electronics) from Syracuse University, New York.
4.	Amit Sharma	CEO and President, Sindh Infotech Pvt. Ltd.	51	Male	He completed BTech in Chemical Engineering in 1977 from the Indian Institute of Technology (Bombay).
5.	Anil Despande	CEO, Tech Writers Inc.	37	Male	After HSC he completed a Diploma in Industrial Electronics from Bharti Vidyapith Polytechnic, Pune and later on, did BE in the same area from the same institution. Afterwards, he completed post-graduation in Marketing Management from the Institute of Management Education, Pune.
6.	Arjun Desai	MD and CEO, Win Infotech Ltd.	47	Male	He completed BSc in 1983 from MES College, Bangalore and, later on, in 1985, he completed MBA from Bangalore University.
7.	Chandan Sivaram	MD, Soft Solutions Pvt. Ltd.	58	Male	He was a BE in Electronics from Veermata Jijabai Technological Institute, Mumbai.

Cont'd ...

...Cont'd

8.	Dinesh Marwari	President, Ryze Softech Pvt. Ltd.	31	Male	He completed BSc Computer Science in 1992 from Loyola College, Chennai. In 1995, he completed M.E. Computer Engineering (with a minor in Business Management) from Cornell University in the USA.
9.	Gautam Apte	CEO, Innovative Web Solutions Pvt. Ltd.	38	Male	He was a BE in Chemical Engineering from Shah and Anchor Kutchhi Engineering College, Mumbai.
10.	Hitesh Patel	MD, Knowledge Software Pvt. Ltd.	47	Male	He completed BCom in 1979 from Narsee Monjee College, Mumbai. Even though afterwards he had joined for a LLB programme at Mithibai College, Mumbai he could not complete it.
11.	James John	CEO, Spaceage.com	35	Male	He completed BSc in Computer Science from St. Xavier's College, Palyamkottam. Later on, in 1993, he completed MSc in Computer Science from St. Joseph's College, Trichi.
12.	Jayant Srinivas	President, Ahead Technologies Pvt. Ltd.	34	Male	He completed BE Electronics in 1993 from Annamalai University, Tamil Nadu.
13.	K. Padma-kumar	MD, Frontech Ltd.	64	Male	He completed BE in Mechanical Engineering from P.H.G. College, Coimbatore.
14.	Kirti Harlalka	Partner, Knowhow	29	Female	She completed BSc in Chemistry in 1998 from Mumbai. Later on, she did MBA from Management Development Institute, Gurgaon in 2000.
15.	Kunal Raman	CEO, Sharp Technologies Pvt. Ltd.	35	Male	He completed BTech in Mechanical Engineering from Indian Institute of Technology (Madras) in 1993. In 1995, he completed M.S. in Operations Research from the same institution. He had joined for a PhD in Operations Research at the business school of University of Rochester, New York, the USA in 1995. However, he did not completehis PhD as, at that time, in 1996, he was more interested in becoming a part of the organization his brother was founding.
16.	Mangalam Srinivas	Chairman and CEO, Global Technologies Pvt. Ltd.	46	Male	He completed Master's in Computer Science from Indian Institute of Science, Bangalore.

Cont'd ...

...Cont'd

17. Naresh Ponnaiah	CEO, Sunshine Technologies Ltd.	33	Male	He completed BCom in 1993 from Kuddalore, his hometown.
18. Naveen Jayakumar	Director, Datamagic Pvt. Ltd.	54	Male	He completed Master's Degree in Physics in 1974 from Andhra University.
19. O.P. Nayar	Chairman and CEO, Accent Tech Solutions	53	Male	He completed BTech in Electronics and Telecommunications from College of Engineering, Thiruvananthapuram.
20. Pankaj Sen	MD, Advanced Software Systems Pvt. Ltd.	50	Male	He completed BSc in Physics in 1978 from St. Xavier's College, Kolkata. Later on, in 1982, he completed BTech in Radiophysics and Electronics from Calcutta University. In 1984, he completed M.Tech. in Electronic Communication.
21. Raj Modi	Director, Softech and Raj Software and Communications	35	Male	He completed BCom in 1992 from Jai Hind College, Mumbai.
22. Rajat Apte	President, Magnatech Inc.	42	Male	He completed BE in Computer Systems Engineering in 1986 from Veermata Jeejabai Technological Institute, Mumbai. In 1988, he completed his Masters in Computer Engineering from North-Eastern University, Boston, the USA. He had also joined for MBA at Babson College, the USA in 1988. However, he could not complete the degree.
23. Ranjan Raghavan	MD, Bangalore Technologies	44	Male	He completed BE (Electronics) from the University of Mysore in 1985. Afterwards, in 1986, he did M.E. (Computer Science) from Indian Institute of Science, Bangalore. Later on, in 1990, he completed his PhD in Computer Science from the University of Nebraska at Lincoln, the USA.
24. Rupa Datta	MD, Infonet Pvt. Ltd.	33	Female	She completed BA in Sociology in 1993 from St. Xavier's College, Mumbai. Afterwards she became a Microsoft Certified Systems Engineer and Microsoft Certified Software Developer.

Cont'd ...

...Cont'd

25.	S. Ram	Director, Integrated Software Solutions	55	Male	He completed BSc in 1972 from Osmania University, Hyderabad. Afterwards, in 1975, he did a BE in Electrical and Communication Engineering (ECE) from Indian Institute of Science, Bangalore. In 1977 he graduated from a ME programme from School of Automation, Indian Institute of Science, Bangalore.
26.	S. Sivakumar	MD, Datainformatics Pvt. Ltd.	44	Male	He completed BE in Electronics and Electrical Engineering in 1985 from Coimbatore, Tamil Nadu.
27.	Sudha Sharma	Principal Consultant, Design Lab	47	Female	She completed BA in Economics in 1981 from Mithibai College of Arts, Mumbai. In 1983, she got a Diploma in Business Management from Chetana Institute of Management, Mumbai. In 2000, she became a Certified Web Master after completing a six months course from World Wide Web Institute of Geneva. In 2002, she became a Certified Usability Analyst after completing a two months course from Human Factors International, the USA. She had acquired the last two certifications from Mumbai.
28.	Ullas Gowda	MD, Knowledge Solutions Pvt. Ltd.	45	Male	He completed BE in Electronics from University Visveswaraiah College of Engineering, Bangalore in 1984. Later on, in 1990, he completed MBA in Engineering Management from University of Dallas, Texas, USA.
29.	Vinay Reddy	MD, Software Consultants Pvt. Ltd.	49	Male	He completed BCom in 1979. He began his BCom at St. Xavier's College, Calcutta and finished it at Vivekananda College, Madras. After that he tried to pursue CA. However he could not complete it. Later on, in 1985 he completed a Diploma in Computer Applications and Programming from Span Computers, Bangalore.
30.	Vishnu Krishna-swamy	Director, Techvision	43	Male	He completed BSc in Physics in 1983 from Madras Christian College. In 1986, he did BE in Computer Science from Indian Institute of Science, Bangalore. In 1995, he had completed his M.S. in Computer Science from Steven's Institute of Technology, New Jersey, the USA.

Table 2

Marriage and Family Background of the Entrepreneurs

No.	Name/Marriage	Family Background in Business	Community/ Regional Background	Details about Family Members and Significant Others
1.	Ajay Aggarwal – Got married after founding the Company	From a business family	From Marwari Hindu family	His father, a graduate, was a trader, and his mother, who was school educated, was a housewife. His wife was a part-time textile designer-cum-Unit Manager at an export house of a friend. He had an uncle, an ICT consultant, who played an important role in the development of his company Netware.
2.	Akhtar Hussain – Got married after founding the business	Not from a business family	Sunni Muslim from Maharashtra	His parents had not completed school education. His mother was a housewife and his father was a technical worker for an automobile products company in India. Like his mother, his wife was also a housewife. However, she had studied till graduation.
3.	Alok Dutta – Married when interviewed	Not from a business family	From a Bengali Hindu family	His father was a graduate in Chemical Engineering and had worked in the Chemical industry. His mother, who was a housewife, was also a graduate. His wife, who had done a Master's degree in Special Education, ran her own school in Mumbai.
4.	Amit Sharma – Married when interviewed	From a business family	From a Punjabi Hindu family	His family was involved in edible oil business. His father went to college, but could not complete the degree. His mother, who was a housewife, was school educated. His wife, who was involved in family business, had an MA degree in English Literature.
5.	Anil Despande – Married while founding the Company	Was not from a business family	From a Maharashtrian Brahmin family	His father, who was school educated, was a Superintendent of Customs. His in-laws were highly educated. His mother-in-law, who provided strong moral support when he decided to become an entrepreneur, was a PhD in Economics and was a faculty member at BMCC College, Pune. His father-in-law, a post-graduate, retired as a senior manager from an automobile company. His wife had completed her graduation from SNDT College, Pune and post-graduation in Sports Science and Nutrition from SVT, Juhu, Mumbai. She was a diet consultant.

Cont'd ...

...Cont'd

6.	Arjun Desai – Married while founding the Company	Not from a business family	From a Hindu Brahmin family	He had a mixed parentage, with mother from Maharashtra and father from Karnataka. He was brought up in Karnataka. His father was an officer in the Department of Agriculture and mother was a housewife. His wife too was a housewife.
7.	Chandan Sivaram – Married while founding the Company	Not from a business family	From a Hindu Brahmin family which traced its roots from TN	His parents were school educated. His father worked as a clerk with a reputed newspaper. His mother was a housewife. His wife, who was a science graduate, was also a housewife. He was born and brought up in Mumbai and was residing in Bangalore since many decades.
8.	Dinesh Marwari – Married when interviewed	His family was in large-scale business for more than last 100 years	From a Marwari family	His father, who was a BTech (Mechanical Engineering) from Anna University, was an entrepreneur involved in manufacturing and real estate industry. His mother, a housewife, had completed her BCom. His wife had a Master's degree in Education from Columbia University Teacher's College.
9.	Gautam Apte – Married while	From a business family	From a Maharashtrian	His mother ran a beauty parlour and his brother looked after the family business in printing started by his grandfather. His father worked as Director of Languages
9.	Gautam Apte – Married while founding the Company	From a business family	From a Maharashtrian Hindu family	His mother ran a beauty parlour and his brother looked after the family business in printing started by his grandfather. His father worked as Director of Languages for the state government of Maharashtra. Both his father and mother were post-graduates. At the time of data collection, Gautam Apte's wife was not working. However, earlier she used to produce and direct television programmes in Mumbai.
10.	Hitesh Patel – Married while founding the Company	From a business family	From a Gujarati Hindu family	His family was involved in textile business. His father, a BCom, was involved in the family business. His mother, an MA and M.Ed., was a Lecturer in Child Psychology at SNDT University, Mumbai. His wife was a BCom.
11.	James John – Married when interviewed	Not from a business family	From a Tamil family	His parents were school teachers, and his wife, an MCA, was involved in software development.

Cont'd ...

...Cont'd

12.	Jayant Srinivas – Unmarried	Was not from a business family	From a Hindu family from Karnataka	His father, a civil engineer, retired as General Manager of a large nationalized construction company. His mother, who was school educated, was a housewife. As mentor he had an ICT entrepreneur who was a PhD.
13.	K. Padma Kumar – Widower when interviewed	Not from a business family	From a Tamil family	His father was a doctor. His school-educated mother was a housewife. His wife, a graduate, was also a housewife.
14.	Kirti Harlalka – Married while founding the Company	From a business family	From a Punjabi family that was located in Mumbai. She was married to a person from Marwari community.	Her father as well as father-in-law was involved in trading: whereas her father was involved in textile trading, her father-in-law was involved in trading multiple products like agarbatti (fragrance sticks), kerosene lamps, etc. Both her mother and mother-in-law were housewives. However, in comparison to her mother-in-law, who, most probably, was illiterate, her mother was highly educated. Her mother was a post-graduate in English. Her husband worked in the corporate sector.
15.	Kunal Raman – Married when interviewed	Not from a business family	From a Tamil family	Both his parents were school educated. His father, who had studied up to standard 10, was a P.A. to the judges in Chennai High Court. His mother, who had studied till standard 8, was a housewife. His wife, also a housewife, was an engineer (Electronic Instrumentation) from Annamalai University. Two of his brothers, with whom he had founded previous business, were highly educated. His elder brother was a PhD from University of Princeton in Electrical Engineering and a BTech from Indian Institute of Technology (Madras) in Electronics and Communication. The second brother had graduated in Electronics and Communications Engineering. During data collection both these brothers were involved with the organizations that they had founded together in 1997.
16.	Mangalam Srinivas – Married while founding the Company	Not from a business family	Not available	His father, an MA in Economics, was an officer in the government sector. His mother, who had studied up to standard 10, was a housewife. His father-in-law, an Electrical Engineer, was an entrepreneur. However, according to him, having his father-in-law as entrepreneur did not influence him to become an entrepreneur. His wife, an Electrical Engineer, was a housewife.

Cont'd ...

...Cont'd

17.	Naresh Ponnaiah – Married when interviewed	His father was into business	From a weaving community in Tamil Nadu	His father, a BSc (Chemistry) was involved in real estate trading. His mother, a housewife, was educated up to standard 12.
18.	Naveen Jaya Kumar – Married while founding the Company	No one in the family was into business	From a Hindu Brahmin family from Andhra Pradesh	Neither of his parents had any formal education. His father was involved in agriculture and also functioned as an Ayurvedic doctor without any formal training. His wife, who had studied up to standard 12, was a housewife.
19.	O.P. Nayar – Married while founding the Company	No one in the family was into business	From the state of Kerala	His father was a farmer who had studied till standard 4. His mother, who had more or less similar educational background, was a housewife. His wife, a doctor, was a housewife.
20.	Pankaj Sen – Married while founding the Company	Even though he was not from a business community, some of his family members were involved in business	From a Hindu family in West Bengal	His father, a school teacher, was an MA in English Literature. His mother, who had studied up to standard 12, was a housewife. His brother ran a business in relation to shipping. His wife, who worked for a large Indian ICT company, had completed MA(English) and MLib, and was pursuing MBA at the time of data collection.
21.	Raj Modi – Got married after founding Softech	From a business family	From a Gujarati Jain family	His father, who had studied up to standard 10, was involved in yarn trading. His mother, who had also studied till school-level, was a housewife. His wife, who was a BCom, was involved in a part-time accounting job.
22.	Rajat Apte – Got married after founding Magnatech	No one in the family was into business	From a Maharashtrian Hindu family	Other than his wife, all his immediate family members including his parents, brother, and sister-in-law were doctors. His wife was a Bachelor in Marketing and International Trade from the USA. She was a wellness consultant/yoga and nutrition expert.

Cont'd ...

...Cont'd

23.	Ranjan Raghavan – Married when interviewed	No one in the family was into business	From the state of Karnataka	His father had completed two Masters' degrees prior to securing PhD degree from University of Minnesota, the USA. His father worked for the Karnataka state government as a Class I officer. He was the founding Director of Administrative Training Institute, Mysore. Both his mother and wife, who were graduates, were housewives.
24.	Rupa Datta – Got married after starting business	Both her father and father-in-law were entrepreneurs	From a Punjabi Hindu family. She was brought up in Mumbai	Her father was a practising Chartered Accountant. Her mother, who was a BA in Home Science, ran a home-based business in jewellery and clothing. Her father-in-law, a BE from Indian Institute of Technology, was also an entrepreneur involved in testing electronic machineries. Her mother-in-law was a housewife. Her husband, a Chartered Accountant, worked as a Vice President for a Call Centre.
25.	S. Ram – Got married after the Company formation	No one in the family was into business	From the state of Andhra Pradesh	His father was a musician. His mother, a graduate in Physics, was a teacher. His wife, a MSc in Statistics, worked for his Company.
26.	S. Sivakumar – Got married after founding the Company	No one in the family was into business	From a Tamil Hindu family	His father, who had studied till standard 7, worked in a textile retail shop in a town in Tamil Nadu. His mother had studied till standard 2. His wife, who was a MPhil from Jawaharlal Nehru University, New Delhi, was self-employed.
27.	Sudha Sharma – Unmarried	His father was into business	From a North Indian Hindu family	His father, who had studied till SSC, was into film production. His mother, a graduate, was a housewife. He had two brothers. One brother, a graduate, was a creative consultant and teacher in higher education. Another brother, also a graduate, was a Chief Manager in a company in the ICT industry.
28.	Ullas Gowda – Married when interviewed	No one in the family was into business	From a Hindu family which belonged to a fisherman caste in South Karnataka	His father, who had studied till matriculation, functioned as a Sales Manager for a large matchstick factory. His mother, who had studied up to standard 5, was a housewife. His wife, an electronic engineer, worked as a technical writer for a software company. His uncle, an entrepreneur, had a Diploma in Engineering.

Cont'd ...

...Cont'd

29.	Vinay Reddy – Married when interviewed	No one in the family was into business	From a family that originated from the state of Andhra Pradesh	His father, who had studied law and hotel management, was a hotel manager. His mother, a graduate, was a school teacher in Madras before her marriage. His wife was a Special Educator for children with Autism.
30.	Vishnu Krishnaswamy – Married while founding the Company	No one in the family was into business	From a Hindu Brahmin family from Tamil Nadu	His father, who had studied till the Intermediate level, was a school teacher. His mother, who did not study beyond standard 10, was a housewife. His wife, who had done BSc (Physics) and BE (Computer Engineering) was a computer engineer for an ICT company.

...Cont'd

Table 3

Professional Details of Entrepreneurs and their Enterprises

No.	*Name/ Location of Entrepreneur*	*Work Involvement before Becoming an Entrepreneur*	*Year of Business Start-up*	*Age of Entrepreneur while Starting Business (In years)*	*Details about the Enterprise*
1.	Ajay Aggarwal – Mumbai	He never joined a full-time job as a professional. Other than working as a temporary research investigator for a large market research organization, he had worked in diamond and financial sector as an apprentice with business owners known to his family members. The purpose of working as an apprentice was to develop skills required for building a business in related sectors.	Netware was founded as a firm in 1996. It was transformed into a company in 2000.	24	Netware primarily provided services related to web designing. It had only one office, located in Mumbai.
2.	Akhtar Hussain – Mumbai	Before starting business he worked for five-and-a-half years as a Customer Support Engineer for a large Indian ICT company.	He began his business operation in 1995. However, he established Communication Networks in 1998 when flow of business increased.	25	Communication Networks provided services in data recovery and ICT infrastructure management. It had only one office, located in Mumbai. It had ten employees and job profile of all the employees was technical in nature.

Cont'd ...

...Cont'd

3.	Alok Dutta – Mumbai	After completing studies in the USA, he had worked for two years in India as a System Analyst in the VLSI group of a reputed Indian ICT company.	1990	28	Silicon Networks was involved in VLSI Designing and Software Development. At the time of the interview, the company had around 100 employees of whom one-fourth were administrative staff and rest were technical staff. The organization also employed consultants. However, the number of consultants kept changing. Silicon Networks had three offices in Mumbai, two in the USA, and one in UK. In addition to having a large number of clients in the USA and UK, Silicon Networks had clients who were located in other countries like China (Hong Kong), Germany, Norway, and Taiwan.
4.	Amit Sharma – Mumbai	Coming from a family involved in business activities, he never worked as an employee for any organization.	He founded the Company in 1985. However, the business operation began two years after registration of the company in 1987.	29	Sindh Infotech was involved in developing software products for export businesses. The organization had 12 employees of whom 9 were technical employees and 3 were administrative employees. Sindh Infotech had two offices, both located in Mumbai.

Cont'd ...

...Cont'd

5.	Anil Despande – Pune	Prior to becoming an entrepreneur, he had worked as a sales engineer for about seven organizations over a period of three-and-a-half years.	1994	25	Tech Writers was involved in technical writing and e-learning. The Company had 26 employees of whom eight were involved in administrative work and rest 18 were involved in technical work. The organization also employed seven technical consultants. Other than having a large number of clients in India, Tech Writers also had clients in other countries like Australia, Denmark, and Greece. Clients belonged to various industry verticals like education, electrical, ICT, ITES, life sciences, logistics, and telecommunications. The Company had four offices globally. In India, one office was located in Pune and the other one was in Bangalore. One of its offices abroad was in the USA and the other in Singapore.
6.	Arjun Desai – Bangalore	After finishing studies, he initially worked with a large Indian ICT company as a trainee software engineer for more than one year and later on with another Indian ICT company as a marketing staff for two- and-a-half years.	1988	28	Win Infotech offered services in ICT infrastructure management and BPO for clients belonging to different industry verticals like legal, financial, manufacturing, and healthcare. Win Infotech had 150 employees of whom around 125 were technical staff and around 25 were administrative staff. The organization also had three technical consultants. Win Infotech had two offices, one in Bangalore and another in Beaverton, the USA.

Cont'd ...

...Cont'd

7.	Chandan Sivaram – Bangalore	Before becoming an entrepreneur he worked for three ICT companies in India for more than 15 years in different capacities like Trainee Programmer, Programmer, and Branch Manager.	1989	40	Soft Solutions was a 40 people strong organization. This included both employees and consultants. Soft Solutions produced software products in the area of ERP and also offered services in the same area. Other than catering to the clients from the ICT industry, Soft Solutions addressed the requirement of clients from different other industry verticals like banking and finance, education, government, healthcare, manufacturing, media, research, telecommunications, and trading. Besides India, clients of Soft Solutions were located in various other countries like Australia, China (including Hong Kong), Indonesia, Malaysia, Singapore, Sweden, UAE (Dubai), UK, and the USA. Soft Solutions has two offices in India (in Bangalore and Chennai), and one office abroad (in Singapore).
8.	Dinesh Marwari – Chennai	After completing studies he worked with a software services company in the USA as a Client Engagement Manager for about three years.	1999	24	Ryze Softech had a total of 490 employees. It had two divisions: the BPO segment had 370 employees and the software services segment had 120 employees. The Company had two offices, one at Chennai and the other at Fremont in the USA.

Cont'd ...

...Cont'd

9.	Gautam Apte – Bangalore	After graduation, he had worked for four ICT companies in different capacities. He had worked for more than 10 years as an employee of which three years he had worked abroad and the rest were in India.	2001	32	Innovative Web Solutions was involved in providing internet services. The Company had one office in India at Bangalore and one abroad in UK. The Company was supported by 140 employees of whom around 130 were technical staff and around 10 were administrative staff. In addition, there were 40 technical consultants.
10.	Hitesh Patel – Mumbai	Before starting Knowledge Software he had worked for his family business for 24 years.	2001	42	Knowledge Software was involved in production of entertainment and knowledge management softwares. The organization had one office, located in Mumbai. It had 30 employees of whom 18 were technical staff and 12 were administrative staff. The Company had also appointed one technical consultant and four legal consultants.
11.	James John – Chennai	After completing education he worked for about nine years in 11 organizations. Three of these organizations were located abroad. Except for two of his employing organizations, which were training institutions, rest were companies in the ICT industry.	2004	32	Spaceage was involved in the development of a product for facilitating software development. Its only office was located in Chennai. The Company had 25 employees of whom 23 were involved in technical activities and two were involved in administrative activities.

Cont'd ...

...Cont'd

12.	Jayant Srinivas – Bangalore	He was one unique entrepreneur, who, despite lacking a business family background, had never worked as an employee before founding Ahead Technologies. He tried to venture into entrepreneurship immediately after completing studies. As that business became successful, there was no reason for joining another organization as an employee.	He founded the Company in 1996. However, he began his business operation three years before forming the Company, that is, in 1993.	20	Ahead Technologies executed software consultancy projects for government departments. At the time of data collection Ahead Technologies had 800 employees of whom around 650 did technical work and around 150 did administrative work. It also had 3,200 technical consultants. Ahead Technologies had quite a few offices. Two offices were located abroad, one in North Potomac, the USA and one in Amsterdam, The Netherlands. In India, the organization had seven offices, two in Bangalore and one each in Chennai, Dehradun, Delhi, Mumbai, and Mysore.
13.	K. Padma Kumar – Bangalore	Before becoming an entrepreneur he worked in three organizations for 24 years. Other than working for a government organization for one year, he worked for private companies in the automobile and ICT industries.	He founded the Company in 1986. However, the operation began in 1988.	45	Frontech was involved in developing products and offering services in the area of technology migration. The organization had 50 employees of whom around 44 were technical staff and around six were administrative staff. Only office of the organization was located in Bangalore.

Cont'd ...

...Cont'd

14.	Kirti Harlalka – Chennai	While studying, she did multiple odd jobs like working as survey research investigator, secretary of a lawyer, teacher in a school on leave vacancy, hostess for product exhibition, and sales person. After completion of studies she had worked with two organizations. Initially, she worked with a company in the pharmaceutical sector as Biotech Business Manager. Later on, she worked as Industry Analyst with a business research organization.	2005	27	Knowhow was involved in business research. Clients of the organization were from different industries like financial, FMCG (Fast Moving Consumer Goods), healthcare, ICT, retail, sports and telecommunications. The organization had about 35 freelancers working for it. Knowhow did not have any employee. Being in the initial stage, founder's residence in Chennai was being used as the office.
15.	Kunal Raman – Chennai	Having joined the founding team of an organization at a very early age, he had very little work experience as an employee. After completing BTech he had worked with a large organization in India as Management Trainee (Mechanical Engineer) for about three months.	He founded the Company in 2004. However, prior to founding Sharp Technologies he was also actively involved along with his brothers in founding two organizations in the same industry in 1996 and 1997.	32	Sharp Technologies developed software products in the area of small network data backup. The Company had one office, located in Chennai. Clients of the organizations were spread out in different countries including Australia, Canada, and the USA. The organization had 30 employees of whom 22 were involved in technical work and rest 8 were involved in administrative work.

Cont'd ...

...Cont'd

16.	Mangalam Srinivas – Bangalore	Before becoming an entrepreneur he had worked for about 17 years as an employee. Initially, he worked for two years with a reputed Indian software company as a Software Engineer. Later on, he worked for 15 years with a reputed multinational electronics company. He joined as a Software Design Engineer and left as MD of the India chapter of the company.	2001	40	Global Technologies developed software products related to Digital Signal Processing. The Company had clients in different countries like France, India, Taiwan, UK, and the USA. Global Technologies had around 200 employees of whom around 185 were involved in technical work and rest 15 were involved in administrative work. In addition, there were 20 consultants involved in administrative activities.
17.	Naresh Ponnaiah – Chennai	After completing studies, initially, he had founded an organization involved in ICT training and software development and operated this organization as the entrepreneur for three years. Afterwards, he worked in India as an employee of two reputed companies for more than seven years.	2003	30	Sunshine Technologies was involved in developing software products in the area of business rule engine. Clients of the Company were from different industries like apparel, banking and finance, electrical, government, ICT, ITES, law, manufacturing, pharmaceutical, printing and publishing, real estate, retail, and trading. These clients were located in different countries like Germany, India, and the USA. The Company had 25 employees of whom 20 were involved in technical work and 5 were involved in administrative work. In addition there were 4 consultants.

Cont'd ...

...Cont'd

18.	Naveen Jaya Kumar – Bangalore	Before becoming an entrepreneur, he worked with three large Indian companies for about 12 years. Of these companies, two were involved in electronic industry and one was involved in aeronautics.	1987	34	Datamagic developed computer-based instruments. The only office of this organization was located in Bangalore. It had 10 employees, all of whom had technical job profiles.
19.	O.P. Nayar – Chennai	After completing studies he had worked as R&D Engineer for an electronics company for one-and-a-half years. Afterwards, he worked for a large Indian ICT company for 15 years. He joined the Company as an engineer and left it as a Senior Manager, Customer Services.	1991	37	Accent Tech Solutions developed software products and offered software services for various industry verticals. The Company had 30 offices in India alone spread over major cities in the country. In addition, it also had offices outside India in Singapore, UAE (Dubai), and the USA. Clients of the Company were from different industry verticals like banking and finance, education, government, healthcare, ICT, manufacturing, media, and telecommunications. The Company, along with one sister concern, had altogether 3,000 employees, of whom around 2,500 were involved in technical activities, whereas around 500 were involved in administrative activities.

Cont'd ...

...Cont'd

20.	Pankaj Sen – Bangalore	After completing studies he worked for six ICT companies for more than 13 years in different capacities like Assistant Manager in the EDP Centre, Consultant, Engineer for Software Quality Management, Manager of Business Development, and Manager of Network Projects.	1997	40	Advanced Software Systems was involved in software product development. Clients of the Company were from different industries like banking, healthcare, insurance, manufacturing, security, and shipping. The only office of the Company was located in Bangalore. The Company had 12 employees; job profile of all the employees was technical in nature. In addition, the Company also availed the services of five consultants.
21.	Raj Modi – Mumbai	Prior to founding Softech, he had worked for six years as a data entry operator for a company in the diamond industry.	He founded Softech in 1995 and Raj Software and Communications in 1996.	25 (While founding Softech)	When interviewed, Softech was already a dead organization, as the only software product which Softech was producing had gone off the market. Raj Software and Communications was involved in offering services for financial market and in developing software products for the same sector. The only office of Raj Software and Communications was located in Mumbai. Softech had no employees. Raj Software and Communications had two employees and their work was technical in nature.
22.	Rajat Apte – Mumbai	After completing education he had worked with an MNC in the USA for three years, initially as software engineer for two years and later on in relation to business development for one year.	1991	27	Magnatech was involved in offering software services. Clients of Magnatech were primarily located in the healthcare industry. Magnatech had two offices, one at Mumbai and another at Westborough, the USA.

Cont'd ...

...*Cont'd*

23.	Ranjan Raghavan – Bangalore	Before founding Bangalore Technologies he worked abroad for seven years for an MNC which was involved in the ICT industry.	1998	35	Bangalore Technologies developed software products targeted towards healthcare sector. However, other than healthcare, the Company had clients who were engaged in financial services, media, member management, performance management, and real estate. The only office of Bangalore Technologies was located in Bangalore. The organization had 85 employees of whom 75 were technical staff and 10 were administrative staff. In addition, there was one company which was appointed as a consultant.
24.	Rupa Datta – Mumbai	Before becoming an entrepreneur she had worked for 14 years in different organizations. This included working for five years as a trustee for a social sector association, for three years as a Systems Engineer for an ICT company, and for six years as a Networking Consultancy freelancer for different organizations.	She founded it as a partnership firm in 2001. Later on, in 2004, she got the organization registered as a company.	27	Infonet offered services in technical writing and accessibility. In its two offices in Mumbai the Company had 60 employees of whom 52 were technical staff and 8 were administrative staff.
25.	S. Ram – Bangalore	Prior to joining Integrated Software Solutions he worked for one ICT company for about three years. Afterwards, he worked as an independent consultant in the ICT sector for about four-and-a-half years.	1982	33	Integrated Software Solutions was involved in offering generic ICT services and developing software products. The only office of the Company was located in Bangalore. However, its sister concern had offices elsewhere. Along with its two sister companies, Integrated Software Solutions had altogether around 900 employees of whom around 810 were technical staff and around 90 were administrative staff.

Cont'd ...

...Cont'd

26.	S. Sivakumar – Chennai	Before becoming an entrepreneur he had worked with an ICT company for two-and-a-half years.	Founded in 1989 as a firm. Later on, it was registered as a company.	26	Datainformatics was into reselling software product for publishing industry. It was also a dealer for products of a reputed multinational computer manufacturing company. The only office of the Company was located in Chennai. The Company had 18 employees of whom six were technical staff and rest 12 were administrative staff.
27.	Sudha Sharma – Mumbai	Before starting Design Lab she had worked with nine organizations over a period of almost 20 years. She worked with those organizations in different capacities like Software Developer, Head of Production, Project Manager/ Visualizer, Design Manager, and Product Manager. One of her key focus areas was Design and User Interface. The companies which she had worked for primarily belonged to two industries, ICT and finance.	2006	46	Design Lab was involved in various activities like design and user interface consultancy, website and web application development, branding and multimedia, and usability and HCI consultancy. At the time of data collection, Design Lab was operating from the residence of the entrepreneur in Mumbai. Five freelancers worked for her, among whom four were involved in technical work and one was involved in administrative work.
28.	Ullas Gowda – Bangalore	Before founding Knowledge Solutions he had worked as an employee for about seven years in four organizations in Electronics, ICT and Steel Casting industry. His last employment was for an MNC and he was posted abroad. In addition, he had also founded two other businesses in electronic goods trading and recruitment sector prior to founding the current company.	2000	38	Knowledge Solutions was involved in e-learning. Clients of the Company belonged to different industries like banking and financial services, business process outsourcing, educational institutions, healthcare, hospitality, information technology, manufacturing, retail, and telecommunications. The only office of the Company was located in Bangalore. The Company had 13 employees. Work profile of all the employees was technical in nature. In addition, there were four consultants.

Cont'd ...

...Cont'd

29.	Vinay Reddy – Bangalore	Prior to starting his first company he had worked for four years as Finance Manager for a group of hotels in India.	He founded Software Consultants in 2003. However, prior to that he was involved with another company which he had founded with two other individuals in 1996.	While founding the previous company he was 38 years old.	Software Consultants developed software products and offered services in website development, website hosting, networking, and Linux. Clients of the Company belonged to different industries like banking and finance, biotechnology, education, electronics, entertainment, event management, floriculture, government, healthcare, hospitality, ICT, logistics, manufacturing, media, pharmaceuticals, printing and publishing, real estate, security, telecommunications, trading, and training. Other than Indian clients, Software Consultants had clients from other countries like Brazil, France, Germany, Malaysia, Philippines, Singapore, UK, and the USA. The only office of the Company was located in Bangalore. The Company had 40 employees of whom 33 were technical staff and seven were administrative staff.
30.	Vishnu Krishnaswamy – Bangalore	Before starting Techvision he had worked in India for three years in one organization and abroad for around 15 years in three organizations. All his employers were ICT companies. He began his career as a Software Programmer. His last job was as a Senior Consultant.	1998	34	Techvision developed software products for the healthcare industry. The only office of the Company was located in Bangalore. The Company had 15 employees of whom 11 were technical staff and one was administrative staff. In addition, there was one technical consultant.

Index